TWENTIETH CENTURY MUSIC

EDITED BY ROLLO H. MYERS

New revised and enlarged edition

CALDER AND BOYARS
LONDON

ORIGINALLY PUBLISHED IN 1960 IN GREAT BRITAIN BY
JOHN CALDER (PUBLISHERS) LTD
17 SACKVILLE STREET
LONDON WI

© JOHN CALDER (PUBLISHERS) LTD, 1960

SECOND REVISED AND ENLARGED EDITION 1968 BY
CALDER AND BOYARS LTD

© CALDER AND BOYARS LTD, 1968

REPRINTED 1969

SBN 7145 0587 0 CLOTH EDITION
SBN 7145 0588 9 PAPER EDITION

PRINTED IN GREAT BRITAIN BY
FLETCHER AND SON LTD, NORWICH

CONTENTS

v

PART II

A SURVEY OF CONTEMPORARY MUSIC IN EUROPE, U.S.A. AND LATIN AMERICA

INTRODUCTION

By The Editor

WE LIVE in an age when nothing can be taken for granted. Values are no longer immutable; change is the order of the day. Ideas accepted yesterday will be rejected tomorrow; everything, in fact, as a Greek philosopher said with great acumen many centuries ago, is in a state of flux.

We have only to look around us to see the changes that are occurring in every sphere of modern life—in the theory and practice of politics and economics, in the pattern of social behaviour and the structure of society, and, above all, in the arts. Above all—but inevitably so since throughout the ages the arts have always been a more or less accurate barometer of the social and intellectual climate at any given period in the countries where they flourish. Music, the youngest of the arts, is perhaps the most sensitive to variations in this climate, one reason being, perhaps, that it is, in a sense, a method of mass-communication, addressing itself to large numbers of people at a time (i.e. collective audiences) rather than to individuals. Thus a picture or statue can only be seen by a very few people at a time and only in one place, whereas it is possible, thanks to the radio and the gramophone, for a piece of music to be heard simultaneously by vast audiences in every corner of the world. Reactions to different forms and kinds of music vary in consequence, in the different countries; creative musicians are consciously or subconsciously aware of these reactions, and the extent to which they are or are not influenced by them is likely to be apparent in their works.

In the past, when facilities for the diffusion of music were extremely limited, styles tended to be more homogeneous. But they always reflected the spirit of the age. Whether in Italy or the Netherlands, in

England or in France, composers at any given time were all speaking the same language. In the fifteenth and sixteenth centuries, the age of new discoveries both physical (geographical exploration) and intellectual (the Renaissance), composers tended to be more adventurous than they had need to be in the staider and more formal seventeenth and eighteenth centuries when society seemed to be established on firm and recognisable foundations, and intellectual speculation was conditioned by the universal cult of reason. The century that followed saw the rise of industrialism and the growth of a society based on wealth. The aristocrat of the age of reason and privilege was replaced by the plutocrat of the era of materialism and opportunity. The arts turned bourgeois to suit their patrons' tastes. But then half-way through the century a reaction set in. In music there was something like a revolution. Berlioz was born, and stormed the Bastille of out-worn conventions and traditions, paving the way for Liszt and Wagner who between them revolutionised opera and the orchestra and engendered the 'new music' that was to be the *fin de siècle* apotheosis of romanticism. It only remained for Richard Strauss to pile Pelion on Ossa, exacerbating nerves and senses with his gargantuan Tone-Poems in which the multiplicity of orchestral staves too often concealed the indigence of his musical thought, for an *impasse* to be reached from which there seemed to be no issue. This was the position when, at the turn of the century, a new voice made itself heard in a series of masterpieces which were to change the whole course of music and usher in a new era of exploration and emancipation which has continued to this day. The voice was that of Claude Debussy, who had been quietly engaged in providing the language of music with a new syntax and a new vocabulary, thus making possible the developments of recent years with which this book is mainly concerned.

The fourth and fifth decades of our century have in fact been marked by new conquests and above all by a new approach to music which would have been unthinkable in any other epoch. In contrast to the formality and solidity of the periwigged seventeenth, the civilised sophistication of the eighteenth and the smug complacency of the nineteenth centuries, we are living today in a society disrupted and disillusioned on the one hand by two major wars in the space of thirty years, and struggling on the other to adjust itself to conditions created by the most astonishing advances in the realm of applied science which are bringing about a revolution in human behaviour and thought, with the emphasis heavily on material rather than spiritual values. As always, this social climate—one of moral and intellectual instability and scepticism combined with a blind and naive faith in material and technical progress—is reflected in the arts, and in none more patently than music.

Creative artists, for their part, including musicians, are torn between a desire to express the spirit of the age and a desire (in some cases stronger) to escape from it. The public, having no standards by which to judge the results of this artistic schizophrenia, will begin by accepting everything and end by believing nothing.

Two further causes contribute to this *malaise*. The first is that while more people than ever before have access to music through the medium of broadcasting and recording, this very profusion of material and the facilities provided for absorbing it tend to produce a mass-receptivity on the part of the listener who is no longer called upon to exercise discrimination and therefore tends to follow the line of least resistance. The second cause, arising out of the first, is that in protest, no doubt, against this state of affairs in which listening is too easy, composers have gone to the other extreme in their desire to make it too difficult. From this attitude springs what we may call the crisis of contemporary music. As composers tend to withdraw further and further into their ivory towers, elaborating new techniques and transforming music into a kind of code-language to which only initiates can have access, the gulf between them and the ordinary public grows ever wider. For the first time in the history of music the technical processes of composition are forced upon the attention of the listener who has to be told whether such and such a work is 'serial' or 'atonal', modal or polytonal, or maybe based on Hindoo or Chinese scales on to which the song of the blackbird has been grafted. All and any methods which may seem good to a composer, it goes without saying, are justified, but these matters are hardly the concern of the listener who nowadays is encouraged to look at the label before being allowed to sample the contents. To make things still more difficult, he is now invited to take an intelligent interest in such things as *musique concrète* and electronic music. To enable him to do so, and to help him to find an answer to some, at least, of the questions I have touched upon, is the main purpose of this book. Somehow or other the gulf between the contemporary composer and his audience must be bridged, but this cannot be done unless a serious effort is made on either side.

Two contributors to this symposium have dealt with the problem of how to keep the channel open between contemporary composers and their public. One, himself a practising composer, discusses the composer-audience relationship and emphasises the importance of establishing some sort of communication between the creator and the listener on whom, in the last resort, the former depends. The other suggests that more care should be taken in the *presentation* of new music, as the apathy and lack of comprehension so often shown by the public is often the direct result of faulty and inadequate performances and inaccurate interpretations. This very question of interpretation is also dealt with by another contributor, this time from the point of view of the conductor.

These are only a few of the subjects treated in this book. The reader will also find, in addition to chapters dealing with the more abstract aspects of contemporary music, a survey of what is actually happening in the various countries of Europe and the two Americas, written either by natives of those countries, or by experts who have made a special study of their music.

I have wished in this way to give this symposium a genuinely international character and to make it as comprehensive as possible in the hope that it may encourage those who are interested in contemporary music but puzzled, perhaps, by certain of its manifestations in recent years, to feel at least that it is a living force and, whether they like it or not, a vital element in the culture of our time.

It only remains for me to express my gratitude to the team of distinguished contributors to this symposium and to thank them warmly for their valuable collaboration.

POSTSCRIPT 1967

AND NOW that a second, revised edition has been called for, this welcome is extended to three new contributors—Professor Wilfrid Mellers, Mr. Colin Mason and Mr. Malcolm Troup—to the former for his illuminating review of the contemporary scene in the United States of America; to Mr. Mason for his valuable postscript bringing up to date the chapter on *Music in Great Britain since* 1945; and to Mr. Troup for his penetrating analysis of the major works of Stravinsky's last period which will always have an assured and unique place in the annals of twentieth-century music.

In Mr. Arthur Jacobs' addition to his original chapter on *Some recent trends in Opera* the reader will find a mine of up-to-date information on the latest developments in the world of Opera; while music behind the 'iron curtain' is lightly touched on by Mr. Goldbeck as an appendix to his chapter on *Twentieth-century Composers and Tradition*. For the rest, I am content to leave my original Introduction unchanged as, though new developments and fresh experiments in compositional techniques have of course been taking place since this book was first published, the overall situation is the same in so far as all these efforts are tending towards the same goal—the extension and enrichment of the language of the music of our time.

I

HOW IT STARTED:
THE NINETEENTH-CENTURY PIONEERS

By Eric Blom

STRICTLY SPEAKING, twentieth-century music cannot be said to have 'started', except in the sense that its earliest appearances coincided with the year 1901. What we loosely call modern music began when sound was first used for conscious artistic expression. We do not know when that was: probably soon after primitive man had discovered that some kind of significance could be conveyed by differences of vocal pitch, which must have been long before he had found speech. An art of music, though of the crudest sort, thus preceded an equally crude use of language, not to mention literature, which, however rudimentary, is infinitely younger as a formally shaped human expression than music.

The first simple patterns of pitched sounds, being a startling novelty, must have been modern music to the rude cave-dwellers of pre-history; and thereafter every step forward was an adventure in modernity. We can no more find any precise points of departure in musical trends than we can in any historical fact: they are not a matter of stops and new starts but one of continued overlappings—monody with descant, descant with polyphony, and so on down to twelve-note composition and indeed—if they are still artistically fruitful media, which yet remains to be seen—electrophonic music and *musique concrète*.

There is no need to show how such overlappings recurred in the course of musical history, but it is perhaps worth saying that twentieth-century music, like any music, has grown like a tree, with seasonal incidents of burgeoning and decline, from a single complex of distant roots; that it is not a detached phenomenon of which one can see the independent beginnings and may foretell an appointed end. Even to pin down the precise origins of particular phases in music is difficult, for although we can trace certain connections and trends, the map shows no great main lines linking one terminus with another distant one and cutting through the intermediate territory without touching other points. There are many stations in between where new stimuli are taken in, like fresh supplies of fuel or water, and where certain features are received and dropped, like passengers coming from or making for some other direction. It may look at times as though, let us say, Maurice Ravel (1875-1937) had come straight from Liszt, or Arnold Schoenberg (1874-1951) from Wagner, but only if we shortsightedly peer at two particular termini. As soon as we stand back and see the whole map in detail, a bewildering criss-cross of lines forming other connections or going off in unexpected directions shows such compli- cated patterns that we grow wary of trusting to appearances that seem to indicate places of origin.

If we see composers like towns on a map connected by railway lines, there are some few who seem to lie apart, detached from any traffic with the world beyond. Berlioz is the classic instance; more relevant to our study, because surviving into the twentieth century, those who immediately come to mind are Leos Janáček (1854-1928), Carl Nielsen (1865-1931) and Ferruccio Busoni (1866-1924), and more doubtfully Frederick Delius (1862-1934), Jan Sibelius (1865-1957), Erik Satie (1866-1925) and Albert Roussel (1869-1937), whose singularity is the first thing that strikes one in their mature work, but in whom influences are easier to trace than in the other three. These too, nevertheless, were of course subject to them, though we have to go to their early and least characteristic and therefore forgotten works to trace them. No artistic manifestation ever came from nowhere.

It has by now become evident that to find 'beginnings' in one composer after another in any systematic or indeed instructive way is a sheer impossibility. The tangled cross-currents are far too numerous and involved. More promising than the study of composers for the present purpose is that of tendencies. Still very difficult, this shows at least a promise of proving reducible to some kind of classification.

What looks like the cleanest break between the music of the nineteenth and twentieth centuries is, of course, the relinquishment of tonality in favour of twelve-note composition or, more broadly speaking, atonal music. But it is actually no more abrupt than the alleged new start of opera and of monodic music in general. Schoenberg's 'invention' of the twelve-note system did not come out of the blue. It came about partly by a process of trial and error in composition begun in an accepted manner, and partly by theoretical reasoning that had nothing directly to do with creative practice. My private notion is that a new way of writing music forced itself on Schoenberg because he realised, probably subconsciously, as detached critics do only too consciously, that what he had written in a more or less Wagnerian or Mahlerian manner (e.g. *Verklärte Nacht* and *Gurrelieder* respectively) was not good enough or new enough of its kind, or at any rate could not have been continued with works of the same quality in the same vein. Thus we see a gradual growing towards tonal emancipation in, for example, the first *Chamber Symphony* and come upon a completely atonal masterpiece in *Pierrot Lunaire*. This is not yet a twelve-note composition, but it contains the germs of that system, no doubt clearly foreshadowed in the composer's perception, if not yet discernible by the critic not wise after the event.

It seems to me that my theory is confirmed by Schoenberg's saying, quite late in his career, that there was still a great deal of good music to be written in C major. But not by him. By C major he meant, of course, any major and for that matter any minor key; in fact simply diatonic tonality as distinct from what he had arrived at far away from it. And indeed, tonality has served many outstanding composers far into the twentieth century as admirably as it had ever served the classics. Masterpieces by Gabriel Fauré (1845-1924) and Edward Elgar (1857-1934), Roussel and Ralph Vaughan Williams (1872-1958), Gustav Holst (1874-1934) and Ravel remain fundamentally loyal to their key-signatures. Béla Bartók (1881-1945) and Igor Stravinsky (1882-) both achieved their mastery in diatonic music, and while the latter departed from it towards serial music quite late in his life, the former returned to it to produce the clarified and ear-easing music of his final period.

As for C major, there is a long stretch of it at the end of Richard Strauss's (1864-1949) *Die Frau ohne Schatten*. But is it good? It is solemn and glowing, but rather emptily and ostentatiously magnificent. No doubt it symbolises a return to natural health and strength (naturals in place of sharps and flats) after a long argument allegorically condemning birth control. And indeed, diatonicism has always meant musical health for Strauss, while his departures from it, chromatic distortions of diatonic scales, not a definite break with them, stood for disease, vice and every kind of perversity. Hence his most fiercely chromatic music is that of *Elektra*. But for technical reasons too he was forced to find some refuge from purely diatonic major and minor, for the sake of contrast and an enlargement of his resources. We then find, in his later and on the whole more mellow music, that he constantly resorts, not so much to chromaticism as to modulation, and modulation effected less by lengthy transitions than by interrupted cadences. From *Ariadne auf Naxos*, where this process may be said to become first a little oppressively noticeable, to the last five orchestral songs, where it is positively obtrusive, though they are perhaps the crowningly splendid examples of his art, one is conscious of a certain impatience with diatonicism, of a constant desire to evade it coupled with an invincible reluctance to break with it; and here again, as with Schoenberg, one suspects that the composer had to find a new way of dealing with tonality because he could no longer do so in the old way without succumbing to staleness and feebleness. Much the same anxiety is also found in Max Reger's (1873-1916) ceaseless use of key-changes, not by interrupted cadences so much as by short-cut transitions or by abrupt jerks into another key without modulation of any kind. The trouble in both his case and Strauss's is that the means of avoiding staleness are all too apt to become stale themselves.

All-over chromaticism, not merely at modulatory points, was other composers' attempt at forging a new idiom and stretching tonality so far as to make it barely recognisable to the ear and hard to analyse on paper, but without abandoning it altogether. What it produced was not often durable, and if sometimes for the moment more than endurable, apt to wear thin before long. The highly charged chromaticism of Karol Szymanowski (1883-1937), for instance, produces a sultry hothouse atmosphere which, together with admiration for his luxurious exotic blooms, soon produces a desire to look for fresher airs. Arnold Bax (1883-1953), less luxuriant, still used chromaticism assiduously, not like Szymanowski in a progressive way, but to give spice to his avowedly romantic imaginings. One must regret that his fine art contained an all too rapidly working germ of mortality. So did that of Delius, so rarely heard already nowadays and, when heard, filling one with nostalgic regrets that one is witnessing a beautiful sunset to which one is afraid that total darkness may succeed. And in general, composers of highly chromatic music who could find no other way out of traditional tonality are apt to look now like artists lamenting a lost innocence of sharplessness and flatlessness, unable to discover new virtues.

Very virtuously conscious of seeking fresh airs were those who pursued folk music as a possible new resource and a salvation. Not so very new, when we come to think of it, since this had already been the way of Smetana, Grieg, the Russian nationalist school, Albéniz and others. And mentioning such names, one is struck by the curious fact that the cultivation of folk music in serious composition was an entirely peripheral European activity, going on in Czechoslovakia, Norway, Russia, Spain, a little later in Hungary and—let us face our geographical position on the musical map—in Britain. To tell the truth, a folky art-music, so often delightfully refreshing, is off the main lines, aesthetically as well as geographically. It has produced many picturesque and characteristic works without which music would be the poorer, but it has not been fruitful, as its most impassioned addicts had hoped. Those among them who became eminent did so in other directions, which is not to deny that folk music helped to advance them before it ceased to have any direct effect on them. Of the two foremost of them in England—foremost both in time and in stature—Holst achieved distinction and Vaughan Williams unquestionable greatness by music in which the folk element is least apparent; and the same is true of Bartók and Zoltan Kodály (1882-) in Hungary. Where, on the other hand, the folk idiom has remained prominent as with Manuel de Falla (1876-1946) or Bohuslav Martinů (1890-1959), it seems to indicate a minor stature and a lack of universality.

Vaughan Williams and Bartók made their impression on music above all by being among the great individuals of the art, as for instance El Greco and Turner are in painting. Such figures appear spasmodically all through artistic history. They are in a sense freaks, or at any rate 'sports', standing out in isolation rather than taking their place in the orderly procession of the majority of greater and smaller figures. They are as a rule not clearly seen to have been influenced by predecessors, and they are seldom followed by disciples, at any rate not pupils reflecting much of their characters or achieving great eminence. They can make an impression with limited technical equipments (Delius, Satie), or they may be technically as well as personally so unique as to be falsely accused of clumsy workmanship, as Berlioz still so often is and as Vaughan Williams was all his life, in spite of the fact that except for certain repetitive mannerisms such as after all few artists are without, his technique has always been adequate to his requirements and in his last years became brilliantly and inimitably expressive.

Where technical perfection was not only joined to uniqueness, but went steadily hand in hand with the development, consolidation and growing versatility of the composer's peculiar gifts, as in Claude Debussy (1862-1918) and Stravinsky, mastery has to be acknowledged by the judicious critic even where the composer's personality as a whole or certain works of his may not meet with his sympathy. He may voice disagreement, even dislike, but he will not be able to withhold a tribute of some sort. These two are by almost universal consent the figures who represent the nearest thing to a new start made by music at the approach of the twentieth century. But although pre-eminent, they are not alone in their class. I would myself place Janáček quite near them, and most of those I have mentioned for their singularity on page 12 not far away, though here personal taste begins to take a hand in one's judgment; nor do I claim to see equal importance in other figures for whom I nevertheless claim a place among the strikingly individual composers, such as Ildebrando Pizzetti (1880-), Frank Martin (1890-), Willem Pijper (1894-1947) and, in the new England, Alan Rawsthorne (1905-) and Michael Tippett (1903-). And I know people who will bitterly reproach me for not including Charles Ives (1874-

1954), Egon Wellesz (1885-), Ernst Křenek (1900-), Kurt Weill (1900-1950), Goffredo Petrassi (1904-) and I know not whom else. But I decline to take sides everywhere, and I must stop somewhere.

The innovations of Debussy and Stravinsky, utterly different, bore rich fruit, in their own work much more than in that of their successors. They had many imitators, but the all-over picture of twentieth-century music is surprisingly deficient in composers whom their example has fecundated, and I cannot think of a single great one who stepped into their shoes. The truth is that the epigoni of great composers tend to be embarrassed and made inarticulate by the very eminence of their models. And I cannot imagine Debussy ever wishing to teach anybody anything, nor does one seem to hear that anyone was ever a direct pupil of Stravinsky. Their new inventions were for themselves, not for a posterity in which, I imagine, they had little interest. Genius has a perfect right to be self-centred, as Wagner was, who never had a pupil and whose imitators are the more shadowy the more closely they tried to work like him. Useful influences often come from artists whose own gifts are relatively small. Ravel and Paul Hindemith (1895-) are exceptional among great twentieth-century figures who taught generatively, and only the latter has done so more than spasmodically.

Many innovators left no mark on their successors for a very different reason: their novelties were ephemeral. I am now faced with the paradox that although they were very much part of the picture I am asked to present, nearly all of them were too insignificant to be allowed to figure in it. They were not uncreative in one sense, for they often originated unprecedented things; but what they actually produced had neither stability nor influence. The most remarkable of them is Alexander Skriabin (1872-1915) who, rather like Strauss and Schoenberg, whose eminence he did not nearly reach, however, was forced to find a new way of expression because he must have realised that in his early pianoforte works he was merely continuing on the lines of Chopin and Liszt. He therefore invented a new harmonic system—nothing less. Not quite as new as people thought at the time, for there is more than a trace of it in the middle of Liszt's first *Mephisto Waltz* (from which I venture to guess that Stravinsky got it independently when he wrote some strains for his *Firebird* that sound exactly like Skriabin). Since nothing ever came out of nothing, Skriabin is not to be reproached with 'cribbing', but what was fatal to his art is that the system worked all too systematically, and that once one had become accustomed to his harmony, one found it applied so rigidly that he might almost as well have endlessly repeated the old subdominant-dominant-tonic formula. This is unfortunate, for Skriabin had immense talent.

Others have worked more fruitfully at twentieth-century music without being, or even wishing to be, striking innovators. Their work is rooted in some tradition or other and derived from certain influences. This is in itself no guarantee of vitality, and a great many composers who belong to the twentieth century only by the accident of birth are not entitled to being mentioned by name in a book which sets itself the task of tracing vital developments.

Much interest, however, is to be had from traditionalists who, on the basis of work dating from before their own generation, have contrived to establish and maintain a distinctive individuality. In this category I would place Francis Poulenc (1899-), Serge Prokofiev (1891-1953), Arthur Bliss (1891-), Arthur Honegger (1892-1955) and Darius Milhaud (1892-)—all of whom were most audacious and experimental at the beginning of their careers, but later settled down to more or less normal and expected conformity to set standards. But they were a set by themselves, and the varied characters that thus developed have helped to enrich the immensely diversified musical landscape of the first half of our century. A slightly later composer of this type is Dmitri Shostakovitch (1906-).

Personalities often equally distinctive who developed on solid traditions of the more or less distant past rather than by early adventure are found particularly in the English school. The great exemplar of a characteristically English conservatism tempered by an uncompromising personal independence is Elgar, it hardly needs saying. William Walton (1902-) is perhaps a border-line case, for he began more enterprisingly than he continued, but his continuation became increasingly impressive. Other English traditionalists who developed into striking personalities are Edmund Rubbra (1901-) and Wilfrid Mellers (1914-). Even Benjamin Britten (1913-), with all his great outpouring originality, is fundamentally rooted in England's musical past. He and Walton shine especially in European music of our time for having put English opera on the international map. This has been done, with considerably less precedent, for Switzerland by Heinrich Sutermeister (1910-), with greater assiduity than Walton's, but with less genuine musicality, while with Britten he can compare only in copiousness of output. German opera has never been off the map for the last century and a quarter at least, but it needed revivifying. This has been done by Křenek and Weill among others, and rather more recently, though he is five years older, by Carl Orff (1895-).

There are some purely national and racial traditions that have produced twentieth-century personalities who count in music. Ernest Bloch (1880-1959) has written eloquently for the Jewish race, and this influence has also been seen, though more intermittently and less strongly, in Milhaud. Then there are the Italian musical patriots, Gian Francesco Malipiero (1882-) and Alfredo Casella (1883-1947), intent on reviving the rich but long neglected non-operatic musical traditions of their country, with no resort to folk music, and apart from his impressive work for the stage Pizzetti also belongs to that group. Other representatives of it, sometimes more intent on Italian picturesqueness and on fundamental values, are Ottorino Respighi (1879-1936) and Mario Castelnuovo-Tedesco (1895-); but both are capable of greater profundity than the somewhat similar Joaquín Turina (1882-1949), whose pictures of Spain are attractive but superficial. The United States have produced several composers who have sought American traditions on which to base their work—folk rather than artistic traditions, naturally enough. Aaron Copland (1900-) is the most conspicuous among them.

To finish with, a brief return must be made to twelve-note composition, since, whether one likes it or not, it is the outstanding new departure in the music of our time to be taken seriously. Indeed, it looks almost like the only radical new procedure in all music since the discovery was made that more than one note heard at the same time could be something better than an accident; but Schoenberg's gradual and probably inevitable approach to it has shown that this is not so.

What is more, the most exclusive user of it, Anton Webern (1885-1945), has shown that as a watertight system it produces an exclusively aristocratic and ultra-refined art almost too tenuous and bloodless to live. We have seen by this time that such vitality as it has is fit to enrich the resources of composers who have not altogether renounced the past. This was indeed shown already by Alban Berg (1885-1935) at the completion of the first quarter of this century, when his *Wozzeck* was produced, an opera which makes use of twelve-note music wherever it suits the composer but is the more richly impressive for not doing so consistently. Others who have since used it partially in some works, or adapted it skilfully to their own individual expression are Frank Martin, Luigi Dallapiccola (1904-), Skalkottas (1904-1949), Matyas Seiber (1905-) and Humphrey Searle (1915-).[1]

The complaint is often heard that the workings of twelve-note music are not perceptible by the ear in performance, that they are therefore interesting only to the score-reader. The composer may reply, as T. S. Eliot, Christopher Fry or Ronald Duncan probably would to those who ask why they write plays in verse if they do not want them to sound like verse-drama, that they impose a kind of discipline on themselves, and for themselves alone, which stimulates their invention and fires their imagination. Serial music—for the 'system' has now developed beyond a necessarily strict employment of twelve-note patterns—may well do the same for composers of genius like Stravinsky, who has now set the seal of his mastery upon it.

But it must be a resource for the wilful use of great composers, not a tyrannical system as such. If it should remain that, it would unquestionably be doomed to self-destruction. This is one of the things that the first half of the twentieth century has taught us, and those living through the second half will do well to remember that what matters is not whether its music is to be diatonic or chromatic or serial, or even something else that may turn up at any time (though we had better draw the line at mechanically produced music), but simply that it should be great music. And the recent heritage left us is rich enough to let us look forward to the future with confidence.

[1]No composer born later than 1915 is mentioned in this essay, but many will doubtless appear in later chapters.

II

TWENTIETH-CENTURY COMPOSERS AND TRADITION

By Fred. Goldbeck

TRADITION, where music is concerned, has no need of a capital T. In the house of music it is neither an idol nor a guest of honour nor even a steward, because here it is at home. Modest and indispensable, musical tradition is the very substance of music. And not only of exotic music, which has no exact notation and depends on practice and oral traditions which remain unchanged for centuries, but of Western music, too, whose history during the last thousand years has shown continual change. For the substance of music is not, as is too often asserted or implied, sounds or notes. Sounds are not the substance of music, because they are only its vehicle, just as light waves are the vehicle of painting. And notes are no more music than telephone numbers are the persons to whom they are allotted. The substance, the matter of music, is tradition. What can a composer compose or a listener hear? Waltzes, symphonies, developments, cadences, continuous or broken melodies, modes, regular or asymmetrical rhythms, diatonic music with seven and chromatic with twelve intervals: nothing, in fact, but things which it would be impossible for the composer to handle or for the listener to grasp if the ear and the brain had not immediate recourse to all the traditions evoked by every page and even by the very words 'waltz' and 'symphony' or by any consonant or dissonant configuration. And not only 'evoked by', because these things are the actual matter and meaning of tradition. And this tranquil and inevitable presence of tradition is something peculiar to music: it is not necessary to know anything about the traditions of pictorial art in order to see clearly the pair of old shoes in the picture by van Gogh; but it is necessary to know, consciously or unconsciously, a great deal—I would even say *everything*—about musical traditions if we are to hear properly the chorale and the waltz, no less worn and damaged than van Gogh's shoes, in *The Soldier's Tale* and *Pierrot Lunaire*.

*   *   *

It is a curious fact that for some time after the appearance of a new work the elements of change it contains, implying a momentary and illusory disobedience to tradition, attract much more attention than those which imply respect for tradition. We can see today that the differences between a Strauss Tone-Poem, a Weber Overture and a Vivaldi Concerto Grosso are much less important than the features they have in common: all three are simple pieces of instrumental virtuosity of a predominantly melodic character. The differences which matter are differences in *quality*, and have nothing to do with the style of writing, but are due, for example, to the fact that Vivaldi was writing for a public accustomed to the architecture of the Piazzetta and the paintings of Carpaccio and Tintoretto, Weber for a public accustomed to reading fairy stories and being devoted to its rulers, and Strauss for a public accustomed to the architecture of the Taverne Pschorr and the paintings of Boecklin and Lenbach. But Strauss's contemporaries who attended first performances of his works only heard—with either delight or indignation—what we today scarcely notice at all, namely the few supplementary dissonances and the various surprises and refinements of writing in which Strauss differed from his immediate predecessors. And the young Strauss, we must not forget, was admired and abused as a radical innovator just as today Pierre Boulez is admired and abused.

*   *   *

Came the Viennese school and with it atonality and the twelve-note row. Schoenberg perceived that post-Wagnerian music—including what he himself had written in the Sextet for strings—was decidedly too derivative and of an inferior brand. And so he began his campaign, not as a reformer, but as a counter-reformer: I know of no figure he resembles so much as Ignace de Loyola. Schoenberg's only creed was the romantic creed; but he was determined to purge the faithful and enforce a far more strict observance of the tenets of the creed. Romanticism favoured an increase in tension and in the number of dissonances. Schoenberg went still further and suppressed all relaxation of tension and all consonance. Consequently he preserved in sonata-form only the development section where tension is at its height, the conflict of themes most acute, and the 'working-out' more thorough than anywhere else. The cadence, and the sonata which is derived therefrom, seem to have been done away with. In fact they are only suspended and maintained in a rarified form. There is nothing, I think, in Schoenberg's theory, or in his or Berg's or Webern's practice, to prevent one from considering a dodecaphonic construction to be a harmonic and contrapuntal construction in which the twelve notes are treated as so many 'leading' notes without, however, (on the principle that the expected is always replaced by the unexpected) ever being allowed to attain the resolution towards which they are naturally inclined by the force of tonal gravitation. Consequently, I think one may consider any piece of dodecaphonic music as being a 'phase of development' which, dismissing as useless and conventional the exposition which should come before it and the recapitulation which should come after, dispenses with both and consigns them to the limbo of the *sous-entendu*. As for the expressive content of this music, it too is romanticism in its most exacerbated form. In it we can sense not only tragedy and the fate of Ivan Karamazov, but the panic and anxiety-complexes of Kierkegaard, of Malte Laurids Brigge and of the hero, whose name I have forgotten, of Sartre's *Nausée*.

Here we have, then, without any doubt, a diabolically anti-traditional art and music. But, equally certainly an art and music which are opposed to tradition in the same way as Sacha Guitry was opposed to women. 'I am all against them', he said, 'you understand, all the time against them.' Similarly, atonality and dodecaphony are against tonality and the cadence. Right up against them; propping them up in fact. For if you take away the background of tradition and tonality, atonality loses both its support and its significance. There is much talk today of a new musical language, and even of a new musical era which is about to open beyond the bounds of tonality—the era of the 'emancipation' of dissonance now on a footing of equality with consonance. But it is not easy to see how not only listeners, but musicians and composers too, can suddenly, or even gradually, train their ears to forget that there is such a thing as tonal gravitation; that a major seventh expresses tension and an octave the reverse, and that a chord of an augmented fifth and a major seventh is a harsher discord than a diminished seventh. The terms consonance and dissonance can be treated in as many different ways as the terms angel and devil. We may prefer the company of devils to that of angels. We may ironically call devils angels and angels devils. We may remember that devils are fallen angels. We may even perversely declare that it is devilish to be an angel and angelic to be a devil. All that may be interesting. But if we try to establish that the terms devil and angel are synonymous, then we shall no longer be understood by either pro-devils or pro-angels or by anyone at all. But no atonal composer has ever thought of that; as is proved by the fact that they all continue to substitute dissonances for consonances and are never tempted to do the opposite. And so, in spite of appearances and currently held ideas, it is not through any change in the condition of dissonances that music in our time has changed. Such profound changes as there have been, although no one has noticed it, have been in the condition of composers.

For a very long time, and until the end of the nineteenth century, the music of everyday life with which musicians were mainly concerned (excluding, of course, the special domain of church music) was new and contemporary, with, perhaps, a sprinkling of music belonging to a very recent past. The music of Louis XIV and his contemporaries was the music of Lully and his contemporaries. For a professional musician like Frederick II the latest sonata of C. P. E. Bach was the music that mattered, and that of John Sebastian a curiosity that one would have to hurry to get to know before it became quite *démodé*. 'Contemporary music' was a sort of pleonasm a hundred years ago. It was what everybody played: Chopin, Meyerbeer, Verdi, Wagner, Rossini, Beethoven, Haydn and Mozart, too, were practically contemporary, for there were many in the audience who were old enough to have known Beethoven and Haydn, and perhaps a few old people who as children had seen the first performance of *The Magic Flute*. In conservative England Handel was not forgotten. And it is true that on the Continent people were timidly beginning to take an interest in Bach. But that was the first preliminary sign of a change.

It follows, then, that the composer in those days was a person who belonged essentially to the present. He did not, like Horace or Stendhal, evoke a far-distant future, and he was not interested in the music of the past. If he were a Gluck he hoped that in composing an *Orpheus* he would do better than his contemporaries, and replace the old-fashioned *Orpheus* of a preceding generation. He had nothing to fear from competition with Monteverdi, of whom very probably he had never heard.

That the situation today is very different is obvious. I would not even mention it were it not for a fact that never ceases to amaze me, and that is that no one has ever taken the trouble to notice that it is here that the key to the 'modern' outlook is to be found. It is here (and not in any isolated phenomena such as dissonant, serial, electronic or any other systems) that we must look for the kind of Copernican change that has affected music. *Before*, music gravitated round the square we call the present and the avenues leading directly therefrom. *Today*, music of the present gravitates round the whole history and tradition of music. To prove this gravitation it is not even necessary for a programme to include works separated by three or four centuries. Beethoven and Haydn will be present at the first performance of any new symphony. No musician can write or hear a fugue, a waltz, an *Orpheus*, a *Marteau sans Maître*, a passage for the violin or a piece for four trombones without thinking of Bach, Johann Strauss or Schubert, Monteverdi, the music of Bali, Paganini and Gabrieli.

Now it so happens that this change, this *volte-face* of music in the direction of tradition coincided with the entry into musical history of a musician who by reason of his originality and the freshness of his imagination could have dispensed more easily than all the others with tradition. And yet it was Debussy who, in his writings and in his music, brought us back to Rameau, to the polyphonic masters of the Renaissance, to modal music and to all the most forgotten traditions, real or poetic, of monody: sirens, the syrinx and Egyptian shepherds. It was

Debussy who broke away from the anti-traditionalist tradition of sonata-form and in doing so emancipated, not dissonance (that had already been done by Beethoven, Haydn, Rameau, Bach, Monteverdi and Gesualdo) but consonance, which needed it far more. For in the hands of the Romantics it had become a momentary interlude, precariously placed, and boding no good, between two strenuous phases of dynamic development. Debussy restored it to its proper status, using it ironically as a 'modernistic archaism', and made it the basis of his static style, proceeding not by development, but by juxtaposition. And this is how irony, archaisms, nostalgia, the strange and the fantastic, allusions and quotations (hitherto only used episodically as a nuance or picturesque touch) became the essential ingredients of a method of composition. Counterpoint becomes a stylised polyphony. Scottish jigs, children's songs, the Marseillaise, Luther's Chorale are woven into polyphonic structures whose novelty and apparent incongruity create an impression of shock and surprise less likely to be weakened by familiarity and abuse than the dissonances, with nothing to contradict them, of the die-hard 'serialists' in the romantic tradition. And when a young musician asks me to show him a model of modern composition, I advise him to study Debussy's *Sonata for Violoncello and Piano* and try to discover how, in this dialogue with every kind of music, the comings and goings between the music of Monteverdi and Mussorgsky, street music, the music of Italian comedy and the music of ghosts have combined to make the music of Debussy.

Not that these new perspectives and this fantastically enlarged horizon were suddenly opened up by Debussy. There are plenty of signs and portents foreshadowing them to be found in the music of the nineteenth century. But we must look for them among all that nineteenth-century music which has been either misunderstood, unknown or had led nowhere. In Berlioz, for example, who, because of his baroque polyphony —a polyphony of planes and styles already—has been dubbed a poor harmonist; in the non-pianistic works of Liszt, mostly unknown; in the finale of the Ninth Symphony, always a target for criticism; in the *Diabelli Variations* which Bülow described as 'a *résumé* of the whole history of music' but which have rarely inspired 'Beethoven's successors'; and finally in the ironic 'banality' of Mahler's songs and lighter pieces which unfortunately was stifled all too soon in the straitjacket of symphonic form.

The case of Busoni, who was Debussy's contemporary but in no way influenced by him, is particularly interesting. In his theoretical writings (which are often quoted) he anticipated electronic music (the dynamophone of Dr Cahill) and hyperchromatic research into thirds, quarters and sixths of a tone; but in his compositions (which are rarely played) he preferred to anticipate the dialogue with tradition; thus, in 1915 his *Arlecchino* foreshadowed the style of *The Rake's Progress*. Wherefore this *Arlecchino* was criticised by the *avant-garde* aestheticians for exactly the same reasons as Stravinsky's opera was criticised. For the *avant-garde* aestheticians often hold extremely conservative views as to what constitutes '*avant-gardisme*'.

After Debussy, with disquieting regularity, the really new music continued to be that which had been either misunderstood, unknown or had led nowhere. Among the music of this description I would cite the last works of Fauré, Janáček and Vaughan Williams. As for living composers, I should be quite prepared to revise this view as being too pessimistic if I could be assured that in the near future the *Canticum Sacrum* or *Agon* will occupy in musical life a position comparable with that at present occupied by *Petrushka* or *The Firebird*. Or if I could be certain that soon the philosophers of modern music will no longer be horrified if anyone should assert that certain baroque musicians of today—a Britten, for example, who, like Stravinsky, follows all the traditions—are at least as up-to-date and no less interesting than those latter-day romantics who worship no other god but Webern, although it is by no means certain that they are any more likely to surpass Webern than the Funeral March in *Siegfried* can be said to have surpassed the Funeral March in the *Eroica*.

Those features in the musical life of the twentieth century that have been fashionable and have supplied the chapter headings to studies on twentieth-century music have always been the crudest simplifications. For example: the School of the 'twenties, neo-classicism and the return to Bach which, recognising the necessity of a dialogue with tradition, reduced the dialogue to the level of a pastiche and tradition to a matter of scales and arpeggios which were fondly imagined to be the material out of which the Brandenburg Concertos were made. Then there were the various schools of 'artisan-composers'—an exaggerated simplification of a reasonable idea which the romantics inflated by turning the composer into a visionary, and which is still an exaggerated simplification, even if the composer's stock-in-trade is complicated to the point of becoming a laboratory full of magneto-phones and the differential calculus applied to passages on the border-line of continuity and discontinuity.

But we must admit that these simplifications are terribly tempting; they facilitate the composer's task, which is becoming more and more difficult. For the traditions which, as I said at the beginning, are the very substance of music, have taken to flight, while still remaining indis-pensable. And the formula by which they can be subdued—a formula composed of intelligence, magic and luck—has to be re-fashioned by the composer in every work, and almost in every bar.

[*Translated from the French by the Editor*]

POSTSCRIPT 1968: TRADITION versus REVOLUTION BEHIND THE IRON CURTAIN

REVOLUTION IN music rarely, if ever, coincides with revolution in politics. Except the *Marseillaise*, that very beautiful, very strange and (Constant Lambert *dixit*) very clumsy composition written by an amateur composer, the French Revolution produced nothing but the most unadventurous music: Grétry, Méhul, Lesueur. Nothing revolu-tionary about Verdi's traditional *bel canto* which fired the Italian revolutionaries of the *risorgimento*. Beethoven's last quartets, on the contrary, were written in Metternich's Vienna; Mussorgsky was one of the Tsar's loyal civil servants; the events of February 1848 were distasteful to Berlioz; Debussy quarrelled with Grieg because of the latter's pro-Dreyfus declarations; and Schoenberg's *Pierrot Lunaire* was first performed in Berlin during the reign of Wilhelm II who strongly disapproved even of Richard Strauss. And today the musical situation in Soviet Russia is a remarkable illustration of this antinomy. Stravinsky did not revisit his country before 1964; Arthur Lourié left before 1920, never to return. Prokofiev went back—and at once ceased to be even the permissive rebel he had been in his youth.

In fact, this antinomy is no paradox. All men are 'political beings', and some are musical beings; and the politically minded as well as the musically minded divide into conformists and revolutionaries—but in very different ways. The plutocrat's concert-going wife who adores the B flat minor Piano Concerto, and the plutocrat's concierge (perhaps a member of the Communist party) who vastly enjoys the same concerto played over the wireless by the latest Tchaikovsky prize winner, share the same conservative and democratic musical taste. The plutocrat's son and the concierge's daughter, who may or may not be of their parent's political convictions but prefer to hear Bartók's 2nd piano-and-violin Sonata, are both members of a revolutionary, and aristocratic, minority of music lovers.

And among the leaders the same dissimilarities are not less striking than among the followers. Successful revolutionary composers in general stick to their revolutionary methods. Beethoven's, de Falla's, Stravinsky's later works are even considerably more law-breaking than their first. Whereas successful political revolutionaries almost infallibly turn anti-individualist and disciplinarian. In consequence the same music, which is kept outside the programmes by the capitalist impresarios because of its unpopular revolutionary boldness, is banned by the Soviet commissars for being 'deviationist', decadent and petty bourgeois. And to justify his musical backwardness the commissar has the advantage over the impresario: in as much as the pretermusical connotations of Romantic and post-Romantic music are on his—the commissar's—side: Symphony, from Beethoven to Mahler, being fraught with the symbols of democratic, 'progressist' ideology. 'C'est l'Empereur,' cried the famous Grenadier, swept off his feet by the finale of Beethoven's Fifth—a C major triumph, musically no more revolutionary than any of Handel's set pieces. And Strauss declared that Mahler's Third sounded 'like a pageant of Sozial-Demokraten on the first of May.' No wonder if the commissar requests his composers to prolong this tradition, and grants his blessing to the stalest 'C'est

Staline' and '*C'est Suvorov*' clichés rampant in Shostakovitch's symphonies and Prokofiev's *War and Peace*.

*   *   *

Yet—such is today the vitality of modernism in music, and so irresistible for the young the powers of seduction of a Webern, a Boulez or a Xennakis, that even the strongest ideological barriers have proved powerless to prevent dodecaphonic, structuralist, electronic and other heretical methods from breaking through the iron curtain.

Except Bulgaria, I have not yet visited any popular democracy. But I have for years, during the last week of May, attended the *Rostrum of Composers* in Paris—an encounter where the representatives of about two dozen broadcasting systems, from Rio to Tokyo, present 40 minutes each of contemporary music written and performed in their respective countries. And no doubt whatever: music in Bulgaria, in Hungary, in Romania, in Czechoslovakia—music accepted or even commissioned by official Radios—appears, with increasing radicalism, dressed after the long-forbidden Boulezian fashion. Moscow remains intractable—but stands ludicrously alone in sending technically excellent sonatas that sound like Lekeu or Arnold Bax, and patriotic cantatas of the same feather.

But Budapest has presented one of the best and boldest Violin Concertos written since Bartók's (by Durkó); Constantin Iliev, the Bulgarian conductor, writes string quartets and orchestral works in the latter-day I.S.C.M. style at its best; and in Poland the success of Lutoslavski, Penderecki, Baird is not confined to their native land: they are, and fully deserve to be, on the international list of the best living composers.

They differ widely in style and temperament: Lutoslavski's aesthetic stems from Bartók; Penderecki's ingenuity and originality is never at a loss in handling all sorts of media, from distorted orchestral sound at its most sophisticated to innocent *a cappella* voices; romantic elements are integrated in Baird's structural devices. But in spite of these differences their music speaks the same language. And this common language is not a Polish vernacular, not a Slav dialect, but the modern, structuralist etc. *lingua franca* respectfully used in Stockholm

as well as in Valparaiso by all the well-disciplined musical revolutionaries of our day.

And it is perhaps for such discipline, for the impersonal, anti-individualist side of their common idiom, that modern composers are
acceptable and accepted east of the iron curtain. And who would not
encourage them to make the best of both worlds—placate the commissars—and reassure *us*—by officially stressing their uniformity
without ceasing to cultivate, *inter se*, their essential differences?

F.G.

III

SERIALISM AND
DEVELOPMENTS IN WESTERN MUSIC SINCE WEBERN

By André Hodeir

AFTER THE last shot had been fired in the war of 1939-1945 and it became possible once more, summoning up what remained of one's *confiance* in mankind, to consider the position of the arts, it seemed as if contemporary music had been struck down by a cataclysm no less destructive than the war. Of all that had been achieved by musicians of the between-wars period, quantitatively enormous, hardly anything remained; we had inherited no undisputed masterpiece to guide us along a road we could no longer see the end of, or even be sure that it was leading anywhere at all.

Official teaching had become a vast machine for smothering talents under which only the strongest were able to survive. Academic tradition could only result in a sterile neo-classicism. In those countries where the springs of the new music, though still hesitant, were running most strongly they had been brutally driven underground in the name of national traditions. It only remained for the dark shadows of war to plunge everything into obscurity.

What, then, could a young musician who had grown up under physical and intellectual privations expect from a world where one was beginning to discover again works by famous composers which had survived the auto-da-fé and where certain names, which could at last be freely uttered, sounded strangely to ears which great care had been taken to preserve from any subversive emotions? Hopes were high, but the disillusionment was even greater. People felt obscurely that in their pursuit of a music that would be authentically modern the great composers of our time had merely been precursors; that they had made mistakes which would have to be wiped out, and that the 'purest' of them all, Anton Webern, who was also the least known, had spent his life in quest of a limpidity which he occasionally attained, but for the sake of which he had to renounce any kind of grandeur and any escape beyond the bounds of reason.

These ruins, however, were covered with signposts pointing, for those who were able to read them, towards a possible future. As no one thought that any fruit could be on the way, how could we have suspected that it was already nearly ripe? And yet certain ill-fated attempts made between the two wars contained the germs of future successes. Not only the work of the three Viennese, but those of Stravinsky, Bartók, Messiaen, and even Varèse and Cage were glowing with an inner flame that a sharper eye than theirs would soon discover.

This historical situation called for an exceptional musical intelligence which appeared in the person of Pierre Boulez. The son of an industrialist from Montbrison, Boulez (1925-), when he was about nineteen, turned from mathematics to music. In 1945, after a few months at the Conservatoire, he obtained a First Prize for harmony in the class of Olivier Messiaen with whom he also studied rhythmics and musical analysis, while he worked at counterpoint under Mme Vaurabourg Honegger. About the same time a Polish pedagogue, René Leibowitz, was explaining serial dodecaphony to young French composers. The revelation of the works of Schoenberg, Berg and Webern had a profound influence on the musical destiny of Boulez.

An extremely precocious artist, Boulez started in 1947 to transform completely the serial universe. His great merit was to have been the first to see that Arnold Schoenberg's thematic conception was in contradiction with his own invention, and in so doing, thereby inverting the established hierarchy according to which Webern appeared as only the third person in the 'Viennese Trinity', he struck a mortal blow at the orthodox Schoenbergian doctrine as taught by Leibowitz. Webern's works, like those of Schoenberg in the 'twenties, were perhaps not so much the fruit of a creative frenzy as a signpost, but they were more significant.

The a-thematic serialism glimpsed by Webern and fully realised in the earliest works of Boulez is not only seen to be a definite step forward but seems, in our opinion, to represent in itself the most radical rupture with the past since Schoenberg suspended the tonal system round about 1910. However, Boulez in his writings has always been at pains to link his own conceptions with the past, and he appears in the role of theoretician and historian when he singles out in the works of his great predecessors the facts, discoveries and tendencies which seem to him to point the way to the music of the future. 'What was there for us to do', he wrote later, 'except to gather up the bundle of new means of expression which the work of our elders had made available to us?'

The genius of Boulez found its fullest expression in the organisation, in a coherent and flexible language, of the various discoveries inherited from the past—Schoenberg's twelve-note series, Stravinsky's a-symmetrical rhythms, Webern's feeling for *timbres* and geometrical sound-spacing—and made subservient to that kind of 'musical poetics' of which Debussy had undoubtedly been the initiator. Thus there came into being, solidly .based on an extended serial system which was gradually to include the various musical parameters—pitch, duration, timbre, intensity, attack, *tempi*—a new dialectical conception of music which Boulez himself has defined as *la folie de l'Irrationnel*.

After the Second Piano Sonata (1947-48) which in its impetuosity and liveliness is still, in our opinion, one of his finest works, Boulez began his occupation of a region purged of any human feeling, sometimes using a free, almost improvisatory style, and sometimes writing in the strictest form. Round about his twenty-fifth year Boulez entered upon a period of intense creative activity. He was not content merely to pour his lyrical content into those new moulds in which, thanks to an extremely subtle system of variations, the a-thematic principle finally blossoms into a fully fledged 'form'. His adventurous pioneering temperament drove him to experiment in various different directions. Like those of Schoenberg, the works of Boulez are packed with indications and ideas which are not always completely realised. In *Le soleil des eaux* for voice and orchestra (1948) he was clearly seeking a 'super-expressive' vocal style which he was to attempt later in *Le*

Marteau sans Maître. In *Le Visage Nuptial* (Boulez is a great admirer of the poet René Char) for soloists, chorus and orchestra (1947-1950), he explores the domain of the quarter-tone. Quite recently, in *Doubles* (1957-1958), he has introduced a new spatial structure of the symphony orchestra resulting in an effective form of stereophony, which would seem to be a more ingenious solution of the problem than that proposed by Stockhausen which involves the use of a triple orchestra conducted by three different conductors. This conception is the logical result, on the symphonic plane, of the work undertaken by Boulez (who was the first twelve-note composer to take an interest in 'music for tape') in 1951-52 at the Concrete Music Research Centre—as an example of which may be cited two brief *Etudes*.

Le Marteau sans Maître (1953-54) is today the best known, if not the most successful of Pierre Boulez' works. It has affiliations, although the instrumental lay-out is rather different, with *Pierrot Lunaire*; indeed, both in style and general conception the influence of the latter is clearly discernible (is there not a passage in *Le Marteau* which recalls the famous voice and flute duet in *Pierrot*?) while the instrumentation, just as in Schoenberg's masterpiece, varies from one piece to another— an idea which Boulez had already adopted in *Le Visage Nuptial*. However, what in *Pierrot* was merely accompaniment (bound up, it is true, with the structure), here becomes a commentary; several sections in *Le Marteau* are purely instrumental.

The preponderant use of percussion instruments, either without pitch or chromatic (e.g. vibraphone, xylorimba), the acidity of plucked strings (guitar and pizzicati on the viola) contrasting with the flexibility of the voice and flute, and the general medium-low *tessitura* of all this instrumental apparatus combine to create a sound-colour recalling that of the Far East. Is this merely a coincidence? Was Boulez seeking, like Stravinsky and Messiaen, an exotic effect? Did he mean to go further and be the first to bring about the fusion of two traditions which some discerning minds consider to be the necessary and ultimate destination of our culture and of the culture of the whole world? If such was his intention (and we know him to be sufficiently ambitious to have conceived such a project) we are obliged to admit that *Le Marteau* falls short of an ideal which, in any case, we doubt will ever be attained by any creative artist in the twentieth century. Nevertheless, thanks to the sheer seduction of its sound, this work has helped to destroy the legend of 'hermeticism' which had grown up round the composer of *Structures* and *Polyphonie*.

After the *Marteau sans Maître* the celebrity of Boulez began rapidly to increase, making him a kind of social phenomenon which some journalists have compared to Bernard Buffet and Françoise Sagan. Until then his name had been better known than his music, which was relatively seldom performed; it was surrounded with an atmosphere of scandal, encouraged by the sometimes excessive violence of his polemical articles and the memory of one or two 'incidents' such as that, for example, which occurred in 1952 at the first performance of *Structures* at the 'Twentieth Century' Congress in Paris. The brilliant but deliberately aggressive spirit of the founder of *Le Domaine Musical*, his swift and penetrating eloquence and the vivacity of his reactions have perhaps contributed more to his reputation than his qualities as a musician. And yet his adversaries admit that this all-round genius, as much at his ease on the conductor's rostrum as at the keyboard of a Steinway concert grand, has a rare knowledge of music and an extraordinary mastery of his art. Consequently his reputation as a supertechnician in composition did not depend on the success of *Le Marteau* for its consecration in advanced musical circles in various countries, where his innovations were already appreciated. Although Boulez had not had much influence on the twelve-note composers of the between-war period (Křenek, Martin, Souris, Dallapiccola), or even on some of the younger men such as the German Hans Werner Henze, all of whom are more or less faithful to Schoenberg, on the other hand the impact of his conceptions was too strong not to make an impression on some of the most gifted composers of his generation. In France, Michel Philippot, Michel Fano, Maurice Le Roux; in Italy, Bruno Maderna, Luigi Nono, Luigi Berio; in Belgium, Henri Pousseur; in Sweden Bo Nilsson—all these have been affected by the aesthetic and teaching of Boulez. With many of them this influence has unhappily remained purely external and subservient, in some ways, to that of the Webern of the *Symphony*, op. 21, and the *Cantata*, op. 31, which has led some young musicians, for example Nono and Pousseur, into a kind of sub-jacent academicism from which one hopes they will one day free themselves.

The combined influence of Boulez and Webern has had a far happier effect on the German composer Karlheinz Stockhausen (born at Altenburg, near Cologne, in 1928) who, after studying with Frank Martin and Olivier Messiaen, came to Paris to be initiated into the mysteries of *musique concrète*. Stockhausen, whose *Kontrapunckte* (1953) for chamber orchestra showed great promise, was one of those whose head was turned by the complexities of the language. Following Messiaen's example, Boulez had hit upon an 'irrational' rhythmic language whose limits could not yet be ascertained. It was therefore tempting to go one better. On more than one occasion Stockhausen has been led to write down combinations of rhythmic values of seductive appearance but which no human brain could grasp as a concrete reality and which no human hand could play in the time indicated by the composer.[1]

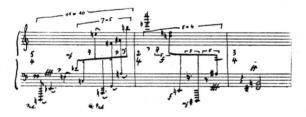

This ultra-complexity inevitably led the young German musician to turn his attention to non-instrumental music, the possibilities of which are theoretically unlimited. More fortunate in this sphere than his French colleagues, Stockhausen was put in charge, together with Herbert Eimert, through the Westdeutscher Rundfunk, of a studio specially equipped for research into electronic music. Here he has made some important experiments, e.g. *Gesang der Jünglinge* (1956). While one can agree as to the praiseworthiness of these experiments, one hesitates to express an opinion as to their purely aesthetic value.

Electronic techniques have not caused Stockhausen to abandon altogether-traditional music. Alarmed, perhaps, at the perspective of

[1]Such an irrational combination of values could only be rendered very approximately in actual performance.

an art confined within a rigorous determinism, the Rhenish composer seems to have been haunted, at a certain moment, by the desire to open a window on to a more 'human' world. To re-introduce spontaneity into this too perfect order was no longer possible on a level of improvisation, as might have been suggested by the Far East; only chance could switch his output on to lines the outcome of which was unpredictable.

The idea of interchangeable elements inaugurated by Stockhausen in the *No. 4 Klavierstuck XI pour piano* (1957) was the musical equivalent of Calder's 'mobile' plastic forms. The work is seen as a juxtaposition of musical fragments; the order in which they are heard is left to the discretion of the performer. The latter is authorised to alter as he pleases, subject to a certain logic in the sequences of *tempo* and dynamic intensities, the order of the elements *suggested* by the composer. Thus the work can be destroyed and built up again continually, each time appearing in a new disguise. This confers upon the executant an active part in the creation of the work such as he had not had since having to deal with the 'ornamentation' of the sixteenth and seventeenth centuries. When David Tudor played this piece for the first time in New York, he gave two performances in which, although the component parts remained the same, the outward aspect of the work was so changed that even its duration was affected.

Is this conception, limited for the moment to solo works, but which could be extended to large-scale compositions, likely really to lead to fruitful results? Boulez seems to think so, and has adopted the idea, with some slight modifications, in his *Third Sonata*.

The Stockhausen of *Zeitmasse* (quintet for wind instruments) and the *Gesang* gives one the impression of a young musician whose creative personality will develop fully during the years to come. Very different is the case of the Frenchman Jean Barraqué, born in 1928, one of the rare composers of whom it can be said that they have had no 'musical adolescence' (or at any rate have not allowed any sign of this to be revealed to the public). A pupil, like Boulez, of Olivier Messiaen, Barraqué has been influenced by no one except perhaps by Beethoven and Debussy (the Beethoven of the late quartets and the Debussy of *La Mer* and *Jeux*) two masters to whom he has devoted some admirable analytic studies, unfortunately still unpublished. Although the two first works of Barraqué—*Séquence* (1950; revised and orchestrated in 1955) and the *Piano Sonata* (1950-52)—were conceived by a composer under twenty-five, to describe them as 'youthful' or 'immature' would be singularly inappropriate. The first, apart from certain risks taken in the purely instrumental writing where the critics have remarked on certain imperfections, has the weight and density of a fully mature work, while the second might well be the last testament of a master who has reached the end of his career; we believe that it will provide commentators in the centuries to come with ample grounds for wonder and astonishment.

These two scores are, in our opinion, the most significant of all post-Webernian music—and this despite the fact that Barraqué, who knows all about Webern, is the least Webernian of all living masters of the serial language. Controversy will rage for a long time round the strange personality of this musician whom we would not hesitate to describe as the most important figure in European music since Debussy. Is he, as he sometimes asserts, a musician who belongs to the past? It is possible—in the same way that Stockhausen's conception of chance, for example, is a typical *avant-garde* solution. But the reason why Jean Barraqué rejects what perhaps he looks on as expedients is because he has gone further than anyone else in the re-creation, though the writing is strictly disciplined, of an improvisatory style of which *Séquence* is the embodiment and which constitutes the major acquisition to date of twentieth-century music.

To achieve the most delirious kind of freedom by the most rigorous control of his pen, to find the most perfect contemporary means of expressing madness without having recourse to neologisms—such is the creative paradox presented to us by this great disciple of Beethoven. (Was the author of the Ninth himself the inventor of a new vocabulary?) Barraqué makes free use of the discoveries of his predecessors. His means of expression are almost always traditional (although he spent months doing research for 'music for tape' which resulted in a strange and captivating *Etude*). In his orchestration he uses everyday instruments, only writes for the brass in groups, shows a predilection for the piano and the voice, accepts the vibraphone but not

Ondes Martenot, and finds a place for all sorts of percussion instruments as used in exotic variety orchestras (the battery in *Séquence* comprises no less than eighteen different kinds). As a serial musician he observes the laws which govern the universe of sound as formulated by the preceding masters of the twelve-note technique, especially the rule which forbids octaves, he uses the serial *grilles d'enchaînement* which Boulez invented (or at least adapted from certain mathematical principles). As regards form, Barraqué, like Debussy, does not admit the pre-existence of any form outside the work itself, which must invent its own form and decide bar by bar how it is going to develop. Boulez made the same choice, and did not shrink from applying to his own music the Sartrian aphorism: 'existence precedes essence'.

It would be difficult to imagine two more contrasting types of artist than Barraqué and Boulez. The latter is an innovator, a discoverer of a new language, a dialectician endowed with an imaginative intelligence constantly on the alert, while the former is an assimilator, a polymorphous genius whose works can be described, to borrow an apt expression of the Austrian writer Hermann Broch, as 'a lyrical commentary on himself'. But let there be no mistake: the personality of Jean Barraqué, powerful though it is on the poetic plane, finds its expression through purely musical means. *Séquence* marks the advent in the history of music of a functional orchestra where each *timbre*, deprived of its individuality, exists only in terms of a liaison, sometimes simultaneous with, but *sometimes following after* the whole ensemble of all the other *timbres* used in the same structure. It is a vast, *unique* instrument with possibilities of sound transformation which, when exploited to the full, result in a perpetual explosion within an absolute unity. The *Sonata*, a most unusual, even terrifying piece, hastens towards its fulfilment, which can only be nothingness—the negation of everything—through a series of 'forgotten' developments, and tacitly implied phases which result in the most monstrous musical ellipses. The progressive apparition of silence plays in all this an inexplicable part which would appear, however, to be of a structural no less than expressive character. (It would be more accurate to say that its expressive potential derives from its structural rigidity, for we are here in the presence of one of those works which, in the same way as the *Art of*

Fugue or the late Beethoven quartets, can only be described as 'pure music'.)

These two works which are structurally connected—both have elements in common, and for that reason ought to bear the same opus number—and which, moreover, belong to the same period since the *Sonata* was begun only a few days after the first version of *Séquence* was completed,—these two pages, each destined to be famous in a different way, are like the two opposite faces of a single heavenly body. One of them, *Séquence*, a sort of 'Concert' for soloists in which the human voice takes its place among the instruments—violin, 'cello, harp, celesta, glockenspiel, xylophone, vibraphone and battery —is a radiant work exhibiting in turn brilliance and seduction, mystery and a Dyonysian lyricism; it might well bear the title of one of Nietzsche's poems that Barraqué has included in the work—*Musique du Midi*. (The other poems used in *Séquence* are: *Trois Fragments*, *De la Pitié*, *Plainte d'Ariane*.) The other work, the *Sonata*, is also Dyonysian, but in quite a different sense. Here the lyrical impulse is severely under control, held back, as it were, under enormous pressure; and if it sometimes explodes in a dazzling rocket display it soon shrinks back again, thus creating a degree of tension unparalleled in music with the sole exception of the *Grosse Fuge*, op. 133, to which, and to nothing else, the *Sonata* owes its origin and of which it seems to be the sole descendant. There is no doubt that this music of the shadows is most difficult to listen to, and its full significance will only be revealed to future generations; for the moment one can only dimly sense its greatness.

In spite of their differences, which it would be idle to deny, there is sufficient similarity between the points of view of Boulez, Stockhausen and Barraqué to provide convincing proof that the myth of a 'national school', encouraged by the wave of nationalism that swept over Europe in the last century, is now discredited. Today Western music is more homogeneous and more unified than it was in the time of Mozart. In the works of a Barraqué or a Boulez the strict Germanic sense of order finds itself at last combined with the Latin's sensuous delight in sound. Thanks to this alliance, the serial dialectic seems to have found that it can also have a sensuous appeal. Better still: the fusion between the architectural concept and the satisfaction of the ear is now complete; each draws its substance from the other. And so, by a curious irony of fate, it is precisely at a time when people no longer speak of the 'supremacy' (entirely invented by the critics) of an alleged French school that an international movement of incomparable strength has come into being, of which the two outstanding personalities happen to be French.

DISCOGRAPHY

JEAN BARRAQUÉ
    Séquence and *Piano Sonata*   Véga C.30.A.80
    Etude (music for tape)   Barclay 89.005
PIERRE BOULEZ
    Le Marteau sans Maître   Véga C.35.A.67
    Etude II (music for tape)   Barclay 89.005
KARLHEINZ STOCKHAUSEN
    Kontrapunkte   Véga C.30.A.66
HANS-WERNER HENZE
    Concerto per il Marigny   Véga C.30.A.65
LUIGI NONO
    Incontri   Véga C.30.A.66

[*Translated from the French by the Editor*]

IV

SERIAL STRAVINSKY:
THE 'GRANITE' PERIOD (1956–1966)

by Malcolm Troup

> Potter nor iron-founder
> Nor caster of bronze will he cherish
> But the monumental mason;
> As if his higher stake
> Than the impregnable spiders
> Of self-defended music
> Procured him mandibles
> To chisel honey from the saxifrage
> A mouth to graze on felspar.
>
> (Donald Davie: *The Sculpture of Rhyme*)

> In the beginning the world was covered with water,
> The great Creator-god then dwelt inside a Rock.
>
> (A. H. Krappe: *La genèse des mythes*)

IN THE decade dividing *Canticum Sacrum* from the *Introitus*, Stravinsky has focused attention in terms of the artistic standards and modes of expression of the present age on the age-old struggle between the fluidity and dissolubility of forms: the wave-like, as perceived by primitive man, and those static aspects of form and geometric determining of shape, the molecular, characteristic of advancing civilisation. Water, as an amniotic liquid, the symbol of birth, and as chrism, the symbol of rebirth, has always been associated with the forces of the Unconscious. In the form of Barcarolles when not in direct tonal representation of millstreams, cascades and oceans, it has long haunted the reveries of composers who, as Schlegel teaches us, to be creative must be half in love with the forces of destruction, the everlasting

45

underworld twins of Night and Flood. The most modern spokesman
of this elemental fascination, according to Bachelard, has been Debussy
—if we don't count stray specimens such as the underwater Dada-play
in John Cage's *Water Music*. But rising squarely from the central
waters of this Flood we behold the equally symbolic and much more
substantial element of Rock, which from earliest Hittite times has
supported the fabric of the Temple, Man's rule of Law founded on
Divine Order. Now if Debussy may be likened to Water, who but
Stravinsky could be likened to the Rock, this material whose sounding
together was perhaps the first music of primitive man and whose
substance has likewise ever epitomised for him identity and perma-
nency—Stravinsky, whose granite-hewn utterances have been undergoing a continuing process of petrification in our time just as his
admirable constitution strengthens and hardens imperceptibly into
the mortal rigour, the final strongman-stance, of Death.

Venice, that shimmering truce delicately poised between Stone and
Water, represents better than anything else the nature of Stravinsky's
precarious achievement, and indeed that of our whole Renaissance-
inspired reason-worshipping civilisation, which has emerged rock-
like from the anonymous waters of the Collective Unconscious.
Stravinsky remains the last great exponent of the lineal approach
which has dominated our way of thinking since the invention of
print. Contained in this approach are automatically built-in beliefs in
human powers of understanding and ratiocination and in the God of
History. A late Stravinsky score may move forward or backward in
time but move it must, from one musical event to the next in an orderly
progression, like the numbers in the bull's-eye of the bathroom
weighing-scales, to be appraised individually and added together
cumulatively in a manner bespeaking that whole classical tradition of
musical structure which is only now being superseded. With him, we
are taking leave of a whole era which runs from the Renaissance down
to our own times, an era all the shifting styles of which it is no
coincidence that he has made so completely his own. We do not only
need to be moonstruck with the coming of the new Aquarian age to heed
the warning of Ruskin and apply it to the Man as to the City: 'I would
endeavour to trace the lines of this image before it be forever lost,

the warning which seems to me to be uttered by every one of the fast-gaining waves that beat, like passing bells, against the Stones of Venice.' Too true it is that Venice, that great patchwork of Byzantine, Latin and Oriental styles, that queenly mosaic of priceless oddments pilfered from a variety of sources, is sinking ineluctably beneath the Adriatic— in the same way that Stravinsky, groaning in a bass clef, under the accumulated weight of Russian cultic, Latin classical and Semitic cabalistical styles, equally embellished with stylistic grafts and encrustations, is slipping down under the new wave, the 'acqua alta' of such apostles of musical 'decontrol' as Stockhausen, John Cage, Morton Feldman and our own Cornelius Cardew. Hence the conjunction of man with his milieu was particularly propitious that thirteenth day of September 1956, when Stravinsky conducted in its first performance, exactly five years after the presentation of *Rake's Progress* in the Fenice theatre, the *Canticum Sacrum ad honorem Sancti Marci Domini*, dedicated to the City of Venice and its Patron Saint, which had been finished in 1955.

The *Canticum* is modelled on a man-made rock, the very temple itself, which in this case is the venerable five-domed pile of San Marco, to which the five main sections of the work correspond. We are reminded of ancient Gothic days when 'spiritualization and abstraction of tone or stone under the sign of abstract number were expressive of the same ideal order of things.' Even more fitting in this spiritual kinship is the conception of San Marco on the part of the original builders as a vast triumphal arch with five openings. This fivefold symmetry is even carried over into the hub of the central movement, the 'Spes' of the 'Ad tres virtutes', in its grouping of psalmodic quotations, where it serves in typical Boulez-fashion as a microcosm of the whole. The fifth movement reveals itself finally as the first movement in reverse, thus symbolising the accomplishment of Christ's behest at the opening of the work 'Go ye and teach all nations.' This chronic rule of Five, already present in the earlier Cantata, will be seen to weave a spell over the composer in the whole of his subsequent production. What makes the *Canticum* so significant for us, apart from its sheer splendour as sound, is that in its internal movement it marks a crucial stage in Stravinsky's burning of his bridges and unashamed espousing of serialism, even though a snide case might still be made out by some determined functional analyst for its being founded on a mighty tonic-dominant arch of D–A–D. This interest was first fanned by his meeting with Robert Craft in 1947, a serial enthusiast, who has since served him as a faithful amanuensis and Boswell, and grew apace following his fateful trip to Paris in 1952 to attend the 20th Century Festival organised by his friend Nabokoff, where he received the full blast of post-war changes. A significant encounter with Boulez at Christmas 1952 led to three years of study on the part of the venerable master to get his serial tools in fine cutting order.

Performed on the same programme with the *Canticum* were the *Canonic Variations* on the Christmas Chorale 'Vom Himmel Hoch da komm ich her' for chorus and orchestra. One of the four Herculean pillars upon which rest Bach's supreme stature as a contrapuntalist, and curiously the most neglected, it served as the master's entry-piece in 1747 into the Mizler Society in the exalted company of Handel, Telemann and some say even Leibnitz, a society whose avowed aim was to enthrone Mathematics as the Queen of Arts and Sciences, an aim doubtless sympathetic to the ageing Bach, who occupied himself towards his life's end more and more with the esoteric and hermetic, what in the Mizlerian sense constituted the philosophic in Music. Stravinsky, setting out on the same road, must have found the work of transcription a grateful tirocinium since the canon, in the working of which these Variations provide almost the last word, is one of the few traditional forms equally valid in the lucubrations of serialists and one which goes far towards assuaging Stravinsky's lifelong need for establishing musical identity by means of repetition.

A still further example of this sort of 'reconstruction' was provided about the same time with the three *Sacrae Cantiones* of Gesualdo, Prince of Venosa, first performed in the Stravinsky version in 1957, and consisting of 'Da pacem Domine', 'Assumpta est Maria', both for six voices, as well as the 'Illumina nos' for seven voices, which may well be Gesualdo's final opus and of which the lost sextus and bassus parts were reworked afresh by Stravinsky. So great was the solidarity between these two musical 'grands seigneurs' that in 1960

Stravinsky took up his pen to pay homage once more to the Genoese master, this time with the *Monumentum pro Gesualdo di Venosa*, comprising two madrigals from the Fifth Book: 'Ascugate i begli', 'Ma tu, cagion di quella atroce pena', and one from the Sixth: 'Belta poi che t'assenti' transcribed for an orchestra of oboes, bassoons, horns, trumpets, trombones and strings.

Following the *Canticum*, the next major work to appear was the ballet *Agon*, concluded in April 1957, though work was begun on it as early as 1953. It represents his largest deployment of the full symphony orchestra since 1945, though applied with a sparing hand. The style is as disconcertingly heterogeneous as was earlier that of *Le Rossignol*, and the ballet, which boasts a choreography correspondingly duodecimal, is based on archaic dance-forms taken from seventeenth-century orchestrions by de Lauze and Père Mersenne. The early parts are in a straightforwardly pandiatonic idiom. Work was then interrupted until 1956 by which time Stravinsky had undergone his dodecaphonic change-of-heart so that an increasing chromaticism makes itself felt as the work progresses until in the *Double Pas de Quatre* we have a definite series taking shape, a very characteristic one for Stravinsky, consisting of many stepwise major and minor seconds. But by far the most uncompromising texture was that of the four Duos, occurring towards the end, and scored for violas, cellos, basses pizzicato and trombones, which, divorced of any rhythmic sophistication, picks away fastidiously at the bare bones of the note-row in its original and retrograde species. A rather lame repetition of the original fanfare brings this most uneven work to a close.

Far superior to this, in monolithic cohesion of style, were the *Threni, id est lamentationes Jeremiah Prophetae*, finished on 21st March, 1958 and performed in Venice on 23rd September, 1958. It is scored for a vocal sextet, mixed choir and fairly large orchestra though eked out grudgingly, so as never to vie with the human voice for precedence. A definite trend in using orchestral support to ornament rather than to accompany the vocal line is getting under way here which will reach such sophisticated lengths in *Abraham and Isaac*. More in the nature of an archaeological excavation than the architectonics of *Canticum* it yet bears many points in common, most especially this growing preoccupation with the foundations as apart from the super-structure, with the subterranean *mise-en-scène* as apart from the terrestrial 'show', which manifests itself in both these works, as in so many of the later productions, in an emphasis on trombones and bass instruments. But whereas the *Canticum*, for all its solemnity, was a hymn of praise, the forbidding *Threni* reveals itself from the outset in a flagellant light. It begins with a juxtaposition of open fifths which steeps us at once in the sprawling forests and gaunt darkling monasteries of the Middle Ages. This perfect-fifth interval, a property of the original series, will imprint itself again and again throughout the work, for instance in the chant-like 'Bonus est Dominus'. The soprano soloists have at the outset a characteristic tremolando on two adjacent notes, what Stravinsky calls a 'melodic-rhythmic stutter', which he says has been 'a lifelong affliction' of his musical diction from *Les Noces* up to the *Concerto in D*. We have already met with it in the archaic Machaut-like cadences in the *Canticum* and it will be conspicuous again in the opening melisma of *Abraham and Isaac* as well as in a phrase which the later Elegy and Introitus share in common. Stravinsky takes over Thomas Tallis' device of leading into each verse by a setting of the Hebrew letter with which it begins, thus creating the aural counterpart of a medieval manuscript with its richly historiated initials.

The Elegies of Jeremiah, which the Vulgate version of the Bible calls 'Threni' and which were written after the sacking of Jerusalem by the armies of Nebuchadnezzar, have received the attentions of many composers before him, most notably Palestrina, William Byrd and Tallis, not to speak of Ernst Křenek in our own times. Stravinsky avails himself of only three of the Elegies, the first, 'How doth the city sit solitary, that was full of people', the third, in three parts: (1) A Complaint—*Querimonia*—'I am the man that hath seen affliction by the rod of His wrath'; (2) *Sensus Spei*—Perceiving Hope—'It is of the Lord's mercies that we are not consumed' and (3) *Solacium*—Compensation—'Oh Lord thou hast pleaded the causes of my soul; Thou hast redeemed my life', and the Fifth Elegy on a prayer of the Prophet Jeremiah, 'Remember, O Lord, what is come upon us'. It is the Third Elegy which contains the greater complexity of workmanship and texture. The *Querimonia*, which is delivered unaccompanied by one male soloist progresses from a two-part canon by way of a three-part one to a double-canon in four parts for the male soloists. The *Sensus Spei* traces a striking root-progression beginning on D♯ and continuing on through E with Heth; F with Lamed (which by the way has something of the quality of a TV jingle); B with Nun and C and G with Samech. The orchestra contains such novelties as sarusophone, alto-trombone, flugel horn, but dispenses with the customary bassoons and trumpets.

The Stravinskian bedrock begins to yield a still rarer sort of deposit in the quartz-like symmetries and crystalline transparencies of the 1959 *Movements*, which Stravinsky has called 'the corner-stone of my later work'. It shows a marked depersonalisation and fragmentation of Stravinsky's usual linear style rather similar to the depersonalisation into corruscating patterns of colour of the faces in late Byzantine mosaics, an echo perhaps of the iconoclastic period or of Moorish influence. Stravinsky is conscious of this Orientally abstract quality and has likened the work to the mathematical patterns of a Chinese carpet. Perhaps because he has come to grips here with rhythmic as well as tonal serialisation, in a more conscious way than in the seminal practices which he instituted in the *Sacre* so many years before, the work begins to have a multi-refractibility, once more as in Eastern mosaics where individual tesserae are often imbedded at different angles in order the better to catch the light. The work lasts a scant twelve minutes and consists again of the eternal five movements, interspersed with minute Interludes, which are said to have been composed afterwards, and which foretell the tempo of the coming

movement. Tempo recapitulations in the fourth interlude and fifth movement give a further feeling of integration to the whole which is earmarked by a pervading symmetry to which the series itself may well testify.

Instances of medieval *talea* and color abound, as witness the iso-rhythmic entries of the piano at the beginning and end of the fourth movement, which contains incidentally the only 'tutti' in the score. At the close of the fifth movement we have a forward- and backward-structure which coincides in its intervals, a real cabalistic permutation of Temurah this!—of the type known as 'atbash'. It is evident that the treatment of the row has become by this time a good deal more inscrutable than in earlier works. Ambiguities between alternative species abound with the result that the work exists not so much on a variety of affective levels as on a variety of structural levels resembling a series of stage trap-doors or sliding panels leading us into a perfect maze of intersecting serial passageways. Stravinsky's well-known love of paronomasia sometimes tempts us to regard his output of recent years as one of the most complete dossiers of punning, albeit serial, in the history of music.

Not only do the 'Movements' depict Stravinsky's 'anti-tonal' purge at its height as well as a desire to eschew classical forms of dramatic contrast. They also reveal him tackling the post-war problem of re-organising the time factor to accord with the changing potentials of an electronic era which has so exercised the minds of Messiaen, Boulez and John Cage. 'The time scale is the vital question,' he writes. 'It must work for every age. Miscalculation is death.' This whittling-away process, the desire to get down to the bedrock of durational necessity, has led in recent years to productions of a perfectly breathtaking concision such as the *Epitaph for the Tombstone of Prince Max Egon of Furstenberg*, which was first performed in 1959 at the Donaueschingen Festival held in the shadow of Schloss Furstenberg, where Stravinsky had been a frequent guest, and whose mere two minutes of duration is made up of antiphonic exchanges between the bass strings of the harp and the treble of flute and clarinet, or the double-canon: *In Memoriam Raoul Dufy* for String Quartet, composed in Venice in September 1959 and which lasts only twenty bars in all.

They dwell in a kingdom of Thule where all is stone and death, symbolised by a rigid use of the series, by an utter dehydration of essence (the total absence of the Waters of the Unconscious) and quartz-like consistency which at once identify the chthonic figure of our study, scuttling between memorial tablet and monument in what amounts to an eerie Japanese-style garden of stones. Indeed with his Nibelungen horde in the shape of the Verigor gold-mines which he owns in partnership with his wife Vera, we are tempted to compare him to a modern-day Alberich.

Not for Stravinsky are the pains of Boulez et Cie. to effect a seamless music. His honest down-to-earth pride of craftsmanship delights in turning up the cuffs and examining buttonholes and lining. 'I want the seams and sutures of my music to show'. *A Sermon, A Narrative and A Prayer*, of 1961, first performed in Basel on 23rd February, 1962, is no 'boneless nude' of the French school of Ingres–Boulez but a quiver-ingly erectile skeleton, a marvel of serial construction which convinces one of the necessity and judiciousness of every device employed. The human pathos and melodic appeal of this music are a far cry from the finespun incorporeality of *Movements* and follow more in the wake of *Threni*. In fact, Stravinsky chooses to regard it as a sort of New Testa-ment sequel to the Old Testament world of *Threni*. It takes the form of a Cantata for Alto and Tenor soloists, Speaker, a Chorus which is silent throughout the 'Narrative', and an Orchestra of flute and alto-flute, 2 oboes, clarinet, bass-clarinet, 2 bassoons, 4 horns, 3 trumpets, 2 tenor- and one bass-trombone, tuba, piano, harp, 3 gongs, 3 tam-tams and strings (8 7 6 5 4).

The first movement, *A Sermon*, is an Anthem on the text of St. Paul's letter to the Romans: 'The substance of things hoped for, the evidence of things seen, is Faith.' It falls into two sections of four parts each, with the first part of the second section reversing the material of its opposite number while the last two parts of each section act as an identical refrain. *A Narrative*, which follows, is the longest movement and tells of the trial and stoning of Stephen, the first of the Holy Martyrs as related in the Acts of the Apostles. It constitutes a sort of musical melodrama for the Alto and Tenor soloists, Narrator and Orchestra. The last of this triptych, *A Prayer*, is a setting of a verse of the early seventeenth-century playwright Thomas Dekker: 'Clothe me in a white robe of righteousness that I may be one of those singers who shall cry to Thee 'Alleluia'.' This movement represents yet another in Stravinsky's celebrated series of epitaphs, being, as it is, 'In Memoriam the Reverend James McLane' (d. 1960).

In this work Stravinsky retreats once more into his special brand of serialism with a tonal bias. *A Sermon* opens with the first note of the tone-row, E flat, spotlighted by the violins, after which the remainder of the row, knotted for the most part tightly into intervals of a semi-tone, can be broken up into isomorphic figures as shown, and it is

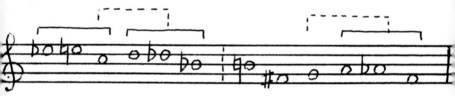

particularly the first trichord of E flat E and C which we will hear over and over again as the work progresses, assuming the function of a cadence. Both hexachords of the series conclude in similar fashion, the second, as it were, at the Dominant—a sort of serial counterpart of fugal subject and answer.

A sort of bird's-eye view of *A Sermon* is provided by *The Dove Descending* of 2nd January, 1962, a tiny three-minute anthem for four-part *a cappella* choir on a verse by T. S. Eliot from Part IV of *Little Gidding* (from *Four Quartets*), originally commissioned by the Cambridge Hymnal.

In dealing with Stravinsky's *oeuvre*, it is important to remember that in the Byzantine as indeed in the Chinese tradition there is no abrupt demarcation between the major and minor arts. The profusion of reliquaries in the shape of perfectly proportioned but miniature churches illustrates concretely what has long been known, that every art, not the least architecture, sought to attain the lapidary precision and completeness of an enamelled reliquary. In the same way, the small-scale but nonetheless exquisitely fashioned works peeping out from time to time between the august ranks of the major works often help us toward a fuller understanding of these latter. Just as the *Cinq Doigts* of 1921 and the *Ariel-Song* of 1953 presaged later serial developments, and the *Dirge Canons in Memoriam Dylan Thomas* of 1954 point the way to *Canticum* as well as to the unadorned style of more recent works, so does this Anthem comment postscripturally on the structure of *A Sermon*.

The Flood, which has been described as a musical pantomime or choral ballet (first produced in June 1962) opens with the Rock of Creation rising from the parting waters of Chaos, a chaos which is stunningly represented by the whole of the twelve-note chromatic scale sounding at once in a wondrous tremolando chord. Moreover, the top half of the chord is a mirror-image of the bottom in a way that would have gladdened the heart of Dr Paracelsus himself. In bar 6 the 'primeval' series begins to heave itself out of the quivering tonal fluid, which also serves as curtain-cue:

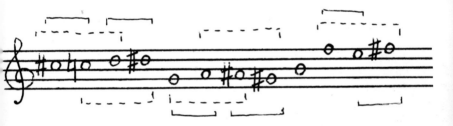

The Prelude ends with the chord representing the earthly half of the original Chaos-chord. So it is that the metaphor of our opening pages is undergoing a veritable tonal transfiguration. The first main section, *Te Deum*, has the character of a 'fast-tempo dance-chorale', with the addition of ritual chanting, and calls to mind similar passages in *Les Noces*. Between this and the closing *Sanctus*—a mirror-reflection of the *Te Deum*—is sandwiched the Miracle Play itself, which recounts episodically the Creation of Man, the Fall, the Flood and its aftermath, the latter recapitulating material from the beginning. Even Satan pops up again, like the Joker at the end of *Jeu de Cartes*, to indicate that the game must go on forever.

Stravinsky has couched *The Flood* in his most unashamedly 'serialism without tears' style, for easy TV viewing, so as to generate a plethora of C♯ cadences, thus providing the listener with what he calls 'a sure sense of topographical location'. In *The Flood* Stravinsky has also released the flood-gates of his own style in a spate of an almost baroque symbolism, although often of a highly recondite nature resembling his younger colleague Boulez, who, in the 'L'Artisanat Furieux' section of *Le Marteau*, uses the twelfth-note of the series to typify the word 'clou'. Some inklings are nonetheless provided of Stravinsky's curiously Gnostic outlook in the syncopated sophistications of Lucifer, a 'high, slightly paederastic tenor' who is 'less sexually sure than God', symbolically singing the series backwards and inverted, which provide a striking contrast to the cavernous featureless Voice of God entrusted to two bass-soloists. The greatest felicity, however, is attained in the depiction of the Flood itself, which Stravinsky describes as 'altissimo not fortissimo, full and high, choked, unable to breathe, but not loud'. It takes place in two tides, in the first of which the time-signatures expand in Blacher-fashion to 11/16 before receding, only to reach the full serial consummation of 12/16 at the second go when the violin ostinato figure, which has been swirling around beginning with the hexachord and appending another note of the series each time, at last carries all before it to attain the same duodecimal perfection as has the metre.

A like absorption in Stone and Death has also determined Stravinsky's choice of vocal texts during most of his life. He has gone so far as to attribute the inspiration for his next work, *Abraham and Isaac, A Sacred Ballad*, finished on 3rd March, 1963 to the actual sound of Hebrew, the accentuation and timbre of which are an indispensable element of the music, and the translation of which he expressly forbids. He has already described his attitude with regard to yet another dead language, the Latin of *Oedipus Rex*, which 'had the great advantage of giving me a medium not dead, but *turned to stone*, and so monumentalised as to have become immune from all risk of vulgarisation.' The words of *Abraham* are drawn from Chapter XXII of the Hebrew

Masoretic text of Genesis and set, in one continuous movement of five sections, for 'Baryton Martin' (high baritone) and orchestra. It is dedicated to the State of Israel, which Stravinsky toured in 1962. One can imagine the nature of the impression left upon him, who has hedged himself about with the most constricting musical laws, by a people for whom the Law is the tutelary divinity of life and religion, and even the secret of historical survival. Symbolic devices are again richly represented here, e.g. the duo for flute and tuba, a double canon by inversion and diminution, which portrays the reprieving angel crying out of the heavens to Abraham below. Only once at the beginning do we have a complete statement of the series, yet another specimen of his persistent stepwise concatenations, since Stravinsky is too much of a sport to deny his analytically-minded listener the benefit of a 'fighting chance':

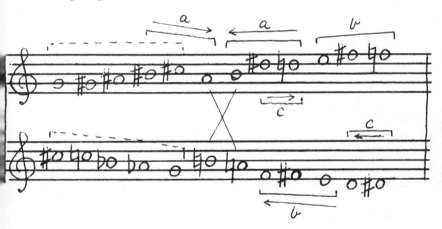

Notice particularly the exceptional number of diatonic scalar steps it includes. The whole work might indeed be construed as evidencing a tonal drift towards A. The same rotation around a 'keynote' by means of permutational concurrences which appears in *A Narrative* finds an echo here in the F-based serial forms for the angel's speech at bar 211 et seq., a concurrence which Stravinsky calls 'serial verticals'. In all these late works, we meet with the use of a hexachord of the series in preference to the complete row, which has come to be known as Stravinsky's 'ritual conservatism' and which reminds us that in Byzantium too, the perfect number was always Six, the Divine Logos, and constituted a bond between Heaven and Earth. This conservatism applies as much to the 'Klangfarbe' use of the orchestra as to the actual texture itself, which is largely monodic or bipartite.

More prayers for the dead and musical obituaries were the bitter fruit of the last years, beginning with the *Elegy for JFK*, the assassinated President of the United States, who died on 22nd November, 1963.

In this, the series is used untransposed throughout and, as in *Abraham and Isaac*, W. H. Auden's words are left to provide their own music. There are two separate versions depending on whether the vocal part is performed by mezzo-soprano or baritone, and three clarinets provide the instrumental commentary. In an interesting sidelight, Stravinsky tells us that the vocal part was finished first and the instrumentation only deduced later from real and implied relationships after the manner of Schoenberg's *Violin Fantasy*. This is not the only point in common between these two tutelary deities of the music of our time. Both came to accept that, in the words of Stravinsky, 'the new function of music must be quintessentially sacred', although Stravinsky interpreted this need in more of a cultic and ritualistic way, less emotionally involved, than Schoenberg, who in typical German fashion sought 'a mystic marriage with the unknowable'. Both accepted the series as a musical epiphany of the immanence of God, even a sort of surrogate for prayer, particularly Stravinsky, who managed to confer on his curiously stepwise note-rows some of the archaic aspect of ceremonial prayer or chant.

On 28th October, 1964 were finished the *Variations: Aldous Huxley In Memoriam*, whom that same fateful 22nd November had carried off as well. These are variations only in the free permutational sense of Webern, whose ultimate Cantatas and Variations seem to constitute the same kind of challenge for Stravinsky as did the *Ninth Symphony* to a Bruckner or a Mahler. More important is their function as a sort of dodecaphonic apotheosis, in which pitch, metre and instrumentation are all subjected at the climax to the co-ordinating rule of Twelve. This climax occurs in the shape of a twelve-part variation distributed in three phases and built on a rotating sequence of time-signatures 4/8 3/8 and 5/8 (=12/8) which encompasses twelve revolutions per phase. These phases have each a twelvefold instrumental identity; the

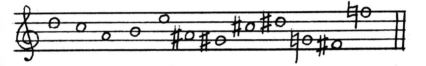

first is scored for 12 solo violins in a high register, which calls to mind immediately the shrill 18-voiced 'Epode' of Messiaen's *Chronocromie*. Stravinsky compares it to 'a sprinkling of very fine broken glass'. The second is for 4 solo violins, 6 solo violas and 2 double-basses while the third is for 12 wind. Different permutations of the basic set are used each time so as to achieve a maximum of independence and non-repetition for all twelve voices. Just as in *Movements*, the rhythmic factor here plays a role of primary importance in articulating the formal structure. This is strikingly brought to our notice in the way that each of the twelve threads, on reappearing, changes character instrumentally as well as tonally; the only thing that remains constant is an isorhythmic identity. Around this triple axis are grouped the remaining 'variations', at either end and in between. The beginning and end are rather more plain spoken and monodic in texture so as the better to throw into heightened relief the more complex contrapuntal threesome. As usual, there is a typical Gesualdo-style homophonic group at either extreme. One such group which rings down the curtain cadentially is constructed from the eleven notes of the basic set while the fugitive twelfth comes only in the final bar on the bass clarinet to plug the gap and allay our expectancy in a serial parallel, much favoured by Stravinsky, of tonal tension and relaxation. Composers as disparate as Cage and Boulez have complained that dodecaphony offers only a discrete note-by-note procedure while leaving the overall structure to the personal recipes of the composer. In this important work, Stravinsky shows us his way of expanding such a system into a megascopic structural principle.

Latest in this splendidly hieratic procession is the *Introitus: T. S. Eliot In Memoriam* from Stravinsky's rumoured 'Princeton' Requiem, destined by the composer as his 'coronat opus'. The appearance of the opening Introitus on 17th February was hastened by the news of the death of Eliot on 4th January, 1965. The scoring calls sepulchrally for tenors, basses, harp, piano, timpani, tam-tams, solo viola and double-basses. Like the Voice of God in *The Flood* it plumbs the depths of pitch with tenors and basses singing the Introitus of the Catholic Requiem Service to the sound of solo viola and double-bass supported by timpani.

This tribute to Eliot reminds us that England can take particular pride in the fact that some of the most positive bonds still holding Stravinsky to the world of the living are furnished by an English cultural orientation with which he has come to identify himself more and more in recent years, not only in his personal life through his friendships with T. S. Eliot, Aldous Huxley, W. H. Auden, and Dylan Thomas but also through his intensive studies of early English music with which his California library is particularly well-stocked. One need only think of *The Rake's Progress*, the three Shakespeare Songs, the Cantata, *In Memoriam Dylan Thomas*, *A Sermon*, *The Dove descending*, the York and Chester Mystery-Plays of *The Flood*, and the *Elegy for JFK* to realise the full extent of this influence. Only Joseph Conrad, who made an equally enriching contribution to our English cultural heritage, can claim the same formative triad of Slavic birth, Parisian melting-pot and English and American spiritual home.

Stravinsky occupies a curious position with regard to present day trends. To borrow a convenient metaphor from Messiaen's rhythmic usage, relating to his concept of active, passive and neutral 'rhythmic protagonists', Stravinsky is neither one of those who wish, as do Morton Feldman, Lamont Young (as in his piece for *Two Sounds* which go on forever) and in part John Cage, passively to contract their

attention to 'one small thing', turning it over and over in sheer hyp-
notic fascination; nor is he one of those who, like Penderecki and
Xenakis, wish actively to reflect in their works the staggering and
indeterminable multiplicity of the expanding universe about them.
Stravinsky is content to remain firmly 'neutral', that is to say, limiting
himself to what can be determined through the use of unaided human
reason, and refuses stoutly 'to cross the gulf from well-tempered
pitches to sounds and noises' and 'to abdicate the rule of my ears.'
Instead he prefers to mount guard on the bulging 'Schatzkammer' of
European tradition, of which he has been conducting tours and nourish-
ing both himself and his Muse for the last half-century.

His music, so 'sweetly reasonable', can be summed up most fittingly
in the words of the twelfth-century Byzantine Nicholas Mesarites
describing the proportions of San Marco, with which our chapter
began, or rather of the church of the Holy Apostles which once stood
on its site: 'It does not please the senses more than it impresses the mind.'

As for what one might call his 'Deucalion fixation', whether one
cares to explain it away as sclerosis and the death-urge on a personal
scale or on a Spenglerian hemispheric scale, it is sufficiently unique to
repay attention.

The musical necrophilia in Stravinsky is no more anachronistic than
those kinky moribund worlds in which move the characters of a
Samuel Beckett play and which provide the same terse comment
on our times. Even Stravinsky's appetite for laws, as manifest in religious and serial observances, is symptomatic of a distancing from the
flux of reality, a reality which continues to gnaw away at the foot of
the rock. Einstein has said 'As far as laws . . . refer to reality they are
not certain; and as far as they are certain, they do not refer to reality.'
Religion and law, monasteries and castles, like ritual and serialism in
the music of Stravinsky, have always seated themselves paternalistically
on Rock. But of one thing we can be sure: that the Stravinskian rock,
like those rocks which figure in so many legends of the Caucasus, is
the dwelling-place of a God!

Postscript

For the sake of completeness the following works, three minor and one major, deserve to be mentioned: *Fanfare for a New Theatre* for 2 trumpets to salute the opening of the Lincoln Center in New York (1964); the seventeen-bar orchestral *Canon on a Russian Popular Tune* (the same that had served him half a lifetime earlier for the nuptials in *Firebird*) of 1965; and *The Owl and the Pussy-Cat*, a setting of Edward Lear's nonsense-rhyme (1966). 1966 also marked the appearance of the Princeton *Requiem Canticles*, six choral movements on Latin texts from the Catholic Requiem with the Responsory '*Libera Me*' from the burial service bound together symmetrically by an instrumental Prelude, Interlude and Postlude with F as the telegonic tonal bias. Like all the large-scale works it is distinguished from the minor ones by a greater wealth of serial pathways furnished by Stravinsky's idiosyncratic hexachordal rotation of the series, supplemented in this case by the unusual presence of a sibling series.

                                                                      M.T.

Special thanks are due to Messrs. Alfred A. Knopf Inc. of New York for permission to quote from Themes and Episodes, Igor Stravinsky/Robert Craft, *New York 1966.*

V

NEW MUSIC AND THE PUBLIC:
SOME PROBLEMS OF INTERPRETATION

By Theodor W. Adorno

No ONE who hears a lot of new music, and particularly works which he knows intimately, will deny, for all his sympathy with the performer who ventures into this uncomfortable and unrewarding field, that very many performances are incomprehensible; not only to the layman, who expects nothing different and indeed almost wants it that way, but even to the listener who is familiar with what is offered and identifies himself with it. Indeed, it often sounds as the indignant philistine imagines it—chaotic, ugly and meaningless. Alban Berg's macabre joke to the effect that he could usually imagine quite well, after a criticism by his arch-enemy, old Korngold, what the music was really like, is well confirmed by such an experience. But belief in the incomprehensibility of new music is so ingrained with the public, and also with many performers, that we scarcely ask any longer whether this incomprehensibility in fact lies in the compositions or in the performance of them; the performers themselves, under the pressure of their obligations—a pressure which is not always forced upon them—are scarcely any longer in a position to judge the quality of their own work. I have seen how a conductor, usually excellent and a man who has grown up in the responsible tradition of new music, has responded to my sceptical glance after the performance of an admittedly exceptionally difficult work, as if to console himself: just one more rehearsal, and it would have gone like a Haydn symphony. On listening to a recording afterwards I was not able to distinguish, in one of the most important, imitative parts of the work, the crucial point in the score when the theme is combined with its augmentation and diminution. But if the sense of musical events is not realised in their performance, no listener deserves reproach if he dismisses the piece as meaningless, since, after all, he only hears the performance.

'It would have gone like a Haydn symphony'; which means to say, it would have functioned well, the ensemble would have been exactly together with every beat of the conductor, nothing would have gone wrong. Performing musicians, and above all conductors, have constantly to solve a dual problem; they have to master the apparatus which translates the score into sound, and to reveal the musical sense, the coherence of what is happening. In time, the first task mostly takes precedence over the second, although in fact the one can hardly be separated from the other. But as a result of the tendency met with everywhere today of concentrating on means instead of ends, also no doubt in despair of the second purpose ever being attained, performers learn to be contented if, as people say, nothing goes wrong; provided, that is, there are no wrong notes and no inaccuracies, and the façade of sound more or less hangs together. It is, however, an illusion to imagine that, in the case of new music, this will ensure that a certain modicum of musical sense will prevail of its own accord. It is possible for everything to function according to the notes (which are not looked at too closely) and for the result nevertheless to be meaningless. A piece of music does not make more or less sense according to the manner of the performance; it is a question of basic quality; unless the meaning is realised completely and every detail is related to this meaning and shaped by it, then in critical instances all will be lost.

Let us take a concrete illustration. Since Richard Wagner introduced the principle of 'division of melody', that is to say, instrumented his scores in such a way that one melodic line after another is brought out in different colours which to a certain extent affect its course, we find in truly differentiated compositions that it is increasingly rare for the melody to be uninterrupted over long stretches. Not only is the practice of allowing the leading themes to pass from one voice to another, already developed in the Viennese classics, now even more firmly established, but even individual melodies are dissolved into

smaller and smaller fragments. Because of this, however, the performer is faced with the task of blending the different instrumental
timbres and, more especially, of bridging the leaps from one instrument or group or instruments to another. In traditional music it was
fairly simple, thanks to the familiar harmonic sequences, to follow the
thread of the procedure, although already Mozart and Beethoven
make far more disturbing demands than the naive listener might imagine; but today this thread has become undeniably a major problem
facing the performer. For instance, if a long spun-out theme starts with
initial notes on the *cor anglais* which gradually mount until the highest
note is taken over by the trumpet, then the unity of the melodic figure
is completely destroyed unless at the critical point the sound of *cor
anglais* and trumpet is blended to such a degree that we feel the trumpet,
for all the difference of timbre, to be the immediate continuation of
the *cor anglais*; should this not be achieved—and what efforts, and how
many individual rehearsals to work out the 'thread' would be needed
in order to solve such problems every time they arise—it is possible,
even in the fourth bar of a theme, for the coherence of the whole
melody to be lost and for the listener to feel himself adrift and conscious
only of the incalculability of musical procedure for which he then
blames the composition. But it may be said without exaggeration that
complex modern compositions consist of innumerable examples of
such a kind; they contain hardly any notes which would not lead to
questions of this kind, and frequently an intense concentration is
necessary in order simply to imagine the right solution, let alone to hear
it realised in sound.

The difficulties caused by the new polyphony, and incidentally also
by the truly polyphonic pieces of Bach, are no less. The more independent voices there are sounding simultaneously, the more necessary
it is to distinguish them clearly from one another so that they are
cogently separate. Schoenberg was so conscious of the difficulty of
achieving this that already at a relatively early stage in his writing he
introduced his own indications for main and subsidiary voices, in
order to make clear what is in the foreground, what similarly is
essential but nevertheless secondary, and what is really in the background. But if the instrumentation itself is not fool-proof, that is, if it

c

does not anticipate and correct the possibilities of misinterpretation—
Mahler was the unexcelled master in this respect—such indications are
not a great deal of use. It is just at the complicated places, which are
what we are referring to here, that all performers become nervous,
unless they are completely sure of the matter in hand. To play ner-
vously, however, means to play too loudly, and in spite of all precau-
tions there looms the threat of a mush of confused *mezzoforte* in which
the most intimate polyphony is lost.

But difficulties arise over quite simple matters, as for example when
single melodies are played by single instruments, such as the violin or
clarinet. We find repeatedly that in new music such melodies do not
sing as they would have to if they were uttered by a living voice; the
inadequacy extends from primitive mistakes in phrasing right up to
subtler shortcomings—insensibility as regards accents, lack of dynamic
flexibility, rigid playing 'to the beat' without musicianly feeling, or a
crude use of *ritardandi*. The effect is comparable to that which may be
observed when someone reads aloud in a foreign language with a
correct pronunciation, but without understanding what the words
mean; the listeners will understand him no better than he understands
himself. However subtle such mistakes may be—and they are probably
the most dangerous in the performance of new music—they can be
detected correctly by the true interpreter; but, in practice, such defects,
or their absence, are usually attributed to the so-called mere natural
gift of musicality, and, protected by such a belief, all sorts of nonsense
will proliferate.

The matter of *tempi* is in no better posture. Schoenberg and Berg
used to talk about 'first performance *tempi*'; they recommended
playing works rather more slowly, before they had become quite
familiar, so as to make it easier for the listener to understand the many
themes heard both simultaneously and in sequence, and also to enable
the composer to obtain a general impression of how his work sounds
and to minimise friction in the actual apparatus of performance. The
superstitious belief in sheer functioning, in letting a piece take its
course, and the deep-rooted fear of losing hold of the listener even
for a second and of boring him if the virtuosity of the *tempo* does not
keep his attention constantly, lead conductors to take a piece at its full

speed although the players, like the listeners too, are not yet up to it; and in the hurry all contrasts are lost. On the other hand the 'first performance *tempi*' too do not give to the musical sense any feeling of security. I once heard a very difficult work performed by a group of young, enthusiastic and infinitely devoted musicians. In their anxiety not to do harm to a single note, they played so slowly and deliberately that the liveliness, which in the first and last movements was essential to the character of the piece, was no longer there, and the piece as a whole left the listener just as confused as if it had been taken at hectic speed; it was a question of disloyalty occasioned by loyalty. Nowadays it is clearly necessary to aim at the right *tempi*, but the difficulty is never one of attaining the *tempo* as such, but rather of seeing that in a quick movement everything that takes place in the composition is articulated quickly, that there is diversity in unity. But how many performers would understand even that element which has been a feature of new music for a long time—the fact that there are melodies which are in very quick time, but still melodies.

Finally, in most performances of new music insufficient attention is paid to the sensuous quality of the sound. It is admittedly true that in a progressively conceived performance tone colour is no longer the stimulus and a purpose in itself, but is by definition functional, a means to the realisation of the musical structure in sound. But this does not mean indifference to the sound of the music, nor an acceptance of the stereotyped conception of many listeners that new music sounds frightful, and that that is how it has to sound. Although authentic pieces of new music are as far removed from late romantic wallowing in sensuous sound as they are from the meretricious voluptuousness which came into its own a long time ago in the musical accompaniments to Hollywood films, the new music does not have to renounce sound-effects as a form of mediation between the musical essence and its appearance in the external world. If genuine works are performed in a faithful and sensible manner, they will also, in a higher sense, sound effective; for sensuous sound is not an isolated phenomenon—though it may appear as such through the meaningless way of listening which the public, trained as it is on saccharine, indulges in—but its beauty depends on the structure of the work; if this sensuous sound is visibly linked to the structure, it will sound beautiful of its own accord. Once one has heard Berg's *Lulu* suite as interpreted by one of the outstanding conductors of Romance origin, such as Sanzogno, one realises how little there is of titivated affectation in the sound-magic of great music, how much it is rather the effect of the composition itself, and how factual just this incommensurable element is; Berg himself has hinted at this when he explained the ideal of musical realism by pointing out that in a well-made table the glue should not smell, nor the nails stick out. The usual performances, however, which do not achieve the unification of internal and external elements, pay no attention to such a need for smoothness and integration, and thus they confirm listeners' prejudices. Because these performances fail to co-ordinate the music as a whole, the façade of sound also threatens to disintegrate, and the result is to do the music a serious disservice. Even if the distinction between traditional and new music is in fact by no means so sharp as is maintained by the division of cultural activities into watertight compartments, all the same these difficulties of interpretation do hold good for traditional music as well. Most performances of this music too are today, in by far the majority of cases, meaningless. It is precisely after we have become familiar with new music that this becomes evident, so to speak, retrospectively. But in the case of the current repertoire, that ever diminishing body of works which nevertheless every musical person knows by heart, we do not notice this. Familiarity, and possibly still more the older diatonic language, carry us comfortably over all the hiatuses and contradictions. The more or less typical and settled phrases establish something like co-ordination, even when the actual integration, the shaping of the individual phrase by means of the structure of the whole, does not take place. But new music turns the inside out, deliberately makes the structure into part of the musical event, and repudiates traditional formulae; therefore the chaos which in the usual Beethoven interpretations is never far below the smooth surface at once becomes obvious. If the coherence in new music is destroyed by shortcomings of the kind outlined above, this leads directly to that kind of confusion which is noticed in performances of traditional music only by someone who already understands it; it is possible therefore even to find that traditional music is more difficult to perform and understand than new music; but the realisation of this and of the idea of true interpretation first needed the stimulus of new music.

In the case of not a few interpreters we shall have to assume lack of understanding as the reason for questionable performances of new music. The contradictions in the relationship of productive musical powers to society also concern the relationship of interpretation to composition. Conductors and performers are let down by their own musical education when they wish to comprehend those very works which are of serious importance. Owing to their calling they are more directly concerned with success than composers and brought into contact with a public to whose intellectual level they often unconsciously adapt themselves. Therefore their own musical taste, however specialised they may otherwise be, does not always keep pace with the development of music itself. Even such significant figures as Furtwängler or Casals could make the most incredibly false judgments about new music in general and the quality of specific works. For the sake of effect the self-righteous traditionalistic interpreters cling to the hackneyed conception of the musician who in close contact with his public lets himself be guided by the sensuous happenings of the music and adds nothing to this except his temperament. Whatever does not fit into this is of no value, according to this school; but they tend to forget that these musicianly qualities are certainly the prerequisite of all worthwhile performances, and prove their worth when they are both maintained and sublimated in an awareness of the structure of the composition. Instead of this, and here we could cite even the most famous names, performances seldom amount to more than a combination of pleasant sound, *brio* and, at best, rhythmical exactitude. Admittedly there are many listeners who sense that something is wrong, but it is precisely these people who project their own insecurity upon something they ought to understand but do not, and therefore upbraid it as 'intellectual'. It is really up to the conductor or performer to stand up for new music and win over the public, unless he wishes to become a mere museum curator. Only too easily, however, does he come to side with the public against new music.

But wrong interpretations are by no means confined to ignoramuses and those who resist new music. The organisation of music-making, in which we are all involved, is more significant, in particular the lack of time for rehearsal. Pieces which even today could scarcely be played decently in much fewer than twenty rehearsals are hustled through in two or three; whatever other misgivings we may have on other counts, it is Toscanini's merit that he put an end to this custom, and it is to this merit that he owes his authority, for all the limitations of his musical qualities. But someone who lacks such authority generally has to accommodate himself to financial demands; social progress, which has turned executive musicians into protected trade-union members whose every minute costs money, acts as a brake on artistic progress by making it impossible to rehearse adequately, as this means being very generous with time, just as presumably large-scale architecture demands a lot of space.

The consequences of all this can scarcely be exaggerated; musical performances, which should bridge in a fruitful manner the tension between the public and a musical work, instead of this deepen the gulf between the two. The gulf is scarcely recognised as such any longer, but has already become petrified into an ideology. People are willing enough to find confirmation in incomprehensible performances of their belief that a work is incomprehensible, while the specialist, who is regarded as the authority in these matters, in fact can understand the nonsense which he has to listen to no better than the outraged regular concert-goer. It should be asked in all seriousness whether the frequent performances of new music which suffer from these defects do not in fact, with the best will in the world on the part of those concerned, do more harm than good. Not for nothing do those who are most responsible tend to hinder rather than to encourage performances of their own works or of those works which have been entrusted to them. There is a long-playing recording of one of the most important contemporary operas, which has been bought by many people with good intentions and by many interested persons; but although the conductor is one of the faithful supporters of new music, this recording makes the course of the music unrecognisable over long stretches. One can only shrug one's shoulders or else simulate an enthusiasm for something which it is impossible to be enthusiastic about because it has so little to do with what it purports to be. At the same time we hesitate to utter out aloud such misgivings, in order not to provide the forces of laziness and reactionary insensitiveness with any excuses for turning away from new music, possibly on the pretext that prevailing conditions do not permit of adequate performances, or of going any further than Tchaikovsky with a clear conscience; whereas in fact what determines the inner tension and justification of an artistic performance is its relationship to contemporary, indeed to the most advanced, forms of composition. If performers, who are the mediators between new music and the broad stream of musical life, were to withdraw entirely, this would only have the effect of neutralising the new art and making it the cultural property of specialists, with the result that indifference towards it would only become more general. Although musical performances must strictly refrain from aiming merely at producing an 'effect' by their nature, performers are not indifferent to response, or lack of response. They would hardly be serious and substantial any more if they were to be weakly resigned in advance to reaching, in spite of all obstacles, only an audience of non-specialists. This would be pandering to existing society and would imply that musical performance was something unconnected with the structure of musical work; this must be avoided by an art unless it is to undermine its own being.

Purists would speak at this point of compromise with conformity, and repudiate care for interpretation as a cowardly consideration for effect. Such purists make it all too easy for themselves. To begin with, a musical work is not only the text of the notes, since the latter needs realisation in sound just as much as sound needs a text; indifference towards performance means indifference to what is to be performed. But then, to re-house new music in an area which is isolated from the public—its most obvious expression is the institution of the B.B.C. Third Programme—has its dubious aspects. However necessary such segregations may be from time to time, in order to protect artistic progress from the rage of the compact majority, such institutions as Third Programmes and cultural cinemas, which avoid the issues and reserve and control new works for the cognoscenti, so that nothing happens, do in fact have the effect that nothing does happen. What is advanced and esoteric about the works themselves always makes its impact on the public; if this impact is blunted, the whole business begins to lose its tension, and those wallpaper patterns and calculations which threaten aesthetic *avant-gardisme* by diluting it, are inseparable from an avoidance of a relationship with the public which should be one not of accommodation but of its opposite. If Wagner's Hans Sachs in *The Mastersingers* demands that the rules of the masters should be judged by the people, he is expressing something of the healthy popular sense which lies in wait to attack intellectuals and other deviationists, but he is also expressing the premonition that a specialisation which is called for for technical reasons endangers the cause which at the same time it is helping. Brecht is perhaps to be respected most for his refusal to draw a line between integrity and success, a division which had long been acknowledged by the entertainment business itself, and because his extremist approach to art—one of his closest friends once called it 'barbaric futurism'—was nevertheless able to intervene in established cultural patterns and to avoid being limited to one territorial reserve. The split between art and society is dictated by society, but the man who on that account bows to it as a decree of fate is being obedient to the dictates of society. Modern painting has been able to establish itself in a hostile society through a peculiar trick of reasoning, namely, the commercial value of the works. Good performances could do something similar for new music. For the true suggestive power of a performance depends on whether it has revealed the meaning of the work performed.

But only radio could help to achieve this. It is silly to stand superciliously aloof from the mass media; the intellectual monopoly of the culture-industry can only be broken by altering its function, not by a retreat into social impotence. Just as radio alone can today offer a refuge to new music which is excluded from the commercial market, and radio alone can represent the cause of new music, which is the cause of a group of people, against the people as a whole, so also only radio should be able to guarantee performances in which this cause comes into its own. The most important thing would be to allow adequate time for rehearsal, that is, considerably more time than is at present available. We know how difficult it is for broadcasting constantly to find enough works to fill up the programmes. Would it not be more sensible to set aside part of this time and use it for rehearsals, rather on the lines of those legendary rehearsals which Schoenberg used to conduct after the First World War in the 'Viennese Society for private musical performances' for his first Chamber Symphony without ever 'officially' performing it? These rehearsal times should not be lost to listeners. Rather, the rehearsals themselves should be broadcast. Any improvement in the delineation of the musical meaning at the same time helps the listener to realise what it is about. The seriousness and discipline with which a musical interpreter brings out the coherence of his work is at the same time evidence for the listener of the seriousness and discipline of the composition, and breaks down the prejudice that the work is wilful and chaotic, and that it does not matter what a note sounds like here or there. Furthermore we can see in the case of Spa orchestras and similar inadequate institutions, how it is precisely the cracks and gaps in ill-prepared performances which allow the inner meaning to shine through and which allow us to get to know pieces as a child gets to know the doll which it pulls to pieces; we should take advantage of the pedagogic function of what is incomplete and faulty, and build on that to offer listeners something that is satisfactorily produced. In such an exercise we should not confine ourselves to the orchestra, where a certain measure of coarseness cannot be avoided, even with limitless time and the greatest mastery— good orchestral works are in a certain sense already composed so that they can allow for such coarsening—but we should also and above all practise chamber-music works minutely, down to the last note, and broadcast the rehearsals. A prerequisite for this would be for the most important broadcasting stations to employ permanently the most highly qualified ensembles, preferably string quartets. This practice should in no way be limited to modern music; it would be equally of service to traditional music.

In this way it might be possible to break down the lethargy of the mass of listeners to new music, and to prevent those who are no longer satisfied with traditional music but not yet capable of mastering new music from drifting together in primitivist cliques. For this purpose admittedly the independence of radio would need strengthening against the organised pressure of that very public taste which it will have to change, if it is going to fulfil its obligations to the public; for the public is also, even today, better than those people who invoke the name of the public in order to hinder the development of what is humanly dignified and valuable.

[*Translated from the German*]

VI

THE COMPOSER AND HIS AUDIENCE

By Roberto Gerhard

IN A QUESTIONNAIRE I was once invited to answer, there was one question which read something like this: 'If, prior to the performance of a work of yours, you were given the opportunity of addressing the audience, what would you like to say?' My answer was: 'Not a word.' This may have had the merit of brevity but it is not perfectly unambiguous; indeed, it lends itself to misinterpretation. Above all, it needs to be made clear that not every inquirer would deserve such a negative reply. It was a matter of addressing, specifically, a concert audience. My answer applied to such a case.

It is an obvious fact that the gap between the composer and his *contemporary* audience has sometimes been wider, sometimes narrower. This depends on a variety of factors not easily assessed. But I think it is true to say that, on the whole, the gap is pretty wide today, wider perhaps than at most comparable periods in the past, and that it shows no signs of narrowing down. This questionnaire was probably framed with some such observation in mind. The idea of asking the composer to address his audience seems to have been inspired by the wish to help in narrowing down the gap, offering the audience some guidance, some listening-aid. And who better than the composer himself—the author of my questionnaire must have thought—to tell the audience what he has been trying to do? Considered from this point of view, my reply must seem distinctly unhelpful. It might easily be taken for a sign of a stand-offish, aloof attitude, as much as to say: as a composer I am concerned with the *making* of a piece of music; audience-reaction is none of my concern. Now, for all its apparent abruptness, this take-it-or-leave-it attitude is, I feel, basically right. It stresses the importance to the composer of the detachment which he knows he must maintain *vis-à-vis* his audience. Only it cannot be denied that it tends to obscure one fact which, I think, is of almost equal importance: namely, the fact that a piece of music is made *for* a listener. It is meant to be listened to by other people besides the composer. There seems to be a conflict here between the demand for perfect detachment on the part of the composer on the one hand, and, on the other, the destination of the work, namely, an audience. Unless the composer is willing to shut himself up in an ivory tower and play there a kind of solipsistic game, he is clearly bound to have in mind some sort of rapport with his potential audience. This relationship is, I think, worth exploring.

Needless to say, the human factor is met with at the very first stages of even the most abstract composition. The composer may be rather hazy as to the precise nature of his rapport with a potential audience, but he has certainly got to reckon with the human factor in the person of the performer or performers of his work, since he is not simply writing for an instrument or group of instruments; his instruments will be played by human beings capable of such and such a length of breath or bow, and with similar limitations in the speed of their reflexes, on which the successful handling of the instrumental mechanics depend. Admittedly, these considerations drop out when it comes to electronic music, since it dispenses with the human performer altogether. Yet even here the quip about music *by* engineers *for* engineers need not necessarily be the last word in the matter, with regard, I mean, to the artistic results which can be achieved in this medium. Which is to say that even in this extreme domain, the necessity of a rapport between the composer and his potential audience remains in full force. Indeed it is significant that no electronic composer worth his salt is (as yet) willing completely to renounce traditional instruments or, least of all, the vocal medium, in favour of the purely synthetic sound. Most significant in this respect is the fact that, in the compositions which the electronic composers are writing for traditional media, the major enterprise afoot now could properly be labelled: *récuperation de l'interprète*—win back the performer! One may certainly argue as to the proposed ways and means for allowing the performer a degree of 'free choice' which is supposed to amount to an almost 'creative' co-operation on his part not only in the rendering but in the actual shaping of the work. Yet what should not be overlooked above all is the awareness of and the sharp reaction against the danger of letting the human factor finally slip away; for these are the preoccupations of precisely those composers who are foremost in the electronic field. One might go as far as to say that the winning back of the interpreter is a good thing in any case—however wrongly one might go about it— if it succeeds. But there cannot be the slightest doubt that the rapport with one's audience remains the crucial issue.

I propose to give the question of 'communication' a wide berth. Whether there *is* communication and, if so, what it amounts to, is evidently very much a matter of speculation. But in that case, what is meant by a rapport between composer and listener? Let me put it like this: to my way of thinking music is, in its essence, dramatic. I am not using the word for its romantic connotations, nor in the purely Aristotelian sense only, but in the larger sense in which any phenomenon that is bound to the *péripétie* of a given temporal cycle or life-span and has, therefore, a beginning, a period of growth and an end, can be said to be dramatic in essence: the life-cycle of a blade of grass, the course of an avalanche, the impact of a drop of rain on a sheet of water, no less than the life-span of a tune or of a symphony. The 'drama' is, of course, in the mind of man, the beholder. This is the level at which the listener's mind must be engaged. I believe in plunging my listener straight away *in medias res* and keeping him there. In other words, the vital affair for me is to hold his attention. This is my work's life-line. The moment it snaps, my work dies.

From a painting hanging on the wall you may take your eyes away, and come back to it as often as you like: it is always there in its whole-ness. Not so with music. A work of music takes shape only in the mind of the listener. It does not exist, apart from this, as a thing in itself. Or rather, it does exist, but as something entirely different. It exists as a catalogue of specifications or directions for use (known as a score) which stands in a far more distantly mediatory relation with regard to the actual sounding work, than that in which the pigments can be said to stand to the image which the roving eye reads on the canvas. Until, and not until, the work of music comes alive in the mind of the listener, my score is but the possibility, the promise of a work. In order to arise in the mind of the listener it must *become*, eventuate, actualise in time. It is never there all of a piece, since it only comes into being as a temporal succession. In order to achieve its particular kind of existence and wholeness, the work has therefore got to be lived through in its total life-span. As long as the listener's attention is held the composer may do anything he likes: the one thing he cannot afford to do is to bore his listener and lose him on the way. Because the moment his attention lapses, be it only for a few bars, there is no knowing what ruin this may cause in the sequel, how many bars may be irrevocably blotted out in the listener's consciousness, as a result of that momentary eclipse of attention.

Whereas in the experience of a work of music 'communication' must remain, probably for ever, an unknown quantity, attention can be directly 'observed'; if it were necessary, it would perhaps even be measured. It is therefore a much more objective datum on which to base and to gauge one's rapport with the listener. But it is far more than that. Attention—deep, sustained, undeviating—is in itself an experience of a very high order. There seems to be a direct relation between the quality of a work of art and the quality of the attention it elicits in the perceiver. We know that it is the works which have held our attention most strongly, that we can bear to experience most often. The work to which I can listen time and again with ever renewed freshness of approach and a seemingly inexhaustible sense of discovery, is also the work which seems to prove my capacity for inexhaustible attention. This is indeed a happy match, and not a little mysterious. I certainly do not profess to know what it takes to achieve this rare captivation. Yet I have often thought that, when it does occur, it is as if the listener in his turn had been able to achieve a degree of detachment in the act of perception matching that of the composer in the act of origination. The listener's mind is emptied of all the petty preoccupations of the day; on exceptional occasions it may even succeed in temporarily suspending that feeling of separateness which we call our individuality. Detachment in the composer, matched by detachment in the listener, thus results paradoxically in the strongest possible bond between the two.

The social side of man has been defined as that part of the person which is entirely 'made up of other people', in other words, of borrowed patterns of behaviour, mostly unconsciously imitative. The feeling of being *different*—an oppressive feeling at most times—is perhaps what drove some people to become artists. Yet in that stage of perfect detachment which a great work of art can induce, both originator and perceiver seem, on the contrary, to find access to that part of ourselves where we are all essentially the same, but where the common ground lies far beyond the plane of superficial social conformity. I believe that this is one of the major aims of every true work of art.

To return to my questionnaire, it might be asked: is not the artist sometimes effectively hindering, if not frustrating, this very aim, as, for instance, when he becomes boldly experimental and upsets accepted conventions by too many or too radical innovations? Temporarily this may indeed be the effect of innovations. Could not the artist then make it easier for his audience to grasp his intentions by explaining what they are? The answer is still: no. If the composer could *say* something that might effectively help to make his intentions clearer to the listener then, surely, something must be missing in the work. *That* by which the work could be explained ought to have been *worked in*. Intelligent listeners and critics know very well that full justice cannot be done to every new, unfamiliar, work at the first hearing. Repeated hearings will almost certainly modify, for better or for worse, their first impressions. Only growing familiarity through repeated hearings can test the work to the full. And I am convinced that no verbal explanations the composer could provide can possibly affect the way in which the listener will finally come to terms with the work, as a result of the immediate and spontaneous experience of his own.

This statement may come as a surprise to listeners who have grown accustomed to the now fashionable technical exordia handed out at the performance of new works. In my opinion this practice has already led to a state of affairs which justifies a word of caution. To begin with, one has to distinguish between the sham and the genuine declarations.

They are not difficult to tell apart. The sham ones are unmistakably *ad usum Delphini;* they are aimed at the listener. The genuine ones, especially when they come from the composer himself and are to be found in technical magazines, are intended mainly for other composers who may happen to be working on similar lines, and whose criticism is implicitly solicited because it may prove useful. The ordinary listener ought to disregard both. The latter are generally couched in a jargon which the layman—happily—will find forbidding. Not that the sham ones are necessarily less so, but there is something more insidious about them. They set out deliberately to foster the fallacy that the more the listener knows about matters of technique, the better will he understand the music. The truth is that a little knowledge can go a long way to confuse the layman, *a fortiori* when the information is false. It appears that among young serialist composers today—I have it from the Trojan horse's mouth—a certain amount of deliberate humbugging is practised on the innocent listener, in the claims which it is now the fashion to put forward as to how many aspects of a composition, how many 'parameters' are being serialised. For some dark reason this is supposed to impress the listener or, more likely perhaps, a certain type of critic. I would have said that what this amounts to is an implicit admission that it matters little if everything is lost, bar some sort of 'intellectual' prestige, even though this should have to be based on false pretences. In point of fact the composer who is advancing such spurious claims can feel quite safe against detection, since none of them can possibly be checked in direct audition and very few people will go to the length of checking by analysis of the score, which is immensely arduous but the only possible means of establishing the truth.

Of far greater concern, however, are the serious misunderstandings that can arise out of genuine claims put forward in good faith by composers, and carefully considered by the student. Once again we are up against the fallacy that music can be *explained*; that more knowledge about how the piece is made will lead to a better understanding of the music. But it is evident that knowledge—here as in many other fields—does not necessarily lead to understanding. The danger is, on the contrary, that more and more knowledge may lead to less and less understanding, particularly where the layman is concerned. Paradoxically, understanding must come first. One must have grasped intuitively the heart of the matter before the factual bits of knowledge can even begin to make sense. And this holds good for all of us, listener, critic and composer alike. It is a case of strict one-way traffic. The direction is from the centre of an intuitive understanding outwards to the factual data, never the other way round. Technique is only illumined from within, from the core of the creative experience, with the composer, or from the core of the perceptive experience, with the listener or the critic. Approached from the outside, the facts that can be known—rules, technical devices, points of method—are barren. They are bound to be read by the outsider in a spirit of literal-mindedness, if I may say so, and, taken at their text-bookish face value, these data have a knack of often turning into the very opposite of what they are really meant to signify. They become then rigid, static formulae. Their inner dynamic and shifting relatedness, apparent to the artist in the act of compositional engagement, is entirely lost on the arm-chair analyst. Hence all the unprofitable quibbling that is going on nowadays on questions of serial technique and methods of composition. The arm-chair analyst has got hold of the wrong end of the stick: technique will never explain the work, but experience of the work could give valuable—indeed invaluable—clues towards explanation of the technique. So, even if that is all he really cares about, he obviously would be better advised to start, as an unprejudiced listener, with the experience of the work pure and simple. 'Pure and simple' is, of course, a manner of speaking, considering all that is involved even in the most elementary act of sensorial perception. What I mean to say is that immediate perceptive experience is the analyst's only chance even from the point of view of his own particular pursuit. Thus it turns out that my argument against answering questionnaires for the benefit of a concert audience goes further than I foresaw; indeed it applies quite as much to the person who looks for technical information, be it professionally or simply for the new dimension which the acquired knowledge may give to his enjoyment of the work. There is no doubt in my mind that to those who have intuitively grasped the heart of the matter, more and more will be revealed, not through conscious straining after knowledge but out of their own genuine experience of the work. Whereas in those who lack this intuitive understanding, even the correct factual information they may gather will, in the end, only serve to increase prejudice and confusion.

If I insist so much on the necessity of first approaching a work of art as an intuitive experience, I must not be thought to advocate, in the composer, an attitude of mere surrender to what, for short, we may call 'inspiration'; nor in the listener a similar surrender to the purely enotional impact of the experience. I believe that there is little to be said, intelligently, against the use of intelligence in any human pursuit. Yet intelligence at its best, or when best trained, *knows its place*. It knows when it is its turn to officiate and when it is its turn to be the handmaiden ministering in the background. Contemporary art, in every field, undeniably shows a powerful accession or increase of intellect. It is not a freak, but a fruit of our time and has got to be accepted as such. But when the extremes are about to meet, it sometimes becomes difficult to tell the cybernetic robot apart from the mystic. It would seem that the artist without faith *must* believe in calculation—that beauty might possibly be achieved by *perfect* calculation. It is the logical creed of the *sceptique créateur*. He has no alternative. The point is, however, that there is no going back from the intellectual rigour which has become our second nature. It would be foolish to expect the contemporary artist to trust to the 'reasons of the heart' with the same naiveté with which it is (probably mistakenly) thought that artists did in other ages. Intellectual rigour has come to stay, at least for our time. It is not in the least surprising, therefore, that given the alternative of being an inspired imbecile or one of the calculating boys of Darmstadt, the young composer today should unhesitatingly plump for the latter. His only mistake is to think that he has got a choice. The truth is that the only way of working out his salvation is to harness both inspired imbecile and calculating boy to the common task.

It is not always realised that all the paraphernalia of rational, systematically organised thought that goes nowadays into the composing of music, is but one very partial aspect of the creative effort. The whole serial technique, for example, is in the end nothing but a kind of cradle of scaffolding which allows the composer to work at certain aspects or levels of the sound-fabric, at which he could not get without this scaffolding. But what matters, needless to say, is the work. Once this is finished we want the scaffolding removed. It is not meant to attract attention. If the work has been successful the props must have become invisible in the end. Correct as I believe the simile to be, it is yet only half the truth. Seen from a different angle, there is another, more important aspect of the intellectual approach and of the constraints to which the artist bends his gift of imaginative invention. By these constraints he endeavours to achieve yet another kind of detachment —undoubtedly the hardest—namely, detachment *from his own work*. In the measure in which the artist can make the work obey immanent laws, conform to a 'programmed' order (randomness taking care of itself), he correspondingly reduces the range of his 'will', of his power of causation. This is the meaning of Valéry's remark: '*il faut vouloir et ne pas trop vouloir*' and Rilke's 'days of enormous obedience'. It seems to me that the artist who directs attention to the disciplines which enable him to approach such an aim is like a man sawing off the very branch on which he sits.

Communication is, no doubt, a function of language. But music is improperly called a 'language'. For all the obvious similarities in their respective structural organisations, it has become an increasingly misleading analogy to call music a 'language'. The sign, or rather the signal, in music never points to a 'signified' beyond and other than itself. On the contrary, it is intransitive, as it were; it arrests and focuses attention upon itself, and yet not so much upon itself as upon the mobilisation of a vast constellation of signals in their courses. The ear, said to be the musician's intelligence, is so very difficult to assess, that I keep on giving it the benefit of the doubt. One of the hardest discoveries for the musician to make, it seems, is that music, contrary to a generally held belief, is not made with notes. The eye leads the ear astray; it easily persuades it that the notes are really there—and nothing but the notes, as far as one can see. The ear, therefore, misguidedly concentrates on locating notes, on disentangling their clusters, on tracing the patterns they form. Yet the basic stuff of music is sonic motion, not notes or sounds. Manoeuvre is the *raison d'être* of the formations. The notes, the actual discrete sounds are but like the bits of straw on the waves in Leonardo's description of the phenomenon of 'tremor': 'the bits of straw are not carried along by the waves in the direction of the spread, but only bob up and down'. The true business of the composer is to release the flow, and shape, and steer the stream of sonic events in time.

Time is the drama; drama is time.

Hans Arp once said that the man who invented the excruciating phrase 'time is money' deserved to be horsewhipped. A society that has adopted this saying has nothing more to learn about devaluation.

VII

MODERN MUSIC AND THE CONDUCTOR

By Norman Del Mar

THE MODERN 'virtuoso' conductor, as he is often called, came into being little more than a hundred years ago. The necessity for such a figure arose during the days of Beethoven and Berlioz principally owing to the rapid increase in size and complexity of concerted and ensemble music which soon reached the point where it could no longer be controlled by one of the actual instrumentalists as had hitherto been the case with the composer or Kappellmeister. This was, of course, especially true of opera where, indeed, the sheer mechanics of ensuring unanimity of execution, let alone consistency of style, had become in itself a skilled occupation. As a result the function and character of the musical director changed utterly and with it the very abilities required by such an artist.

As the position had called into being men capable of fulfilling it, so in their turn these men reacted upon composers (many of them were indeed themselves composers of importance, such as Mahler) who very soon found themselves writing music in the larger forms which was becoming increasingly impossible of performance without some controlling influence. Thus the conductor became established, a figure who alone amongst his performers makes no sound whatever yet exercises absolute authority. In time this trend spread rapidly to all forms of music both vocal and instrumental from chamber music to grand opera until the métier of the conductor came to demand an unprecedented degree of versatility in knowledge as well as technique. This state of affairs was aggravated by the preoccupation of late nineteenth- and twentieth-century composers with evolutions and experiments of

85

style, leading naturally to extremes of every conceivable kind: of harmony; of contrapuntal or polyphonic texture; of rhythm; of tonality with the attendant techniques of atonality and serialism; of instrumental resources; of melodic subtleties including the use of intervals smaller than the semitone; of unusual vocal techniques; of popular idioms including jazz and the exotic folk music of distant countries; of theatrical devices and the cinema—all these, and many others, have been exploited by modern composers in their search for a personal manner of self-expression, and all or any of these may fall to the lot of the conductor of today who may be expected to take them all in his stride together with the wide varieties of human emotion (or deliberate lack of it) and spirituality that these techniques may be summoned up to express.

Whilst it can be misleading to over-categorise the qualifications of any artist, let alone that most controversial of figures, the conductor, certain requirements can be pointed out which, although constantly overlapping, are called into operation in especial degree in certain kinds of contemporary music. This is best done by means of a few contrasted illustrations which will throw some of the outstanding problems into sharp relief.

In the *Three Orchestral Pieces*, op. 6, by Alban Berg, for example (a post-Romantic work in idiom yet standing on the threshold of what is understood by the term Modern Music), the conductor is faced with an unusual degree of textural complexity: see Ex. 1, page 64.

The page chosen for reproduction is by no means exceptional in this work, which is accordingly a particularly difficult score of which to form a clear mental impression before the first rehearsal. This is not because any of the individual contrapuntal strands are particularly exotic in their formation, or because the orchestral tone qualities employed in their production are in any way unusual (except possibly in their technical difficulty). Orchestral music exists today in which both of these are also true. In the present instance, however, it is the sheer juxtaposition of so many melodic lines, each in its own variant of the main rhythmic pulse, which offers the initial difficulty, together with the music's freedom from any framework of traditional harmonic progression. It is often affirmed that a conductor should be able to hear

Alban Berg: from *Drei Orchesterstücke*, op. 6
I. Präludium

(*By permission of Universal Edition, Vienna and London*)

a score in his mind before facing an orchestra. In the case of classical
and romantic works he may even be considered a charlatan if he is
unable to do this. As so often in art, however, so sweeping a condemna-
tion may be unjust, and indeed when one reaches the music of more
recent times it is not going too far to say that in many cases of more
complex and advanced techniques an honest fulfilment of this require-
ment is virtually an impossibility! Nor can all such scores be learnt
adequately at the piano (one important method of learning a new
work).

Nevertheless the conductor must be able to form a clear impression
of the substance of the music together with an intimate knowledge of
its salient features: in the present example, for instance, the main
subject (indicated by the Schoenbergian symbol H indicating 'Haupt-
thema') on clarinets, xylophone and trumpets announced together
with its diminution and double diminution on flutes and harps, and
violins and glockenspiel respectively (the latter treated by Berg as the
subsidiary theme—hence the symbol N for 'Nebenstimme'); the broad
syncopated figure on trombones reinforced by timpani, this derived
also from the main subject; the horns with their trills and snap chords
hurled apparently at random into the melos; all these elements must
be vividly present in the conductor's mind with a careful realisation
of their relative importance if the passage is not to dissolve, as it can
all too easily, into a meaningless jumble of unco-ordinated ideas.

As the page progresses, moreover, the basic rhythm itself becomes
subject to subtle deviations. Nor are these always in the same direction
—this alternation of *rit.* and *accel.* which continues into the following
bar is, of course, a specified and exaggerated form of rubato, always a
very hard effect to achieve with a large orchestra even without the
additional onus of so many conflicting rhythmic patterns.

Rhythmic complexity naturally calls Stravinsky to mind and of all
the many works of this great composer which present immense difficulties to the conductor the *ne plus ultra* is still the *Sacre du Printemps*
with its notorious *Danse sacrale de l'élue*. The illustration on page 66
presents a typical example of its particular snares.

As in Ex. 1 an enormous orchestra is employed, though the difficulties
are not this time so greatly affected by this factor. Similar problems

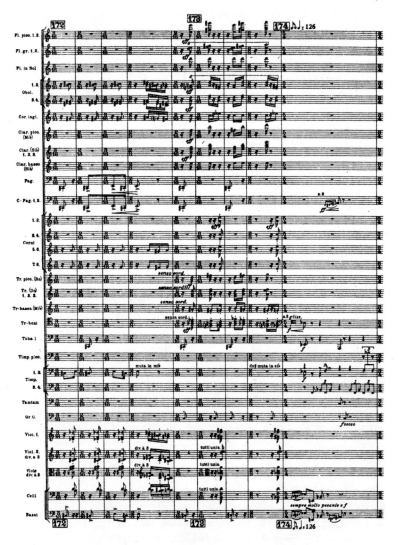

Igor Stravinsky: from *Le Sacre du Printemps*
By permission of Boosey and Hawkes, London)

are to be encountered in *L'Histoire du Soldat* in which the orchestra
numbers a total of no more than seven players. Nevertheless these
seven instrumentalists are as dependent upon a skilful conductor as
the one hundred-odd of the *Sacre*.

If both examples quoted above use a large orchestra, these orchestras
are by no means identical, as can be seen at a glance. Stravinsky uses,
for instance, a small trumpet in D and a bass trumpet in E flat as well
as the three more usual members of the species. Berg used four of the
noble but practically extinct trumpet in F. This in itself may present a
problem to the conductor of an orchestral society, though not so
great as that of the percussion in these two works. Berg calls on the
hammer which Mahler first used in his *Sixth Symphony*, without ever
specifying in detail precisely what the hammer should smite, a very
serious practical consideration and scarcely helped by the single proviso
that it should not make a metallic sound! Stravinsky uses the South
American *guero rapo*, a very unusual instrument. Contemporary
composers are apt to include many such special instruments which are
often entirely new to Western concert halls. In the case of Villa-Lobos
the publishers reckon on sending the numerous percussion instruments
he calls for, together with the hired material, since few orchestras can
boast a *xucalho* or a *réco-réco*. Yet the conductor risks a humiliating
situation if he cannot at least identify the instruments in his score!
With the numerous gourds (Copland, etc.), bongos (Boulez), Chinese
tom-toms (Gerhard), iron chains (Schoenberg), and so on, the list
could be extended almost indefinitely, while up to now no reference
book on music in general or orchestration in particular has yet been
written to provide exhaustive answers in the case of specialised knowledge of this kind, which no musician of any era has ever before
required in such detail and profusion. Occasionally an unusual term
hides a familiar instrument; hence Respighi's *raganella* and *sonagliera*
prove to be no more than rattle and sleigh-bells, while the *arpaliuto*
in Falla's *El Retablo de Maese Pedro* is simply a harpsichord!

To return to the specific problems of the page of Stravinsky quoted,
the outstanding feature of the music is its irregular rhythm calling for
a high degree of skill and clarity in the conductor's actual stick technique. This cannot, however, be an end in itself even here where at

first glance the purely motivic structure of the music appears to be relatively simple. In fact this page shows in close proximity no less than three entirely independent thematic sections; the first consists of bars 1-4 (the main subject of the movement), bars 5-8 (the closing figure of the principal theme which dominates the music in the last pages of the work), and bar 9 which is the first bar of a new and extended episode in an entirely different rhythmic pulse based on the crotchet instead of the quaver or dotted quaver.

Here the conductor must have a crystal clear understanding of not only the rhythmic relationships between the irregular bar lengths (often confusing in themselves), but a profound realisation of the architectural scheme. In particular this will prevent his representing to the orchestra the only two adjacent bars in an identical time value as two bars of momentarily rhythmic regularity. (In fact the first of these is the second of a two-bar phrase $5/16$ in total length, while the second is the first of a balancing two-bar phrase extended to $7/16$ in total length.) But in the wider sense a true perception of the gigantic scheme of the work will prevent an all too easy preoccupation with the incidental difficulties from producing a frenzied and thus puny interpretation of its immense potential grandeur, as I have witnessed on more than one occasion.

My next example on page 69 shows again the greatest possible contrast with the two previous quotations. It is a page from the *Orchestral Variations*, op. 30, by Anton Webern and is in a style which is particularly in favour with the most recent *avant-garde* developments in modern music.

For spareness of texture one can scarcely go further, as can be seen at once. The chief problem lies in the fact that no instrument contains more than a few notes of the thematic strand which weaves in the usual manner of Webern's mature work up and down the score. If the conductor is not fully acquainted with the idiom and technique of this kind of music he can be no guide to his players in a sincere interpretation, be his gestures never so clear! Moreover, his sense of pitch and colour must be far more acutely developed than in either of the earlier examples if the music is not to become utterly fragmentary and incoherent. In particular, sympathy for the difficulties (both musical

Anton Webern: from *Variations, op.* 30

and technical) of each instrumentalist is essential if during the numerous and strenuous rehearsals, indispensable with this kind of work, the conductor is not to antagonise his players in the face of their preposterous and individually meaningless parts.

In fully serial and dodecaphonic works a detailed knowledge of the method and working of the Tone-row and its mutations may be required for the establishing of the correct text. I myself encountered this problem when preparing Schoenberg's *Suite*, op. 29, for performance since it transpired that the parts and score differed from one another repeatedly. The only way of answering the practical queries raised by players was through reference to the forty-eight possible note formations on which the work was contrived.

The human voice may be thought to be less capable of elaborate development than instruments, but here too composers have shown astonishing resourcefulness. Wordless choruses and Vocalises have become almost commonplace since the days of Skriabin and Debussy, and are often used in a variety of ways, including pitchless declamation as in Ex. 4 on page 71.

This gives a page of *Les Choéphores* by Milhaud in which a number of different syllables are declaimed rhythmically by the chorus. Later the tenors and basses also take up whistles of both fixed and varying pitch. Such passages occur frequently in Milhaud's work and are usually, as here, accompanied by a vast array of percussion instruments.

Naturally enough the crucial problem in modern vocal music is that of pitch, and this becomes acute as soon as the harmonic palette is stretched to and beyond breaking point. Nevertheless, composers have not hesitated to write music for voices which is excessively difficult for singers to hear and pitch accurately. Here, too, the conductor must be able to help and, if necessary, correct his singers even if he does not have that otherwise doubtful asset known as 'absolute pitch'. Moreover, a further important consideration enters the conductor's orbit with vocal music in the shape of language problems. The suddenly increased speed of travel during the present century and the prevailing taste for works to be presented in their original language have created the situation in which the conductor may find himself shouldering the responsibility of correcting diction and pronunciation in tongues which

Darius Milhaud: from *Les Choéphores*
(*By permission of Heugel et Cie, Paris*)

are not his own and which he does not necessarily speak fluently. He must still be able to suggest the words and manner of singing since a chorus, even when fully professional, needs even more confident encouragement than an orchestra at each lead if it is to enter at all, while expecting the conductor to keep a constant watch on intonation and the exact placing of syllables.

Modern composers also require choruses to do other things than sing. In his *In the Hall of Mirrors* the Swedish composer Blomdahl directs the chorus to clap their hands off the beat while actually singing surrealistic words to a jazz tune! Some choruses find this novel effect tricky and it may well be necessary for the conductor to demonstrate personally how this should be done.

Where the single voice is concerned the most difficult and problematic development is undoubtedly Schoenberg's invention of the *Sprechstimme*, an attempt at realising and evoking by means of musical notation the natural rise and fall of the speaking voice. The success of this device is still far from accepted generally, and its fallibility is to some extent demonstrated by the recording of *Pierrot Lunaire* in a performance conducted by Schoenberg himself, in which the 'singer' rarely approaches to within a fourth of the pitch indicated in the score. Here again a great understanding of the intention of the composer and of the literary content of the text, in whatever language, is necessary for the conductor in his tactful guidance of the vocalist faced with a task which is almost impossible to accomplish satisfactorily.

I have so far dealt specifically with extremes of stylistic complexity, but this is naturally only one aspect of contemporary music. The worth of a conductor is often far more apparent when faced with the vast variety of personal styles to be found in the more accessible yet utterly individual composers such as Bartók or Britten. In Bartók, the problems of rhythm and colour may so put the conductor on his technical mettle as to blind him to the profound spiritual qualities of the music. In the case of Britten the apparent simplicity of texture and idiom in some of his finest works hides severe pitfalls, as in his chamber operas, where taste and practical skill in their presentation are as important to the conductor as musicianship.

It is true to say that the conductor of today may find himself in need of a wider knowledge of all forms and styles of music than ever before including, it is important to stress, the music of early periods. Not only may he be required to handle in the same programme the music of, for example, Machault or Gabrieli and that of late Stravinsky, but Stravinsky himself will draw on a composer such as Pergolesi for his *Pulcinella* and Hindemith will incorporate ancient plain chant and folk-song in his *Mathis der Maler* and *Der Schwanendreher* respectively. At the other end of the scale Křenek will draw on jazz for his *Jonny spielt auf*, and a knowledge of popular music (a highly fluid and constantly changing idiom) together with a feeling for the many jazz styles is necessary to interpret to the best advantage some works by such composers as Walton, Milhaud, Liebermann or Blomdahl.

At one time it was regarded as a failing on the part of any artist to be able to appreciate too general a range of music, as if such an ability reflected a lack of critical judgment and personality. This can even remain true of a composer who, if too ready to accept the music of others can come to lack consistency of style in his own work. A conductor on the other hand genuinely needs the power constantly to absorb new styles of every conceivable kind, many of which may at first be inimicable or actually incomprehensible to him. This has become especially true in recent years with the arrival on the scenes of a new extremist group of young musicians led by Boulez, Nono and Stockhausen, the latter with his experiments in electronic music. Some of the music of this group is as hard to absorb as Chinese to a scholar of hitherto exclusively Western languages. Nevertheless the conductor has a responsibility to try and keep abreast of such developments which is becoming ever more assumed by contemporary opinion. Unless the course of his career has made it plain that he is essentially a specialist he may be required to handle, often at short notice, any of these widely varied intricate styles which are the particular feature of the contemporary musical scene.

VIII

SOME RECENT TRENDS IN OPERA

By Arthur Jacobs

TO BE SURPRISED because so few new works become established successes in the opera house is like being surprised because so few people,
these days, travel by Zeppelin. The opera houses of the world's capital
cities are not institutions called into existence to accommodate the
modern composer. Supported at considerable expense for reasons of
social prestige, they are primarily mausoleums for exhibiting a historic
nineteenth-century type of romantic spectacle. In such works the
heroic-romantic situation of nineteenth-century novels and plays was
matched by heroic-romantic music. Moreover nineteenth-century
opera, like the 'legitimate' drama of its time, presented its romantic
vision as a naturalistic slice of life, into which the audience was permitted to penetrate through the 'fourth wall' formed by the proscenium
arch.

Such opera had its distinctive place in the cultural pattern of nineteenth-century society. Though frequently answering local or nationalistic passions, it was couched in a form that won it universal appeal.
A successful opera went quickly across frontiers—and, moreover,
penetrated society vertically too. Operatic tunes reappeared on the
drawing-room piano, in the ballroom, and even in the repertory of
street musicians. But in the twentieth century opera no longer provided
'hits'. Rather, with the growth of a new American-inspired popular
music, the process was reversed. German and Austrian opera houses
found after the 1939-45 war that their audiences made a favourite of
Cole Porter's *Kiss Me, Kate*.

Moreover, the twentieth century saw a revolution in the diffusion

D

of serious music. Thanks to the radio (and, less so, to the gramophone) new music for the concert hall achieved rapid international circulation —while opera houses acquired deposits of mud on their wheels. It took twenty-six years for Berg's *Wozzeck* (not just 'an' opera, but one which musicians everywhere recognised as a masterpiece) to come from the opera stage at Berlin (1926) to Covent Garden (1951). Janáček had died in 1928, but it was not until two decades later that his operas became staple fare in Germany. Prokofiev completed *The Angel of Fire* in 1920-2, but it was never staged until 1955.

A composer today is not expected to write symphonies like Brahms' or Tchaikovsky's, and there is no more reason to think that he will naturally be drawn to the form of the traditional opera and the meeting-point of the traditional opera house. He will probably not feel, as some of his predecessors did, that opera is the great, the all-enveloping form, the queen of the representational arts. Vaughan Williams, in remarking that 'the film contains potentialities for the combination of all the arts such as Wagner never dreamt of',[1] was stating no more than literal truth. No creative mind today would expect to realise a 'total work of art', Wagner's *Gesamtkunstwerk*, within the resources of an opera house. Indeed, Wagner's own heirs at Bayreuth, stripping his works during the 1950s of Wagner's own type of representational staging, implicitly confessed themselves a good deal *moins royaliste que le roi*.

Instead of opera as the all-enveloping form, we have seen the boundaries of opera broken by the invasion of speech. In Schoenberg's unfinished *Moses und Aron* (1957), one of the principal characters, Aaron, does not sing. Speech also invades the operatic setting of Shakespeare's *The Tempest* (1956) by Frank Martin (1890-). We may note, however, that like many another modern composer, Martin avoids the actual word 'opera' on his title-page. And in *Jeanne d'Arc au bûcher* (1938) by Arthur Honegger (1892-1955) the domination of the non-singing role of Joan of Arc is such that we may consider ourselves out of opera's domain—despite some indubitably 'operatic' touches.

Most of the great nineteenth-century operas (and we may extend

[1]Quoted by Muir Matheison in *Winchester's Screen Encyclopaedia*, 1948.

this generalisation up to Puccini) were tragedies. If the twentieth century has seen a revival of comic opera, we need not imply that its composers take a funnier view of life. The truth is more likely to be that they have relished the overt artificiality of comic opera—its deliberate invitation to the audience not to identify itself with pathetic characters but to stand apart and watch from a quasi-moral viewpoint. Thus Bohuslav Martinů (1890-1959) could marshal his characters in *Comedy on the Bridge* (originally for radio, 1937) with the precision of puppets for purposes of satire, not sympathy. Sometimes modern opera, rejecting romanticism, evokes the spirit of eighteenth-century comic opera instead. Stravinsky, in *The Rake's Progress* (1951), displayed a chain of self-contained musical numbers linked by recitative in a general back-to-Mozart diatonic stylisation. Moreover, he exactly paralleled *Don Giovanni* by presenting a 'sad' tale in a comic-opera framework, even to having the cast address the audience in a direct moral sermon at the end.

A similar direct address from the cast to the audience—who are told to go home and have babies—is made in *Les Mamelles de Tirésias* ('The Breasts of Tiresias', 1947) by Francis Poulenc (1899-). Moreover, Poulenc here brings French comic opera very near the spirit of French revue. The temptation to come to terms with the 'popular' musical theatre is, as we shall see, strongest of all for the American composer. But no composer anywhere can have failed to observe how the public which cultivates the 'musical' is much more eager for new works and much less wedded to the past than those who frequent the mausoleum of the opera house.

And yet the mausoleum of the opera house also attracts the composer. Since such an expensive team of skilled musicians and stage people is maintained there for the servicing of dead bodies, what a pity not to be able to insinuate a live one occasionally! Moreover, the mausoleum also has its regular congregation of worshippers who, though crippled by the plagues of snobbery and the cult of 'great voices', might possibly like to see a change of offering on the shrine. The living composer sneaks in to try. A characteristic case is that of Hindemith. He early split open the whole 'naturalistic' convention of opera with his *Hin und zurück* ('There and Back', 1927) in which the music is played straightforwardly through and then is heard in reverse to accompany a similar reversal of the action on stage (like the re-winding of a cinema film). But he also felt the pull of old-fashioned opera with its romantic hero-against-the-world and music to match. After *Mathis der Maler* ('Mathis the Painter', 1938) he again attempted the form, with somewhat less success, in *Die Harmonie der Welt* ('The Harmony of the World', 1957), of which the hero is the astronomer Kepler.

It would be too easy, of course, to say that modern attempts at 'old-fashioned opera' are reactionary and therefore bad, and attempts at a new, non-romantic, and specifically twentieth-century musico-dramatic form are good. We prudently recall that a genius may nominally use an old framework for vitally new content. Is not Berg's *Wozzeck* written for the traditional resources of an opera house? Has it not always been staged in such a theatre? Yet what it proceeds to do is to turn the conventions of such a theatre inside-out—with a multiplicity of short scenes precluding the building-up of romantic tension, with normal tonality and normal canons of 'good singing' overthrown, and with a hero who is unheroic. We need not doubt that a composer with a powerful modern musical style can still create a moving musical drama within an old-fashioned 'heroic' handling of the stage. Such a work as *Pallas Athene Weint* ('Pallas Athene Weeps', 1955) by the twelve-note composer Ernst Křenek (1900-) might be so described.

But other composers apparently find it fatally tempting, in order to gain an entrance into the opera house, simply to fill a traditional bottle labelled 'grand romantic opera' with what they imagine to be never-failing ingredients. They perhaps do not think of asking why the public, which apparently can *never* see too many performances of *Butterfly*, should go to try somebody else's mock-*Butterfly* instead of the kind they already know to be the Old Original Brand. There is in *Troilus and Cressida* (1954) by Sir William Walton (1902-) an inevitable feeling that here a very clever modern composer is *manufacturing* music with big tunes 'just like Puccini' in it, tunes linked with the heroic treatment of things like love and death and treachery. (It is no wonder that this music seems to lack the 'bite' of Walton's own radical period of a quarter of a century before.) Poulenc chose a French revolutionary setting for an old-fashioned grand opera, but *Les Dialogues des Carmélites* (1957, produced in Britain as 'The Carmelites') failed not so much through the archaism of its form but because its musical material was so weakly realised.

In Italy itself the idea of 'doing another Puccini' is not quite dead: a recent example is *Il Vortice* ('The Vortex', 1958) by Renzo Rossellini (1908-). Busoni died in the same year as Puccini (1924), but never made much impact on Italian musical life with such an anti-romantic conception as that of *Arlecchino* (in German, 1917), which cocks a snook all round and then tosses the matter over the footlights to the music critics. Yet there is something of Busoni's dryness and avoidance of romantic afflatus in harnessing music to speech, and something of his preference for obliquely symbolic rather than naturalistic meaning in opera, in the work of Gian Francesco Malipiero (1882-)—for instance, in the recent one-act pieces *Venere Prigioniera* ('Captive Venus', 1958), and *Il Capitan Spavento* ('Captain Terror', 1958).

Malipiero's fellow-veteran, Ildebrando Pizzetti (1880-) has continued to prefer the almost literal setting of heroic plays—for instance, of D'Annunzio's *La Figlia di Jorio* ('The Daughter of Jorio', 1954) and of T. S. Eliot's *Murder in the Cathedral* (1958). He has kept the shape and feeling of romantic opera without the so-called 'excesses' of romanticism, but restraint is not a positive tool, and one is left wondering what operatic compensation is offered for a certain loss of dramatic subtlety from Eliot's original play. A more modern feeling is given by two Italian works first produced in 1950 which, though very different, verge on oratorio in their moral approach to the audience: *Morte dell'aria* ('Death in the Air') by Goffredo Petrassi (1904-) and *Il Prigioniero* ('The Prisoner') by Luigi Dallapiccola (1904-).

It is a provoking paradox, however, that the most successful opera composer to be born in this century in Italy settled in America—which, of all musically advanced countries, appeared to be most firmly dedicated to the proposition that opera reaches its height when consisting of music by dead composers sung by foreigners in foreign languages to rich people. Gian-Carlo Menotti (1911-) has lived in the United States from 1928. Apart from *Amelia al ballo* ('Amelia Goes to the Ball', 1937), all his librettos have been written in English by himself.

Moreover, he is invariably the stage director (never the conductor) of his own works.

Only in limited respects, however, can Menotti be considered a 'rebel' or 'modernist' in opera. There is in fact only one work in which he has thrown over the traditional form of operatic presentation. This is *The Unicorn, the Gorgon, and the Manticore* (1956), in which the action is expressed in mime and dance, while off-stage a chamber chorus accompanied by a chamber instrumental ensemble takes charge of both narration and dialogue. Menotti calls the work a 'madrigal-fable' and its construction is indebted to Orazio Vecchi's *L'Amfiparnaso* ('The Amphiparnassus', 1594)—which, however, was never intended to be staged. Menotti's piece is a clever, lucid, civilised enter-tainment.

But with *The Consul* (1950), in which the heroine is driven to defeat between evil totalitarianism and stupid democratic red tape, Menotti was doing little more than bringing Puccini (especially *Tosca*) up to date—and doing it very well. Not only did he set the scene in our own times; he also increased the operatic pace to suit an audience brought up on films; and he stirred in a fashionable dream sequence. In *The Saint of Bleecker Street* (1954) and *Maria Golovin* (1958) he also gave traditional romantic opera an up-to-date touch. In the delightful two-character squib of *The Telephone*, in which the comic musical handling of everyday dialogue is so assured, Menotti is also not so much putting forth something new as paralleling the skits of Offen-bach a century before.

But in one respect Menotti *has* shown his inclination to break away from the world of traditional opera. Organising his own companies, he has sensibly tried to fit into the live American world of 'show business'. *The Medium* (1946) must be the only opera which was filmed, with its composer as film director, within five years of its stage produc-tion. *Amahl and the Night Visitors* (1951) is a simple Christmas legend (the capacity to sneer at it is the touchstone of musical hyper-aestheticism) which was not only the first opera written for television; it also has an intimate dramatic shape and simple musical form that ensured its being presented repeatedly by school and college groups—in whose charge is the seed of genuine operatic appreciation in America.

But in America, which had given the whole world a new and lively kind of popular music, would not opera immeasurably enrich its appeal if it could meet that popular music half-way? The idea of basing a short opera on actual American folk-songs and on other songs specifically composed in 'folk' style was most poetically realised by Kurt Weill (1900-50) in *Down in the Valley* (1948); and two of the most successful operas by native-born Americans also made use (though not exclusively) of American folk-melody—*Susannah* (1955) by Carlisle Floyd (1926-) and *The Ballad of Baby Doe* (1956) by Douglas Moore (1893-). The sharper, urban accents of jazz had been harnessed to leftist social criticism by Marc Blitzstein (1905-) in *The Cradle Will Rock* (1936) and other stage works; and Leonard Bernstein (1918) not only used popular idioms in such works as the satirical opera *Trouble in Tahiti* (originally for television, 1952) but found attractions in the form of the American musical itself (and the filmed musical). Bernstein's *On the Town* (1944, later filmed) and *West Side Story* (1957) were conspicuously successful. Nor was he, of course, the only seriously trained musician to cultivate the Broadway musical: among others, Kurt Weill produced notable music in *Lost in the Stars* (1949), based on Alan Paton's novel *Cry, the Beloved Country*. Against these successes by composers deliberately trying to meet the popular taste in music, only one operatic work by a composer from Tin Pan Alley itself achieved a widely-recognised standing: *Porgy and Bess* (1935) by George Gershwin (1898-1937), with some touching music not quite satisfactorily integrated into dramatic shape.

It is too easy to use emotive labels here—to think of serious composers as 'slumming' when they cultivate jazz and its derivatives. But this is perhaps to misunderstand the current situation which confronts the composer who wishes to unite music and the stage. To 'compose opera' in the old sense may mean, concretely, to fill a three-act romantic scaffolding with romantic music in an attempt to please people who will *not*, in the last analysis, desert Wagner and Puccini for you. But the theatrical public which goes to the 'musical' expects something new (as did opera-goers when opera was in its prime); and the serious composer has the craftsman's tools which can make that new thing for them, often with considerable freedom in the use of theatrical resources.

Of course this is to postulate a composer who feels himself a craftsman in this way, not a romantic artist with a 'message'.

We have twice mentioned the name of Kurt Weill, and here we must do so again. Weill not only tackled the Broadway musical (*Street Scene, Lost in the Stars*) and the 'folk-opera' (*Down in the Valley*); he had also, among several earlier works, written for the German stage *Die Dreigroschenoper* (1928)—which, more than two decades later, as *The Threepenny Opera* enjoyed an astonishing wave of success in Britain, America, and elsewhere. *The Threepenny Opera* has a libretto by Bertolt Brecht, who became one of the most influential men of the European theatre as playwright, producer, and manager. Its tale of low life was inspired by the idea of bringing *The Beggar's Opera* (1728) up to date. But it stands as a basic new model in opera. Its characters are not real or naturalistic, but the expression of social attitudes; composer and librettist give the audience the constant idea that they are all (creators, audience, characters) playing a game or enacting a meaningful ritual together, rather than that the audience is gazing at a pretended slice of life. Moreover, the music, borrowing the idioms of the street and dance-hall, is music that helps to express the characters' individual identities and the links between them, rather than music which in some way contrives to reproduce real feelings. In other words the opera-composer here has ceased to feel that he must 'write great music'. Instead he is writing music for a modern stage, in a functional, craftsmanlike and amusing manner.

We may quote Brecht himself: 'Opera should be a spectacle made up of clearly definable components, rather than an illusory image of a magic super-world, and the spectacle should convey an explicitly demonstrated meaning for those beholding it, instead of being merely expensive entertainment or glorified dope.'[1] We may add that such a conception, when realised, may appear without the label 'opera' on it—and that, in America, such a work is more likely to spring up almost anywhere else than at the Metropolitan, where such old-fashioned romantic vehicles as *Vanessa* (1958) by Samuel Barber (1910-) are felt to fit the plush and the seat-prices. In England, it is perhaps not

[1] Quoted by D. J. Grout, *A Short History of Opera*, 1947.

realised how well Benjamin Britten has fulfilled the desiderata of Weill and Brecht with *Noye's Fludde*.

The position of Britten is a curious one. Like Menotti, he partly broke away from normal opera channels in respect of organisation. It was fortunate that the economy involved in writing for small casts and for chamber orchestra, which allowed him to form his own 'English Opera Group', evidently corresponded to a deep artistic need of his. But partly he accepted not only the traditional opera house but the traditional opera conventions. *Peter Grimes* (1945) is a romantic opera, though stronger in its 'atmosphere' (especially through the orchestra, perhaps) than in the operatic delineation of character except in the hero. The structure of romantic opera is preserved in the later (and less striking) *Billy Budd* (male characters only, 1951) and *Gloriana* (1953). All these are on 'grand opera', not 'chamber opera', scale. *The Turn of the Screw* (1953), for the small English Opera Group, tautly and evocatively written, treats an unusual story of ghostly 'possession' through a fundamentally old-fashioned operatic use of 'heroine' and 'villains' in naturalistic presentation.

In *Billy Budd* the story is presented as a cinematic 'flash-back' in the mind of one of the characters; in *The Turn of the Screw* a dramatically and musically superfluous 'prologue' starts: 'It is a curious story . . .' as if putting the whole operatic action in quotation marks. *The Rape of Lucretia* (1946), a chamber opera, includes two characters called Male and Female Chorus who stand outside the plot and who, with seeming obtrusiveness, embellish a pagan plot with a Christian moral. But is this seeming obtrusiveness really a clumsy interference with the business of opera? It is more tempting to see all the devices in all these three operas as showing dissatisfaction on Britten's part with opera presented merely through a 'fourth wall'. And indeed in *Let's Make an Opera!* (1949) he quite demolished the 'wall' by presenting the 'construction' of an opera and making the audience join in. There survives in this work one 'pathetic' aria which is a little out of place. But in *Noye's Fludde* ('Noah's Flood'), produced in 1958, Britten created a completely consistent opera-as-a-social-gesture (instead of the old opera-as-a-romantic-spectacle). The audience again takes part, singing traditional hymns, and the gesture-opera is enacted in a functional place, namely a church. This is ritual, not make-believe. We are not asked to pretend that the baritone voice behind a pillar really *is* the voice of God. There is the feeling not of 'great music' but of good tunes assembled with masterly craftsmanship.

Of other post-war British operas, none seems to show Britten's clear vision of the possibilities of a modern operatic form. Michael Tippett (1905-) in *The Midsummer Marriage* (1955) was a victim of his own muddled thinking. Instead of opera enacted *as* a rite he made an opera *about* a rite—or rather about a sequence of ritual gestures and 'naturalistic' gestures, the relation between which was insufficiently clarified. Not even the lyrical inspiration of much of the music (particularly the *Ritual Dances*) could save the matter. Ralph Vaughan Williams (1872-1958) had earlier found a poignant but dramatically limited operatic language for *The Shepherds of the Delectable Mountains* (1922) and *Riders to the Sea* (composed 1926-7, produced 1937), each in one act, but the idiom was not successfully stretched to cover the full-length structure of *The Pilgrim's Progress* (1951), in which *The Shepherds of the Delectable Mountains* was incorporated. Romantic comedy proved stillborn in *The Olympians* (1949) by Sir Arthur Bliss (1891-). Alan Bush (1900-) chose historical themes of Leftist significance in *Wat Tyler* (1953) and *Men of Blackmoor* (1956)—operas with old-fashioned 'heroic' and 'popular' dramatic components. Both had their first productions in East Germany and have not been staged in Britain.

Lennox Berkeley (1903-) also chose the old-fashioned heroic type of opera in *Nelson* (1954) but failed to make it spark. He was more successful with the comedy of *A Dinner Engagement* (1954) with its deliberate artificiality—matching a plot of modern social embarrassment to a succession of self-contained musical numbers. Even more successful in the vein of deliberately artificial comedy is the one-act opera by Arthur Benjamin (1893-), *Prima Donna* (composed 1934, produced 1949), with an eighteenth-century setting which allows musical pastiche to show its head very agreeably. Benjamin evidently writes from a real feeling for stage effect, and his *A Tale of Two Cities* (1957) has the real meat of romantic opera in it. (The 'clouding-over' of Dr Manette's mind and the big soliloquy of Sydney Carton are master-strokes.) It will be interesting to see if it can survive the obsolescence of its form. After all, it arrived sixty years after theatregoers had first seen Sir John Martin-Harvey in *The Only Way*.

In Germany, Austria, and German-speaking Switzerland (which may, operatically, be considered as a unit with a particularly active network of theatres) there has been a good deal of variety in the evolution of modern types of opera. A straightforward comedy, constructed in virtually self-contained musical numbers and tricked out with a dream sequence, achieved success in *Der Revisor* ('The Government Inspector', after Gogol, 1957) by Werner Egk (1901-). A more artificial type of comedy, with obeisance towards eighteenth-century opera, was accomplished by Rolf Liebermann (1910-) in the one-act opera *School for Wives* (in English, 1955, afterwards extended to three acts in German). In *Penelope* (1954) Liebermann had successfully essayed a different sort of artificiality, intertwining a modern and a classical Greek story (and, characteristically, bringing boogie-woogie into the score). This disruptive treatment of myth is to be contrasted with such a straightforward older setting as that in Richard Strauss's *Daphne* (1938).

Gottfried von Einem (1918-) had, with a thoroughly modern technique, successfully tackled a de-romanticised historical drama in *Dantons Tod* ('The Death of Danton', 1947); but the abstraction of Kafka's novel 'The Trial' did not suit him so well (*Der Prozess*, 1953). Meanwhile a still younger composer furnished the remarkable example of modern opera embracing the world of magical and moral symbolism created by the Italian eighteenth-century dramatist Carlo Gozzi.[1] *König Hirsch* ('King Stag', 1956) by Hans Werner Henze (1926-), is a powerful score of great complexity and variety, partly following twelve-note methods. It incorporates certain closed 'instrumental' forms—like Berg's *Wozzeck*, a work which also influenced Henze's earlier modernised treatment of the 'Manon' story, *Boulevard Solitude* (1952).

But among German composers there is an older one who has deliberately sought a new conception of opera, removed not only

[1] Whose work also furnished the plot for one of the best and most significant inter-war operas, Prokofiev's *Love for Three Oranges* (1921).

from romantic impersonation on the stage but from all feeling of writing 'great music'. Carl Orff (1895-) writes diatonic, strongly rhythmical music which is simple enough for the schoolroom. With ludicrous misunderstanding, some writers have described this as 'watered-down Stravinsky', alluding to the percussive patterns of such works as *The Wedding* (1923)—as if there were not a world of emotional difference between the inward tension of Stravinsky's irregular repetitions and the mere cumulative effects of Orff. Whether in *Carmina Burana* (on medieval, mainly Latin texts, 1937), in which the action is mimed to off-stage singing, or in more normally 'operatic' works such as *Der Mond* ('The Moon', 1939) and *Die Kluge* ('The Clever Girl', 1943), or when touching both genres in *Antigone* (1949), Orff is a liberator of modern opera. That he is a great composer is not necessarily implied.

At the beginning of this essay it was remarked that the mobility of operas between countries is less and not greater than formerly. We are reminded of this in comparing the stimulation which pre-1914 western audiences received from contemporary Russian opera with the wall which has confined Soviet opera. After the sensational denunciation and suppression of Shostakovich's *The Lady Macbeth of the Mtsensk District* (1934), Russian officialdom has apparently frowned on any attempt at 'modernism' in opera, and the news of such new operas as have apparently established themselves in Russia indicates that they are heroic, semi-political dramas—such as Prokofiev's *War and Peace* (concert performance, 1946) Shaporin's *The Decembrists* (1953) and Kabalevsky's *The Family of Taras* (1950)—or romantic moral comedies. For lack of the evidence of a score, one is left speculating whether the venture of Shostakovich in writing a musical comedy (*Moscow-Cheremushki*, 1959) marks a parallel to the enterprises of serious American composers in the field of the 'musical'. The psychological dramas of Janáček perhaps provided the main model for the most successful of recent Czechoslovak works, *The Whirlpool* (1949), by Eugen Suchon (1908-).

Thus opera lurches, rather than marches, on. We need not yet write its obituary. The use of music as a psychological prime mover in the representation of action is doubtless capable of new metamorphoses yet. Perhaps the hardest obstacle to the recognition of the validity of such metamorphoses is the use of the term *opera* itself, redolent of fossil-collecting and the cultivation of hot-house blooms. No wonder that modern composers themselves so often fight shy of the term on their title-pages! While so-called connoisseurs of opera, with the subtlety of medieval theologians, sit comparing the performance on gramophone records of two dead sopranos in the trivialities of *Lucia di Lammermoor*, a new and unspoilt audience is perhaps waiting for a clear summons along paths that spirits as bold as Orff, Weill, and Britten have at least begun to clear.

POSTSCRIPT ON RECENT OPERATIC DEVELOPMENTS

By Arthur Jacobs

IN FEBRUARY 1966 the Hamburg State Opera brought to the stage a work described not as an opera but 'a report for electronic devices, instruments and singers'. Sign of the times! This was Boris Blacher's *Zwischenfälle bei einer Notlandung* ('Incidents at an emergency landing'). Though born in 1903, Blacher evidently shares the feeling of many younger composers that 'opera' itself is an old-fashioned word and that the newest technical means are properly applied in seeking to renovate the old art.

Fortunately for such renovation, Hamburg possesses an opera house where electronic sound reproduction in up to six channels is available. No less fortunately, the Administrator of the theatre is a composer himself, Rolf Liebermann, who—resisting a general tendency to make 'first-class' opera depend on internationally peregrinating, un-attached 'top stars'—has maintained at Hamburg the principle of a large, permanent company or ensemble. Only such a combination of circumstances has enabled Hamburg to stage so many 'advanced' operas in recent years, and not all by German composers: others represented have included the expatriate Italian, Antonio Bibalo (born 1923) and the American, Gunther Schuller (born 1925). Their contributions have been, respectively, *The Smile at the Foot of the*

Ladder (1965; after Henry Miller) and *The Visitation* (1966; after Kafka).

Which is to say that 'modern opera' (using the adjective as it is used in the phrase 'modern music') tends to flourish these days only in a very special social and theatrical context. Hamburg has also launched the two most recent operas by Giselher Klebe (born 1925), *Figaro lässt sich scheiden* ('Figaro petitions for divorce') and *Jacobowsky und der Oberst* ('Jacobowsky and the Colonel', after Franz Werfel's play), dating from 1963 and 1966 respectively. These, with such other works as *Alkmene* (1961; the first new work to be given at the rebuilt West Berlin Opera) have established Klebe as an important operatic composer of today, in an idiom firmly post-Berg and post-Webern. Another German composer aiming, similarly, at a 'total theatre' and an 'advanced' musical expression is Bernd-Alois Zimmermann (born 1918), whose most notable opera *Die Soldaten* ('The Soldiers', Cologne, 1964) incorporates electronic sound. More celebrated internationally is Hans Werner Henze (born 1926), who has progressively sought a greater clarity of utterance, finding it partly in a return from twelve-note to tonal music. His comic opera *Der junge Lord* ('The Young Lord', Berlin, 1965) and his Greek-mythological *The Bassarids* (Salzburg, in German translation, 1966) are less 'dense', musically, than his *Elegy for Young Lovers* (Schwetzingen and Glyndebourne, 1961) —though it must be said that the two-and-a-half hours uninterrupted span of *The Bassarids* is in itself likely to prove an obstacle to receptive listening. In both this and the *Elegy*, Henze's libretto was by W. H. Auden and Chester Kallmann (who wrote *The Rake's Progress* for Stravinsky).

A successful German example of opera of a more traditional type— the music not too 'difficult', the drama straightforwardly melodramatic —was Egk's *Die Verlobung in San Domingo* ('Betrothal in Santo Domingo'), produced at Munich in 1963. Meanwhile Carl Orff has further explored his conception of theatre as a kind of quasi-magic ritual. His *Oedipus der Tyrann* (1961), a literal setting of Hölderlin's translation of Sophocles' *Oedipus Rex*, follows the starkly declamatory manner of the earlier *Antigone*. The Christmas musical play *Ludus de nato infante mirificus* (also 1961) has a percussion-orchestra typical of the composer: the instruments include two tam-tams one inside the other, the hollow space being filled with small pebbles and the sound produced by gyrating the instrument.

But it will not have gone unnoticed that the composer regarded as the high-priest of German musical modernism, Karlheinz Stockhausen (born 1928) has not attempted opera. Nor has his French counterpart, Pierre Boulez (born 1925), though he has proved a very successful opera conductor—at Bayreuth, among other places! As for the leading modernists of Italy, little effect beyond a 'political' first-night scandal at Venice was made by *Intolleranza 1960* (the '1960' was later dropped) by Luigi Nono (born 1924). The Piccola Scala, little sister of Milan's famous theatre, ventured in 1963 to stage *Passaggio* ('Passage') by Luciano Berio (born 1925) which has only one character (female) on stage but a 'speaking choir' as well as an orchestra in the pit. All these four representatives of the 'vanguard', however, can hardly be blamed if they feel their music more welcome in the concert-hall (and, even more so, in the broadcasting studio) than in the opera house. Not that the older, more 'traditional' composers in Italy have enjoyed much more of a welcome: *succès d'estime* is as much as seems to have been accorded to Mario Castelnuovo-Tedesco (born 1895) for his setting of *The Merchant of Venice* (Florence, 1961) and to Pizzetti for his *Clitennestra* ('Clytemnestra'), given at Milan in 1965; he died in 1968.

As previously indicated, Menotti has had a career that prevents him being considered simply Italian, and has written nearly all of his own librettos in English. But he reverted to Italian for the original libretto of the work which eventually received its first performance in Paris in 1963 as *Le Dernier Sauvage* ('The Last Savage'), and which attempts, not unsuccessfully, to revive the formal Italian *opera buffa*. Menotti's other side ('realistic', conversational setting of melodramatic text) is represented, and very weakly, by *Martin's Lie*, given in Bristol Cathedral as part of the Bath Festival in 1964.

Despite its place of performance, this work preserves theatrical 'illusion' and is not a 'church opera' in the sense that we may so style Benjamin Britten's *Curlew River* and *The Burning Fiery Furnace*, presented in Orford Church as part of the Aldeburgh Festival in 1964 and 1966 respectively. In both these works the small orchestra, as well as the cast, enter robed as medieval monks and join in the enactment of a dramatised parable. Indeed, 'parable for church performance' is the composer's own description of the works themselves. Musically, both works are remarkable for using male voices only (including boys') and for their debt both to plainsong and to Oriental percussion and heterophony (melody simultaneously given with slight, non-harmonic differences). *Curlew River* with its Japanese story (taken from a traditional Noh-play) is more difficult to accept in its 'church' context but is perhaps the stronger work: the male 'Madwoman' is a particularly striking figure.

Britten still dominates the English operatic scene. But Michael Tippett's *King Priam* (1962)—much stronger, dramatically, than *The Midsummer Marriage*—had an originality and melodic force that perhaps would have won it better fortune in a less museum-ish environment than Covent Garden. Of younger composers, Malcolm Williamson (born 1931) achieved a success with *Our Man in Havana* (Sadler's Wells, 1963) which led to the commissioning of *The Violins of Saint-Jacques* for the same theatre (1966); *The Mines of Sulphur* by Richard Rodney Bennett (born 1936), greeted enthusiastically at Sadler's Wells (1965), was remarkable in harnessing 'serial' procedures to a very singable and easily comprehensible idiom. It was later staged at La Scala (Milan) and elsewhere. Favourable attention was also received by Nicholas Maw (born 1935) for *One Man Show* (London, 1964) and by Gordon Crosse (born 1937) for his one-act *Purgatory* (Cheltenham Festival, 1966). The last-named work was also produced on B.B.C. Television in that year: in general, it must be said that television services in various countries have both assisted the dissemination of operatic classics and encouraged modern composers to tackle operatic forms.

With *Aniara* (Stockholm, 1959) by Karl-Birger Blomdahl (born 1916) a Swedish opera won international notice. It was modern both in its subject (the title is that of a space-ship which has gone off course) and in its use of electronically-distorted, taped sound. But when he essayed a more traditional dramatic subject in *Herr von Hancken* (Stockholm, 1965), Blomdahl proved less convincing. Perhaps a more important Swedish contribution to opera came in the spatial experiment of *Drömmen om Thérèse* ('Dreaming about Thérèse') by Lars Johan

Werle (born 1926), written for the Rotunda, a large circular room in the Stockholm Opera, where it was staged in 1964: the orchestra surrounds the audience, who in turn surround the central platform stage. Electronic sound from loudspeakers is also used. A genuinely singable line and dramatic structure is linked to this novel presentation of sound. Mention should also be made of Gunnar Bucht's operatic version (on his own libretto) of Ibsen's *The Pretenders*, produced at the I.S.C.M. Festival at Stockholm in 1966.

Modern opera continues to proliferate in Czechoslovakia without any recent examples of successful transfers to the non-Communist world (although, happily, there is no longer any political barrier in the way of such intercommunication). In Hungary, two composers who have won prominence are Emil Petrovics (born in Yugoslavia, 1930) with his *C'est la guerre!* (title in French), originally broadcast in Hungary in 1961 and then staged by the Budapest Opera, and Sandor Szokolay (born 1931) with his opera *Blood Wedding* (on Lorca's play), staged in Budapest in 1964. Although the Soviet Union continues to encourage new opera both in Russia proper and (in their various languages) in other regions, it is ironic that the only Soviet opera to make a recent world conquest has been *Katerina Ismailova* by Shostakovich. This is the opera formerly called *Lady Macbeth of the Mtsensk District* (see above, p. 108). Contrary to what is generally believed in the West, the re-naming took place soon after the original production in 1934. But the version newly released in Moscow at the very end of 1963 (according to some accounts the first 'official' performance was early in 1964) embodied various revisions modifying not only the music but also the crude erotic element in the original plot.

American opera has also failed to 'travel'. But three American composers whose names might be added to those mentioned above (p. 103) are Samuel Barber (born 1910), whose *Vanessa* was staged by the Metropolitan, New York in 1958 and whose *Antony and Cleopatra* (on Shakespeare's play) was chosen to open the Metropolitan's new theatre in 1966; Robert Ward (born 1917), whose setting of Arthur Miller's *The Crucible* (New York, 1961) exemplifies a readiness of certain Americans to seek inspiration in subjects of strong national or historical appeal; and Hugo Weisgall (born in 1912 in what is now

Czechoslovakia) whose more European outlook is shown in his recourse to Strindberg and to Wedekind for his one-act operas, *The Stronger* and *The Tenor*, both produced in 1952, the one in Lutherville, Md., and the other in Boston. Of South American operas, *Don Rodrigo* (Buenos Aires, 1964) by the Argentinian Alberto Ginastera (born 1916), shows a careful matching of scenic form with 'fixed' musical forms which doubtless stems from Berg's *Wozzeck* and *Lulu*—those two works which still (a generation after their composer's death) stand as landmarks on the modern operatic scene.

IX

MUSIC AND THE RADIO

By Anthony Milner

I

THE UBIQUITY of radio and mechanical sound-reproduction is a commonplace of contemporary civilisation. Its chief consequence, however, is generally ignored, probably because the greater proportion of mankind is by now unaware of it: the fact that from infancy our aural perception and imagination are profoundly (because unconsciously) influenced and even modified by the timbre of sounds produced by the combination of valves, amplifiers, and loudspeakers. By upbringing and experience, therefore, most men are favourably predisposed to radio and gramophone listening. They believe two dogmas: one, that radio sound is 'almost as good as the real thing'; two, that its approximation to 'real' sound will increase continually as further technical improvements are discovered. These, surely, are harmless beliefs. Or are they? While radio is rightly regarded as one of the chief amenities of modern life, it is nevertheless necessary to recall its inescapable limitations before beginning any discussion of its place and value in musical culture.

These limitations begin in the studio or concert-hall. A studio-manager's task requires great skill in balancing the demands of a sensitive ear with the power of his equipment to reproduce what he hears. The transmission of music ideally needs a knowledgeable and professionally trained musician; to watch such a man at his work reveals the talent and care involved. Anyone who has taken part in broadcast performances and listened to studio rehearsals in the control-room will know how much adjustment it takes to secure a satisfactory balance of sound where merely three or four performers are concerned. The position of a microphone, and the blending of the sound picked up by several microphones in different positions, can severely distort the original sound. Such problems increase in difficulty with larger ensembles. Generally, the engineers are successful in solving them, though they recognise that there is a limit to the amount of detail that can 'come over' at a given moment, and there is (at the present time anyhow) a limit to the range of frequencies that can be broadcast. Most radio music, even when heard on the best equipment, lacks bass; inevitably, it also lacks 'background', that subtle colouring which music receives from its surroundings, which the listener recognises as the effect of music in an ample space, and which, although the music may be broadcast from a large hall, disappears very largely when the sounds have been collected by the various microphones, blended in the control-room, disseminated as radio waves, and received by the average radio-set. It is wonderful that so much survives! Good transmission of a large body of sound achieves its effect partly by illusion, a fact amply demonstrated by the broadcast of a solo concerto; we accept the result, but the equation of soloist and orchestra is not that of the concert hall. In other words, radio music is a business of diminishing returns: *something* (though it may be very little) is lost at each stage of the technical process. Some sounds broadcast less well than others: those of an unaccompanied choir, the piano and the harpsichord seldom sound quite enough like 'the real thing'. Even under the most favourable conditions and with the best receivers, broadcast music is never mistaken for 'live' music.

Nevertheless, despite these intrinsic limitations, radio has transformed the musical world. For those who desire it, the musical wealth of our civilisation is available at the turn of a knob. Broadcasts have awakened thousands to an interest in music which, but for radio, they might never have had. Radio provides for those music-lovers who live far from concert-halls or who cannot afford frequent concert-attendance the means for renewing and enlarging their delight. Since most radio corporations are financed by the state, their music directors can avoid the restrictions of the popular classic-romantic repertoire. Listeners are encouraged to take interest in medieval and renaissance music and

the music of the East. From the end of World War II the great radio
stations of Europe have tended more and more to take the place of
the aristocracy of the previous centuries in patronising the contemporary composer: they introduce new composers to their potential
audience (many young composers nowadays owe their first recognition
to a successful broadcast), they encourage contemporary music by
commissioning works of every sort, and the fees they pay for performances provide a considerable part of composers' incomes. Radio
has stimulated the great increase in the number of professional musicians
by creating new opportunities for performance and by the formation
of ensembles, choirs and orchestras devoted to broadcasting.

Composers and performers (while grateful for activities which bring
them so much of their livelihood) are perhaps more likely than the
rest of the world to be concerned at the possible misuse and abuse of
music that may stem from radio. So long as broadcast music (whether
'light' or 'serious') is truly listened to and enjoyed, so long as it does
not oust contact with live performance and serves chiefly to lead the
listener to more fruitful and first-hand acquaintance with the art, its
influence is entirely beneficial. But the mass-distribution of music has
called forth the passive listener, a listener who, says Hindemith, 'by
his very nature can never be reached by any sincere endeavour of
a musician; a listener who never existed in earlier times . . . of the
most degenerate type, who is surrounded by music every minute of
his daily life. When he first came in touch with this continuous stream
of music, he enjoyed it as a musical treat. Then he got used to the
permanent outpour of sound, and now he does not listen at all. Yet he
wants to have this lulling noise, and the only time he feels uncomfortable is when by some mechanical defect his sound distributor
ceases to emit its gifts. There is no question of quality, of characteristic
expression, of ethical aims, of moral effects. Everything else disappears,
if the one condition is accepted: a non-stop flow of faceless sound. . . .
Our musical drunkard's only meaningful move is to turn the faucet on
in the morning and shut it off at night.'[1] Such men prefer their music
'canned'. This preference is shared by some uneducated radio-fans
who, while not so degraded as Hindemith's example, avoid the

[1] *A Composer's World*, p. 211. pub. Harvard.

concert-hall, averring that they enjoy music more via the loud-speaker: they resemble the unfortunates who eat tinned salmon rather than fresh from choice. Both types have been so conditioned to the machine flavour of a 'processed' adaptation that the true thing seems insipid. The same love of loudspeaker timbre appears in the widely increasing use of amplification for variety theatres, dance-halls, out-door bands and the like; the audiences do not need it, but they are so accustomed to it that it makes any listening easier. Mental laziness is the root of these abuses. But even on intelligent listeners, radio tends to have at least one bad effect: since music can be obtained merely by turning a knob, the proportion of music-lovers who approach music by the hard and creative way of learning, singing, and playing it themselves becomes smaller every day. (Sometimes these receive spurious support from persons who might be expected to know better: a music-critic wrote recently that he preferred hearing Wagner on the radio with a score beside him.) Yet the greatest danger of radio is not to be found in perversions of taste, but springs from the well-known truth that what is obtained easily is often little valued. When some of the greatest achievements of humanity can be approached in so unimpressive a way, there is a likelihood that familiarity may breed contempt, that the greatness and the beauty may not be perceived with an adequate sense of their glory and grandeur, and the vision of the artist be obscured in the mists of half-interest.

II

The use of the gramophone presents similar problems. In his stimulating lectures entitled 'The Musical Experience' Roger Sessions points out its chief disadvantage: 'It cannot be made too clear or understood too thoroughly that music, just because it is an art in which time and movement are the basic elements, needs constant renewal. This principle is extremely difficult to formularise and is full of pitfalls; but it is none the less real for that reason. Perhaps we can understand it most clearly if we consider a certain inherent limitation of that most useful instrument, the gramophone. I need not dwell on the fact of its usefulness, nor expatiate on the incredible advantages won through its invention and development. Any musician could add to the list of those advantages; and we of the mid-twentieth century are acquainted enough with the ordinary facts of technology to take it for granted that purely technical limitations can either be ignored or overcome. . . . But what will never be overcome are the diminishing returns inherent in mechanical reproduction as such. We can listen to a recording and derive a maximum of pleasure from it just as long as it remains to a degree unfamiliar. It ceases to have interest for us, however, the instant we become aware of the fact of literal repetition, of mechanical reproduction—when we know and can anticipate exactly how a given phrase is going to be modelled, exactly how long a given fermata is to be held, exactly what quality of accent or articulation, of acceleration or retard, will occur at a given moment. When the music ceases to be fresh for us in this sense, it ceases to be alive, and we can say in the most real sense that it ceases to be music.'[1]

There are discophiles who know only one recording of any particular work. This becomes for them the authentic performance: all others that they hear are judged by it (frequently, in my experience, adversely), and, if they have made their first acquaintance with the music through a disc, they may prefer the recording to a concert performance. This is an extreme example; *abusus non tollit usum.* But precisely *because* everyone recognises the value of the gramophone it is thereby all the more important to be aware of the possible corruptions of musical experience that its use may produce. Like radio, disc reproduction is influencing our listening and our taste. Whether that influence be good or bad, we should acknowledge its existence.

Recording has imposed exacting standards of musical accuracy. The making permanent a transient thing renders all errors highly undesirable: a small blemish, which may occur in the most masterly performance, becomes intolerable when repeated. Hence, many recordings are mosaics to a greater or lesser degree. The various movements of a symphony may be recorded separately, thus giving the performance a polished correctness but so often depriving the whole of that indefinable continuity which comes from a play-through. There are worse practices. Modern techniques make it possible to add corrections to a recorded performance: for example, faulty bars, chords

[1]p. 70, pub. Princeton University Press.

even, may be removed and their correct versions, performed separately, may be inserted instead. Since recording is expensive, difficult and elaborate works are not infrequently touched up in this way. The result, of course, is not a true *performance* at all, yet it easily convinces the unwary listener that its perfection is possible for all occasions. Critics who hear a singer for the first time on disc may be unreasonably disappointed when they hear him in the opera-house. Quite recently several English critics wrote of a famous American quartet that the high hopes aroused by their discs were heavily dashed by their 'live' performances. Obviously their discs were mosaics of the sort I have described. In such a situation, everyone concerned is at fault. The quartet for passing such concoctions off on a gullible public; the recording company, who abetted them; and the foolish critics who made discs a foundation for estimating concert work.

Sometimes the composer unwittingly encourages such practices by expressing a desire that performances of his works should possess what is really a machined accuracy. The latest trends in *avant-garde* experiments have pushed this to its logical conclusion. Since the human element is always risky, since performers have limitations, a new music is desired from which all such uncertainties and handicaps are removed. Electronic 'music' (if it can properly be so described) is the apotheosis of mechanical reproduction in music: the sounds are synthetic and the instrument that produces them is the amplifier. Thus we have music 'untouched by hand': the art of a technological mind. The attitude that generates such forms is one shaped and conditioned by the impact of radio and disc on musical culture. Electronic music would not have obtained the small success it has had were not men already accustomed to the sound of music via the amplifier.

III

One of the more disturbing factors in the dissemination of music by disc and radio is the insensitiveness of the majority of listeners to the quality of the sounds produced by their instruments. Most commercial radio sets and gramophones are quite incapable of reproducing everything contained on the wavelength or disc-groove since they cover an insufficient frequency-range and distort gravely above or below a small range of dynamics. Far too many listeners are deluded by an elaborate cabinet and control-buttons. Good reproduction can be achieved quite inexpensively by building sets privately, but few have the necessary knowledge for this. Naturally the vendors of the sets, while emphasising the superior value of their most expensive instruments, endeavour to persuade the public that even the cheapest models give satisfactory results.

This would seem to cast a little doubt on the value of the musical education achieved by radio and gramophone. Music is brought to a vast public that never had it before, but the increase in 'musical appreciation' is not accompanied by a corresponding discrimination and sensitiveness in aural perception; if it were, it is inconceivable that so many listeners would acquiesce in inferior reproduction. Of course, even the cheapest sets incorporate some of the main improvements that are continually being discovered; nevertheless, the gulf between their performance and what is possible and desirable is still disquietingly great. Far too often, professional musicians are ignorant or careless of what can be done, taking the standpoint that no mechanical reproduction can ever be truly satisfactory. Their complacency encourages the amateur in his delusion that he receives adequate performance.

In considering questions such as these the fundamental involvement of music with the world of business enterprise (which is perhaps the most noticeable musical development of the century) must perforce be taken into account. With the growth of a 'mass-audience', to quote Sessions again, 'the purveyors of music, however disinterested, found themselves obliged to count costs and to concern themselves with profits. . . . In order to understand the situation as it has developed it is necessary to assume this disinterestedness. For the situation has not been made by individuals at all. It is the result of economic facts the like of which have never existed before; and these facts are far too large in scope, too intricately interwoven with the very bases of contemporary life, to be influenced one way or the other by the decisions of individuals. When music or any other product is furnished to millions of individuals, it is bound to become necessary to consider the tastes of those individuals in relation to the product offered them. Those who furnish the product are obliged to produce as efficiently and as cheaply as possible the goods which they can sell to the most people; they are obliged, furthermore, to try to persuade the people to whom they sell that it is preferable to buy the goods that are most cheaply produced; it is furthermore necessary to do everything possible to enhance the value of the goods sold. If they fail to do these things they are taking foolish economic risks. These facts are elementary . . . and the "listener" has become, in relation to them, the "consumer".'[1] Whereas the gramophone is immediately subject to such considerations, radio, in most European countries, is less directly concerned by reason of varying degrees of public financial support. But we in England, who have recently seen the reduction of the Third Programme in favour of television, know that state aid is no protection against majority views. In a democratic society it is still assumed that the majority will, eventually, 'love the highest when they see it', a belief which, however optimistic and charitable it may be, has almost no evidence to support it. Nevertheless, it now forms the justification for continuous support of music and musicians by public funds. Doubtless much improvement in the general appreciation and understanding of music is still possible (and we can only proceed on the assumption that it is) and radio and the gramophone have proved and will certainly continue to be powerful instruments in the task as long as they remain subordinate to the furtherance of 'live' music of every sort. If I have drawn attention to their limitations and abuses in this article rather than to their generally admitted advantages, it may serve as a reminder that even the best machines must be properly used if men are not to become their slaves.

X

MUSIC AND THE CINEMA

By Frederick W. Sternfeld

FILM MUSIC is an art of the twentieth century. The first public programme arranged by the Lumière Brothers in a Paris basement café was accompanied by a piano (28th December 1895) and, similarly, in London (20th February 1896) the Lumière programme was accompanied by a harmonium. From the earliest projection of a story upon a screen it was deemed desirable to have a running musical accompaniment, and the reason is not far to seek. The very scope of the camera, its unlimited range in moving from wide panorama to close-up, and its tendency to prowl in byways, are qualities that tend to slow down the plot, in time, if not in interest. With music to underline an expression or deepen suspense audience attention can be sustained, and here, in a very real sense, music becomes a functional part of the new dramatic art.

As this art developed, it became clear that, given a composer of stature and imagination, the musical accompaniment was by no means restricted to mere 'background'. Prokofiev's 'Battle on the Ice' from *Nevski* and Vaughan Williams' 'Climb Music' from *Scott of the Antarctic* are emphatically foreground, that is to say, the music is a primary agent of expression. It addresses itself to the audience in a manner that does not detract from the drama; on the contrary, it enhances the effect and makes the drama soar. Compared with opera, films provide such opportunities at less frequent intervals, but it is a measure of the composer's dramatic acumen and adaptation to modern times to be sensitive to these potential musical climaxes, if and when they occur.

That the early films were accompanied simply by a piano or a harmonium was merely part of their unassuming beginnings, before the days of cinema palaces. It was a case of expedience, the music itself an opportunely devised scissors-and-paste job. Excerpts taken from our so-called 'popular classics' were accommodated to the episodes of the film and joined together by the music director of the producing studio in what was considered a plausible sequence. This method of devising a musical accompaniment continued, but for some notable exceptions, until the talking films were developed, and even after their introduction. But as early as 1907 the French, who have been pioneers in all phases of film production, commissioned one of their established and recognised composers, Camille Saint-Saëns, to compose an original score for a full-length film, *L'Assassinat du Duc de Guise*. It is the first of the silent films to have an accompanying score of musical significance (see the film chronicle at end of this article). French producers continued to commission composers whose reputations rested on serious works outside the cinema. To their credit it may be said that the native wit, elegance and imagination that distinguished the films are also present in the film scores of their musicians.

In 1922 Honegger provided the score of Abel Gance's monumental *La Roue*. The real hero of this film was not a human being at all, as the title implies. The machines that dominate our century—railways, airplanes, cranes and other industrial apparatus—come in for a fair share of treatment in the cinema. Gance claimed that 'the cinema is the music of light' and, accordingly, trains were photographed as fluidly mobile machines on the shunting tracks of the Nice railway station. Preparing himself to compose the music for Gance's long masterpiece (four sessions of three hours each) Honegger studied the contents of the music library of the Gaumont studio. A symphonic fragment by Alfred Bruneau, whose periodic rhythm seemed exactly right for *La Roue*, supplied the melodic germ from which Honegger was able to develop one of the main themes (which he later also employed in the symphonic piece, *Pacific 231*, its première given under Koussevitzky at the Paris Opéra in 1924). This machine music, with its rhythmic drive and steely character, was born out of the composer's great fondness for his subject, in his own words, 'aimant les locomotives comme d'autres aiment les femmes ou les chevaux'. Its traces are to be found not only in Honegger's later film scores (of which his biographer M. Delannoy lists thirty-five) but in some of the best works of American composers. The mechanised civilisation of the New World was bound, sooner or later, to be reflected in their works. There are machine sequences in Thomson's *River* and *Louisiana Story*, in Copland's *City*; in Kubik's *C-Man*, and in John Cage's music for Alexander Calder's mobiles in *Works of Calder*.

Perhaps the most important teacher of the younger film composers in Paris was Erik Satie. He influenced Honegger, Milhaud, Auric and Sauguet, as well as the Americans, Thomson, Copland and Antheil. In 1924 Satie wrote the score for René Clair's first film, *Entr'acte Cinématographique*, an interlude in Picabia's surrealist ballet, *Relâche* (also with music by Satie). In it Satie's notion of 'musique d'ameublement' played a large role. This fanciful appellation had its origin in a remark by Matisse who had postulated a new art without any distracting subject matter, 'something analogous to an easy chair'. When applied to music, the theory called for a new kind of listening that did not distract from the screen but framed, as it were, the visual images on the screen. Music was not to be absolute, it was to be functional, devoid of artificial dignity or self-consciousness. And the relationship between the visual images and the music should not be mere naive illustration but of a subtle and sophisticated nature. To say that music framed the visual element was one way of putting it, that it counterpointed it was another. Satie's music aimed at not diverting an audience from René Clair's performance; paradoxically, though, there was no slavish adherence to the screen's movements and never—to use a Hollywood term—any 'mickey-mousing'. A further distinguishing trait in Satie's music lent itself well to dramatic exigence, the clever use of popular tunes, sometimes merely quoted, at other times ironical or counterpointing the action.

Satie's influence could be seen across the Atlantic as well as at home. There are, for instance, the works of Charles Chaplin and Friedrich Hollaender. Chaplin's sophisticated and unexpected use of popular tunes in *Modern Times* and in the 1942 version of *The Gold Rush* is of great dramatic eloquence. In the latter work, his spoofing of Wagner's

'Serenade to the Evening Star' from *Tannhauser* is more than a joke.
In its negative way, it enhances the scene between a character starved
to the point of delirium and the comedian who in his companion's eyes
suddenly takes on the form of an enormous, hunger-satisfying rooster.
The dream-like quality of the music raises a comedy joke to the stature
of true pathos.

Hollaender has practised this technique on both sides of the
Atlantic. His use of a theme reminiscent of Mozart's bird-catcher
Papageno to accompany certain of Emil Jannings' movements in
The Blue Angel has the virtue, despite its brevity, of illuminating this
pathetic character. Upon his migration to Hollywood, Hollaender
continued to use these methods in comic quotations from *Rosenkavalier*
and *Lohengrin* for the film *Talk of the Town*. Indeed, the third *Lohengrin*
prelude for underlining the scene where Ronald Colman shaves off his
beard, once heard, is never forgotten.

Virgil Thomson's fugue in Flaherty's *Louisiana Story* is another piece
of seeming non-relevance. Thomson, also a pupil of Satie, had the
task of accompanying a tussle between an alligator and a small boy.
The camera moved consistently from boy to alligator and now and
again to the anxious father. The visual and auditory impressions are
not synchronised but are projected at different points, with the result
that the sections of the fugue do not dovetail or coincide mechanically
with the boy and father sequences. By this procedure of overlapping
the music succeeds in creating a third dimension in the same familiar
pattern as those blurred outlines and contours unrealistically separated
from the areas they surround in modern painting.

These few instances must suffice to show that the lessons taught by
the pioneer film composers in France in the twenties continued to
exercise their influence after the advent of the sound film in 1929.
During the first decade of the sound film the initiative taken by certain
directors yielded various benefits to the industry as a whole. The
French led off by providing both superb entertainment by René
Clair and *avant-garde* creations by Buñuel and Cocteau. Georges Auric
(*A Nous la Liberté, Le Sang d'un Poète*) and Armand Bernard (*Sous les
Toits de Paris, L'Age d'Or*) were associated with both schools. It is the
genius of the French that their chic does not come to a stand-still in

the commercial sphere. The choice of the sentimental music-hall song to complement Clair's *Sous les Toits* elicits our admiration still today. But the masterpiece of the period is *Le Sang d'un Poète* of 1931. It is this work that was then (and still is) cited as proof that the cinema is an art in its own right, not merely a vulgar relative of the age-old theatre.

Satie's death in 1925 removed from the film scene a composer who might have been immensely useful and sympathetic to Jean Cocteau. As it was, Cocteau asked Georges Auric (one of the group 'Les Six') to write the music for his surrealist film. Auric was destined to become France's most famous film composer.

The scenes where music not only accompanies the visual image but also counterpoints it in *Le Sang* are many and usually speak for themselves. The film owes a great deal to René Clair's *Entr'acte*, both in attitude and technique. Cocteau's images and Auric's melodies have a strong immediacy because they are, as it were, naked. For much of the film the photography speaks for itself, without narration. And much of the melody is without chordal accompaniment. 'If a single line is eloquent, why muddy it with a chord?' queries Auric. As a result the orchestra has practically no string section. (Auric also used this modern texture and percussive sonority in the score for the Sartre film, *La Putain Respectueuse* in 1952.) Cocteau and Auric have also seen to it that the silences are as eloquent as the musical passages. In the second of the four episodes music mirrors the soul of the poet as he stalks through the corridor of the haunted hotel, but there is no music as we peep with him through key-holes and regard the scenes on the other side. In an opera, this sort of occasion would provide the composer with a fine opportunity for expressive orchestral music. But the images of the poet's subconscious must speak here *qua* images. There are similarly moving silences in the final episode, and there are effects reminiscent of the *musique concrète* to come, such as the noise of the aeroplane propeller and the high whistle accompanying the guardian angel; also the drum beat for the poet's pounding heart, as we see him in close-up. And the gay theatre music which frames this final episode is Satie's *musique d'ameublement* in the best sense of the word.

But the high promises of the early French works were never quite fulfilled. There is an excitement and a stylistic unity about them that one misses in the later creations of Cocteau and Clair. Have they been contaminated by a commercial world which invited films that were more gaudy (and expensive) but less true to the real nature of their creative genius? On the other hand, the sound film is barely thirty years young, and it is rash to make predictions after so few decades.

The German and Russian films during these years exhibit, as one would expect, a good deal of social satire. There were Weill's *Threepenny Opera* and Prokofiev's *Lieutenant Kijé*. However, Eisenstein's and Prokofiev's *Nevski* of 1938 is patriotic rather than satirical. Today this work is deservedly regarded as a classic for, thanks to Eisenstein's enlightened attitude, the composer was allotted more leeway than is habitual in the average entertainment film. The famous 'Battle of the Ice' was filmed to the music and the resulting integration, while by no means mechanical, is impressive. In fact, in *Nevski* (as later in *Ivan*) Prokofiev's music plays such an important role that these Russian films may almost be regarded as the cinematic equivalent of operas. The work is remarkably free from dialogue.

The American scene presents a rather curious dichotomy. Hollywood is, after all, three thousand miles away from New York City. With the studio musicians in the one place and the concert-hall composers in the other, there is bound to be a good deal of divergence. Hollywood feature films at their worst are shoddy and stale; at their rare best they are surprisingly good. *The Informer*, directed by John Ford in 1935, is dramatically a great film. Its musical score is by Max Steiner, a composer who has written music for well over two hundred films. Though undistinguished apart from the screen, the music of *The Informer* is competent and craftsmanlike. It is interesting to note that Steiner has remarked that only once in his career as film composer was he 'consulted about music by the scriptwriter, prior to the finished product'. The film was *The Informer*, and it is not surprising that this is one of the best film scores Steiner has produced. As a rule a Hollywood film (or a Rank film for that matter) is written and filmed before the composer is permitted a look-in. Once the composer *is* called in, the music must frequently be supplied in less than three weeks. Some cutting then takes place, without re-recording the music, so that the composer has very little to say about his contribution to the total product.

The strength of the American documentary films, largely made in New York City, is that their directors have more respect for the composer and they have, in the East, a large number of good composers available to them. Here the collaboration of Virgil Thomson and Pare Lorentz (Appendix A 1936, 1938) commands our especial respect. The *Spanish Earth* (1937) is also interesting because it brings in Ernest Hemingway, another American strongly influenced by his sojourn in Paris.

The British scene between 1929 and 1938 offers a confused picture. It is true that there were three significant newcomers in 1935: Bliss, Britten and Walton. The great film scores of Walton were yet to be written, but the contributions of the other two were of great importance. About that time John Grierson invited Cavalcanti to come from France to help with the sound-tracks of documentaries, and Muir Mathieson became music director for the Korda feature films. The result was that in England, as in France, the leading composers have been given the opportunity to work for the films, with financial advantage to themselves and artistic advantage to the medium. Bliss scored the H. G. Wells film *Things to Come*, of which Wells wrote that 'music was a part of the constructive scheme of the film'. (After the war Thorold Dickinson gave Bliss an even more challenging assignment in *Men of Two Worlds*, which the composer handled with considerable imagination.)

Two pre-war scores by Britten, both with verse by W. H. Auden, are particularly to be commended. One regrets that, with the exception of Muir Mathieson's teaching film, *Instruments of the Orchestra*, Britten never returned to the medium. But it is fair to say that since Cavalcanti's and Grierson's *Coalface* the British documentary has not lagged behind the French.

In approaching the war years one is hampered by an *embarras de richesses*: the earlier developments bore fruit, and patriotism and urgency frequently overcame bureaucracy. France continued to produce superb documentaries, among which were Sauguet's *Farrébique*, Baudrier's *Bataille du Rail*. What is even more remarkable is that these French composers contrived to inject a breath of fresh air into lengthy

E

star feature films, of which Delannoy's *Volpone* and Kosma's *Enfants du Paradis* may be noted. The latter score deftly underlines the unforgettable acting of Barrault and Arletty and proves that the commercial attitude of film makers need not preclude music with some degree of merit.

The English scene is dominated by two circumstances that were important in English music apart from the films: Vaughan Williams discovered a new medium, and William Walton established his true stature as a dramatic composer. On the basis of his *Henry V* one does not hesitate to acclaim him among the greatest film composers to date. The music for the Battle of Agincourt (available on gramophone records but not in score) holds its own with Prokofiev's 'Battle on the Ice' and is, indeed, a great achievement of English music.

The significant American development was the emergence of Copland as a film composer. Following Thomson's example, he wrote distinguished documentaries such as *The City*. He then invaded Hollywood and wrote successful feature films: *Our Town* and *Of Mice and Men*. The first of these is remarkable in that both the dramatist, Thornton Wilder, and the composer were able, by their joint effort, to evolve a truly American classic, without obvious backward glances to their Paris schooling; no foreign artifice here, but a truly native product.

In speaking of the post-war years only time will determine the soundness of our critical intuitions. In France one is impressed by the continuing artistic development of the documentary: G. Bernard's *Guernica* and Auric's *Picasso* are not holding operations, they signify progressive growth of the art. But the important step forward to this observer is Cocteau's and Auric's *Orphée*. In many respects this film is an extension of *Le Sang d'un Poète* of 1931 but it is also a fuller development. Cocteau said: 'I had already developed this theme twenty years ago, but in *Le Sang* I played it only with one finger; in *Orphée* it is orchestrated'. The use of quotations, such as the D-minor Trio from the Dance of the Blessed Spirits in Gluck's *Orphée*, is extremely deft. Its initial introduction as it emanates from the wireless is innocent enough, but its subsequent appearances are psychological rather than obvious, in the best Satie tradition. The transitions from noise, such as Morse code signals or drums, to full-fledged music are beautifully handled, and Auric's diatonic tune for the Princesse (Maria Casarès) has great dignity; it is never exploited in the tiresome manner of endless leitmotif repetitions. The use of jazz in the café scene, and the super-imposition of the drums from Katherine Dunham's band on to the sound track when Orpheus is killed by the Bacchantes, is very eloquent.

In the U.S.A. Thomson and Copland solidified their positions by composing for full-length films, Thomson with Flaherty's *Louisiana Story* and Chayevsky's *Goddess*; Copland with Milestone's *Red Pony* and Wyler's *Heiress*. Of these, *Louisiana Story*, with its poetic use of French folk songs from the Bayou country and its dodecaphonic chorale, promises to become a classic in the repertories of film societies. Among the work of resident Hollywood composers, Antheil and Hugo Friedhofer should be noted. Antheil had done remarkable work in Europe as early as 1924 when he provided music for Fernand Leger's *Ballet Mécanique*. The discovery of the period was Gail Kubik, whose feature film *C-Man* and cartoon *McBoing Boing* showed an imaginative and effective application of modern, percussive sonorities to Hollywood films. That *McBoing* was a great commercial success was a delight to serious musicians.

The Italian film, both documentary and feature, made considerable strides. The work of Rota is not particularly novel, but shows a dramatic flair; Roman Vlad has written many features, but his documentary *Leonardo* for Luciano Emmer is probably his best work to date, imaginative and tasteful.

Last in this résumé of the post-war years, but by no means the least, we come to England. The scores of the younger composers, Alwyn, Arnold, Frankel and Rawsthorne, have established a high tradition of craftsmanship, and the work of Vaughan Williams is justly a matter of national pride. Alwyn has a lively imagination for sonorities and will use modern microphone techniques to great advantage. His overture to *Odd Man Out* is recorded on three different sound-tracks, for whole orchestra, strings, and horns, and the resultant total effect is eloquent. In *The Rocking Horse Winner* the inter-play between the rhythm of the speaking voice in crucial passages of the script and that of the music is so subtle that the audience is not aware of it, but the film gains as a whole in unity and style. Arnold, born in 1921, is a prolific and quick worker, whose rise has been rapid. His music for David Lean's *Sound Barrier* is yet another instance of the imaginative way in which the film creators of our century have handled the machines of their time, here aeroplanes flying at supersonic speed. The conventional sonorities for the love of the young couple, the use of piccolo flute and celesta for the dangerous 'sound barrier' which the young wife rightly fears, the waltz-like transformation of certain themes when the new method of flying succeeds, all testify to the sure-footed way in which Arnold uses old means to new ends. Frankel's scoring is economical, but precisely because of this it is the best sort of counter-part to Alec Guinness's comedy style (*The Man in the White Suit*). Of Rawsthorne's music one likes best his work for documentaries; in *The Drawings of Leonardo* it is the perfect complement to Michael Ayrton's script, spoken by Laurence Olivier. It fades out when functional sound or significant spoken passages dominate, but speaks with quiet dignity when the camera focuses on contemplative details in the painting of the Virgin and Saint Anne.

But the delight and pride of England in this field is the work of Vaughan Williams who, at the age of seventy-five, wrote *Scott of the Antarctic* and, at eighty-five, *The Vision of William Blake*. The documentary on Blake was one of the composer's last works, and in scoring the Blake songs for voice and oboe only, that is, dispensing with chords, the composer made splendid use of his great melodic gift. His masterpiece, however, remains the feature film *Scott*. As it infrequently happens in the case of functional music, the film score is better, that is, truer to its own artistic nature than the *Sinfonia Antarctica* which is derived from it. The Penguin Scherzo is brilliant in the film, but too slight in stature or originality for a symphonic movement. The demands of a film are altogether different from those of a symphony. What would be monotonous in the concert hall makes the strongest effect in this film, the repetition of the 'climb music' when Scott's party, exhausted and doomed to death, are on the return trip. This repetition has an epic eloquence. But it is the quality of the music that elicits our admiration. Here the bleakness of the polar landscape, the quiet determination of the explorers, and the possibility of disaster are all caught perfectly in the score. In a tradition where snippets of music of one minute or less are the rule, this sizeable, continuous piece of orchestral writing is a delight. The composer himself commented, in a general discussion of the topic, '. . . ignore the details and . . . intensify the spirit of the whole situation by a continuous stream of music'.

APPENDIX

Appendix A.   Selected Chronological List of Film Scores

		Composer	Director
1907	*L'Assassinat du Duc de Guise**	C. Saint-Saëns	H. Lavedan
1915	*Birth of a Nation* (U.S.A.)	J. K. Breil (with Griffith)	D. W. Griffith
1922	*La Roue*	A. Honegger	A. Gance
1924	*Ballet Mécanique*	G. Antheil	F. Léger & D Murphy
1924	*Entr'acte*	E. Satie	R. Clair
1925	*Potemkin* (U.S.S.R.)	E. Meisel	S. M. Eisenstein
1925	*L'Inhumaine*	D. Milhaud	M. L'Herbier
1927	*Le chapeau de paille d'Italie*	J. Ibert	R. Clair
1927	*Berlin* (Germany)	E. Meisel	W. Ruttmann
1929	*Sous les Toits de Paris*	A. Bernard & R. Moretti	R. Clair
1930	*Blue Angel* (Germany)	F. Hollaender	J. Von Sternberg
1930	*L'Age d'Or*	arr.: A. Bernard	L. Buñuel
1931	*Le Million*	A. Bernard & G. Van Parys	R. Clair
1931	*A Nous la Liberté*	G. Auric	R. Clair
1931	*Le Sang d'un Poète*	G. Auric	J. Cocteau
1931	*Threepenny Opera* (Germany)	K. Weill	G. W. Pabst
1933	*Don Quixote*	(Chalyapin singing)	G. W. Pabst
1934	*L'Idée*	A. Honegger	B. Bartosch
1934	*L'Hippocampe*	D. Milhaud	J. Painlevé
1934	*Lieutenant Kije* (U.S.S.R.) ('The Czar wants to sleep')	S. Prokofiev	A. Feinzimmer
1934	*New Earth* (Holland)	H. Eisler	J. Ivens
1935	*Coalface*	B. Britten	A. Cavalcanti & J. Grierson & W. H. Auden

*Country of origin is not indicated when England or France.

		Composer	Director
1935	*Things to Come*	A. Bliss	W. C. Menzies & H. G. Wells
1935	*Escape Me Never*	W. Walton	P. Czinner
1935	*The Informer* (U.S.A.)	M. Steiner	J. Ford
1936	*Night Mail*	B. Britten	B. Wright & H. Watt & W. H. Auden
1936	*Plow that Broke the Plains* (U.S.A.)	V. Thomson	P. Lorentz
1936	*Midsummer Night's Dream* (U.S.A.)	arr. E. W. Korngold (Mendelssohn)	M. Reinhardt
1936	*Modern Times* (U.S.A.)	C. Chaplin (with A. Newman)	C. Chaplin
1936	*As You Like It*	W. Walton	P. Czinner
1937	*Les Perles de la Couronne*	J. Françaix	S. Guitry
1937	*La Grande Illusion*	J. Kosma	J. Renoir
1937	*The Spanish Earth* (U.S.A.)	V. Thomson (with M. Blitzstein)	J. Ivens & E. Hemingway
1938	*Pygmalion*	A. Honegger	L. Howard & A. Asquith
1938	*The River* (U.S.A.)	V. Thomson	P. Lorentz
1938	*Nevski* (U.S.S.R.)	S. Prokofiev	S. M. Eisenstein
1939	*Roads Across Britain*	W. Alwyn	P. Rotha
1939	*Le Jour se lève*	M. Jaubert	M. Carné
1939	*Volpone*	M. Delannoy	J. de Baroncelli
1939	*The City* (U.S.A.)	A. Copland	R. Steiner & W. Van Dyke
1939	*Of Mice and Men* (U.S.A.)	A Copland	L. Milestone
1940	*Our Town* (U.S.A.)	A. Copland	S. Wood & T. Wilder
1941	*The 49th Parallel* ['The Invaders']	R. Vaughan Williams	M. Powell
1941	*Major Barbara*	W. Walton	G. Pascal
1941	*Next of Kin*	W. Walton	Th. Dickinson
1941	*The Land* (U.S.A.)	R. Arnell	R. Flaherty
1942	*Coastal Command*	R. Vaughan Williams	J. B. Holmes
1942	*The People's Land*	R. Vaughan Williams	R. Keene
1942	*The First of the Few* ('Spitfire')	W. Walton	L. Howard
1942	*North Star* (U.S.A.)	A. Copland	L. Milestone

		Composer	*Director*
1942	*Gold Rush* (U.S.A.) [Silent version 1925]	C. Chaplin	C. Chaplin
1942	*Talk of The Town* (U.S.A.)	F. Hollaender	G. Stevens
1942	*Citizen Kane* (U.S.A.)	B. Herrmann	O. Welles
1943	*Flemish Farm*	R. Vaughan Williams	G. Dell
1943	*Le Voyageur sans Bagages*	F. Poulenc	J. Anouilh
1944	*Memphis Belle* (U.S.A.)	G. Kubik	W. Wyler
1944	*Les enfants du paradis*	J. Kosma & M. Thiriet	M. Carné
1944	*L'Eternel Retour*	G. Auric	J. Cocteau & J. Delannoy
1944	*Henry V*	W. Walton	L. Olivier
1945	*The Stricken Peninsula*	R. Vaughan Williams	P. Fletcher
1945	*Caesar and Cleopatra*	G. Auric	G. Pascal
1945	*Farrébique*	H. Sauguet	G. Rouquier
1945	*Ivan the Terrible*, Part I (U.S.S.R.)	S. Prokofiev	S. M. Eisenstein
1945	*Tuesday in November* (U.S.A.)	V. Thomson	J. Houseman
1945	*The Cummington Story* (U.S.A.)	A. Copland	H. Grayson
1945	*La Bataille du Rail*	Y. Baudrier	R. Clément
1946	*Man of Two Worlds*	A. Bliss	Th. Dickinson
1946	*Odd Man Out*	W. Alwyn	C. Reed
1946	*Instruments of the Orchestra*	B. Britten	M. Mathieson
1946	*La Belle et la Bête*	G. Auric	J. Cocteau
1946	*Symphonie Pastorale*	G. Auric	J. Delannoy
1946	*Best Years of Our Lives* (U.S.A.)	H. Friedhofer	W. Wyler
1946	*Spectre of the Rose* (U.S.A.)	G. Antheil	B. Hecht
1946	*Strange Love of Martha Ivers* (U.S.A.)	M. Rosza	L. Milestone
1947	*Loves of Joanna Godden*	R. Vaughan Williams	C. Frend
1947	*Fiddle-de-dee* (Canada)	N. McLaren	N. McLaren
1947	*L'Aigle à Deux Têtes*	G. Auric	J. Cocteau
1947	*Red Pony* (U.S.A.)	A. Copland	L. Milestone
1947	*Private Affairs of Bel Ami* (U.S.A.)	D. Milhaud	A. Lewin
1947	*Le Tempestaire*	Y. Baudrier	J. Epstein
1948	*Scott of the Antarctic*	R. Vaughan Williams	C. Frend
1948	*Hamlet*	W. Walton	L. Olivier

		Composer	*Director*
1948	*Les Parents Terribles*	G. Auric	J. Cocteau
1948	*Louisiana Story* (U.S.A.)	V. Thomson	R. Flaherty
1948	*Dreams that Money Can Buy*	P. Hindemith, D. Milhaud, J. Cage, E. Varèse, P. Bowles, L. Applebaum	H. Richter
1949	*Dim Little Island*	R. Vaughan Williams	H. Jennings
1949	*Rocking Horse Winner*	W. Alwyn	A. Pelissier
1949	*Third Man*	A. Karas	C. Reed
1949	*Les Enfants Terribles*	P. Bonneau (Vivaldi)	J. P. Melville & J. Cocteau
1949	*Guernica*	G. Bernard	A. Resnais & P. Eluard
1949	*Pacific 231*	A. Honegger (composed 1923)	J. Mitry
1949	*Heiress* (U.S.A.)	A. Copland	W. Wyler
1949	*C-Man* (U.S.A.)	G. Kubik	J. Lerner
1949	*La Beauté du Diable*	R. Vlad	R. Clair
1950	*Orphée*	G. Auric	J. Cocteau
1950	*Gerald McBoing Boing* (U.S.A.)	G. Kubik	S. Bosustow
1950	*Macbeth* (U.S.A.)	J. Ibert	O. Welles
1950	*Works of Calder* (U.S.A.)	J. Cage	H. Matter
1951	*Man in the White Suit*	B. Frankel	A. Mackendrick
1951	*Le sel de la terre*	G. Bernard	G. Rouquier
1951	*Goya: Les desastres de la guerre*	J. Grémillon	J. Grémillon
1951	*Voyage en Amérique*	F. Poulenc	H. Lavorel
1952	*Sound Barrier*	M. Arnold	D. Lean
1952	*Cruel Sea*	A. Rawsthorne	C. Frend
1952	*La Putain respectueuse*	G. Auric	M. Pagliero & J. P. Sartre
1952	*Leonardo da Vinci* (Italy)	R. Vlad	L. Emmer
1953	*Crin Blanc*	M. Le Roux	A. Lamorisse
1953	*Drawings of Leonardo*	A. Rawsthorne	A. de Potier & B. Wright
1953	*Moulin Rouge*	G. Auric	J. Huston
1954	*La Strada* (Italy)	N. Rota	F. Fellini
1954	*Romeo and Juliet* (Italy)	R. Vlad	R. Castellani
1954	*On the Waterfront* (U.S.A.)	L. Bernstein	E. Kazan
1955	*Ship That Died of Shame*	W. Alwyn	B. Dearden

		Composer	Director
1955	*Richard III*	W. Walton	L. Olivier
1955	*Les Mauvaises Rencontres*	M. Le Roux	A. Astruc
1956	*Le Ballon Rouge*	M. Le Roux	A. Lamorisse
1957	*Les Mystères de Picasso*	G. Auric	H. G. Clouzot
1958	*Vision of William Blake*	R. Vaughan Williams	G. Brenton
1958	*The Goddess*	V. Thomson	P. Chayevsky

Appendix B. Alphabetical Index of Composers in Appendix A

Alwyn	1939, 46, 49, 55	Friedhofer	1946
Antheil	1924, 46	Grémillon	1951
Applebaum	1948		
Arnell	1941	Herrmann	1942
Arnold	1952	Hollaender	1930, 42
Auric	1931, 31, 44, 45,	Honegger	1922, 34, 38, 49
	46, 46, 47,	Hindemith	1948
	48, 50, 52,		
	53, 57	Ibert	1927, 50
Baudrier	1945, 47	Jaubert	1939
Bernard, A.	1929, 30, 31		
Bernard, G.	1949, 51	Karas	1949
Bernstein	1954	Korngold	1936
Bliss	1935, 46	Kosma	1937, 44
Bonneau	1949	Kubik	1944, 49, 50
Bowles	1948		
Breil	1915	Le Roux	1953, 55, 56
Britten	1935, 36, 46		
		McLaren	1947
Cage	1948, 50	Meisel	1925, 27
Chaplin	1936, 42	Milhaud	1925, 34, 47, 48
Copland	1939, 39, 40, 42,		
	45, 47, 49	Poulenc	1943, 51
		Prokofiev	1934, 38, 45
Delannoy	1939		
		Rawsthorne	1952, 53
Eisler	1934	Rosza	1946
		Rota	1954
Françaix	1937		
Frankel	1951	Saint-Saëns	1907

Satie	1924	Vaughan Williams	1941, 42, 42, 43, 45, 47, 48, 49, 58
Sauguet	1945		
Steiner	1935		
		Vlad	1949, 52, 54
Thomson	1936, 37, 38, 45, 48, 58		
		Walton	1935, 41, 41, 42, 44, 48, 55
Varèse	1948	Weill	1931

Bibliography

Annuaire Biographique du Cinéma. Paris: Contact Organisation. (This trade annual gives full listings of composers.)

L. Chiarini, ed. *La Musica nel Film*, Rome: Bianco e Nero, 1940.

H. Eisler. Composing for the Films. New York: Oxford Univ. Press, 1947. (London: Dobson, 1951.)

Grove's Dictionary of Music. Ed. E. Blom, 5th ed. Vol. II (London: Macmillan, 1954), pp. 93-110.

Georges Hacquard. *La musique et le cinéma*. Paris: Press Universitaires, 1959.

J. Huntley. *British Film Music*. London: British Yearbooks, 1947.

J. Huntley & R. Manvell. *The Technique of Film Music*. London: Focal Press, 1957.

K. London. *Film Music*. London: Faber, 1936 (tr. E. S. Bensinger).

C. McCarty. *Film Composers in America*. Glendale, Calif.: Valentine, 1953.

Musik in Geschichte und Gegenwart. Ed. F. Blume. Vol. IV (Kassel: Bärenreiter, 1955), pp. 187-202.

L. Sabaneyev. *Music for the Films*. London: Pitman, 1935 (tr. S. W. Pring).

XI

EXPERIMENTAL MEDIA: I

Musique concrète—Electronic Music

By Humphrey Searle

Musique concrète was the invention of Pierre Schaeffer, who has been pursuing researches into the subject since 1948; in this he has been given technical assistance by the studios of Radiodiffusion-Télévision Française. In collaboration with Pierre Henry he has produced a number of works in this medium, some of which have become world-famous, and two commercial discs of *musique concrète* have been issued by the Ducretet-Thomson company under the auspices of U.N.E.S.C.O.

The principle of *musique concrète* is fairly simple; sounds, whether musical or natural, are recorded on magnetic tape and are then put through various processes before being combined with one another to form a piece of 'concrete music'. The sounds may be distorted by being put through various kinds of filters which remove different frequencies from them; they may be played backwards, or at any speed or pitch—an instrument called the Phonogène has been invented which allows the speed to be altered without affecting the pitch—or short sounds like string pizzicati may be artifically prolonged by means of another instrument called the Morphophone. It will be seen that the possibilities of *musique concrète* are enormous, the only limiting factor being, at one end, the choice of the sounds to be recorded, and, at the other, the creative imagination of the composer. The making of *musique concrète* is a long, elaborate and laborious task, and this may account for the fact that up to now very few composers of repute have made experiments in this direction; they have simply not had the time to learn and assimilate the technique properly. As a result the main works of *musique concrète* so far have been produced by technicians like Schaeffer and Henry rather than by professional composers; and though in France Boulez, Messiaen, Sauguet and others have made a few *concrète* pieces, these have remained by-products of their main activity.

This is not to say that the works of Schaeffer, Henry and other technicians are artistically valueless; indeed they have produced a number of extremely interesting compositions in this medium, some of which are of definite musical importance. Up to now, however, and in spite of the claims advanced for it in some quarters, *musique concrète* has been most successful in the evocation of dramatic atmosphere in background and incidental music; it has not yet been able to produce works which are musically self-sufficient. Schaeffer himself admits this when he says: 'The first works of *musique concrète* could call themselves "symphony" or "cantata"; nobody has claimed to be able to make a quartet'.

In fact one of the best-known works of Schaeffer and Henry—here working in collaboration—is the *Symphonie pour un homme seul*, but this is certainly not a symphony in the classical sense; its ten short movements represent the sounds which a man walking alone at night might hear round him, and its lack of self-sufficiency as music is underlined by the fact that it has recently been turned into a ballet, with choreography by Maurice Béjart, who has specialised in the use of *concrète* scores for his ballets. But it undeniably evokes a powerful atmosphere, and as such is one of the most successful productions in this medium. Another important work of Schaeffer and Henry is the 'opéra concret' *Orphée 53*, first produced in that year at the Donaueschingen Festival. As well as sounds which give the effect of choral singing, this work actually uses a human voice reciting an Orphic hymn in Greek; however this is split up and distorted by the use of echoes, filters, different speeds and other devices so that it becomes more or less unrecognisable as human speech except in one or two moments—this type of treatment of the human voice is fairly common in *concrète* works, which tend to avoid realism as far as possible.

Another work which has been successfully staged is the ballet *Haut Voltage*, again with choreography by Maurice Béjart. Here the music was shared between Pierre Henry and Marius Constant, the former providing *concrète* sounds and the latter music for normal instruments; of the two, Henry's contribution was immeasurably the more effective. *Musique concrète* has also been successfully used in films; typical examples of this are Schaeffer and Henry's scores for the big documentary *Sahara d'aujourd'hui*, in which the sounds are mainly used to provide a discreet background, and Boulez' music for *Symphonie mécanique*, a short film in which shots of various machines in action are neatly matched with *concrète* noises; there is no commentary, and the film is left to speak for itself. Another possibility of the combination of *musique concrète* with visual images was demonstrated at the 1958 Brussels Exhibition, when the 'Audio-Visual Research Foundation' of San Francisco presented a programme of *musique concrète* and electronic music accompanied by visual images which were partly inspired by the architectural features of the dome of a planetarium.

There are however a certain number of works dating from the earlier period of *musique concrète* which can fairly well stand on their own feet as music. One of these is the *Concerto des ambiguités* of Pierre Henry, which evokes an unusual, menacing atmosphere in many passages; here again there is no question of the classical concerto form, and the work seems to have been so called chiefly because it contains a number of piano effects. There are also a number of shorter studies which each illustrate some technical point, such as Schaeffer's *Variations sur une flûte mexicaine*, based not only on normal flute sounds but also on the effect of striking the wooden part of the instrument, and Henry's remarkable *Vocalise*, which is entirely constructed from the sound of one human voice singing the syllable 'Ah'. An agreeable light-weight work in this genre is the *Boîte à musique* of Philippe Arthuys.

The 1958 Brussels Exhibition also presented the first performances of a number of works of *musique concrète* composed in the last few years which show rather more abstract tendencies than those with which this medium first began. Pierre Schaeffer sums up the change in these words: 'As a result of an evolution which is logical rather than surprising, the recent works, which are infinitely less spectacular than the older ones, are in fact more "serious". . . . The prolonged effort of these last few years has allowed us to enter into the knowledge of sounds, to reveal their characters and analyse their "contexture". From this we get results which are less expressive but more reasoned, and are the only way to a music "without adjectives".' Schaeffer implies that in future *musique concrète* will in general renounce the use of effects which arise fortuitously from the nature of the electro-acoustic instruments employed and will make less use of the devices which distort the natural sounds. This new development may lead to a kind of *musique concrète* in which the composer has a greater conscious control of his material, and this would certainly be a good thing; but at the moment there are not sufficient data to evaluate this subject properly. However it is interesting that among the composers who were represented by new works of this type in Brussels were Edgard Varèse and Henri Sauguet. Varèse, a pioneer of experimental music, shocked the twenties with his *Octandre*, *Intégrales*, *Ionisation* (for percussion only) and other works. These pieces were all written for normal instruments, though these were handled in a very extreme way; but Varèse has been experimenting with electronic music for some time, and his *Déserts* of 1954 is a pioneer work in the combination of music recorded on magnetic tape with music scored for normal orchestra—a device which has since been taken up by a number of younger composers. Sauguet has a long experience as a dramatic composer, particularly in ballet; but his *Trois Aspects Sentimentaux* of 1957 appears to be his first work of *musique concrète*. The composer regards the work as a kind of symphonic poem in which *musique concrète* is used as an extension of traditional music. Other composers represented in Brussels with new works of *musique concrète*, apart from Schaeffer and Henry, were the young Frenchman Luc Ferrari, a pupil of Messiaen, and the young Greek Yanis Xenakis, who is an architect as well as a composer and is at present one of Le Corbusier's collaborators.

Though *musique concrète* originated in France, composers of other countries have not been slow to take it up and exploit it in various ways; similarly electronic music, which originated in Germany and was given technical support by the studios of the West German Radio in Cologne, is now also being made in other studios such as those of R.A.I. Milan, Philips at Eindhoven and Apélac in Brussels. This is not the place to enter into a technical description of the methods used in making electronic music—those who are interested in this aspect of the subject will find a good deal of information in the booklet *Electronic Music*, published in English and German as No. 1 of the series 'Die Reihe', by Universal Edition Ltd.: this also contains the reproduction of a page of electronic score—but one can say briefly that the sounds are produced by an electronic oscillator which can be adjusted to any given frequency, pitch or tone-colour. In addition to single tones it is also possible to produce 'fat sounds', caused by the use of several adjacent frequencies, and numerous other effects; also, of course, the traditional division of the octave into twelve semitones no longer applies, and in theory any kind of subdivision is possible. This means that the sonorous possibilities of electronic music are even greater than those of *musique concrète*, with the added advantage that they can be exactly determined in advance and even written down in the form of a score. The preparation of such a score, however, needs a good deal of mathematical and scientific knowledge on the part of the composer, and electronic music is not a medium which can be quickly mastered: in addition, the composition of each piece takes a considerable time. The composers working in Cologne and Milan have, naturally enough, concentrated on the production of new sounds which are unlike anything which can be produced by normal instruments: those in Holland and Belgium have been more conservative on the whole, and many have written 'normal' music for electronic means—not a very satisfactory procedure. Of course it is possible to write music in the style of, say, Tchaikovsky for electronic instruments, but what is the purpose of that?

The first recital of electronic music was given in Cologne in October 1954, and consisted of works by Herbert Eimert, the originator of the medium, the young German composer Karlheinz Stockhausen, the young Belgian Henri Pousseur (who is now working independently in Brussels) and two other composers. In Milan the leading figures have been Luciano Berio and Bruno Maderna—the latter is also well known as a conductor—and in Holland the electronic composers are headed by Henk Badings, perhaps the leading Dutch composer of today. In Germany and Italy electronic music can be regarded to a considerable extent as an extension of the post-Webern school of composition for normal instruments, in which not only are the notes themselves treated serially, but also their dynamics, octave pitch, instrumentation, rhythm and duration; the principal exponents of that method of writing are Pierre Boulez, Luigi Nono and Karlheinz Stockhausen. Of these three it is Stockhausen who has gone the furthest in applying mathematical principles to electronic music; though Boulez has made some works of *musique concrète*, Nono does not appear to have used electronic media at all. It is obvious that electronic music gives far greater possibilities of mathematical arrangement and subdivision than any music written for normal instruments and scales can; but up to now the difference in sound between Stockhausen's electronic works and those for normal instruments is not so great as might be imagined, the same mathematical principles apparently holding good for both. He has even combined electronic music with the use of the human voice partly distorted as in *musique concrète*, in one of his best-known electronic works, the *Gesang der Jünglinge*, based on the story of Shadrach, Meshach and Abednego. Similar processes have also been used by Luciano Berio, for instance in his *Omaggio a Joyce*, which is officially described as follows: 'It is entirely composed of vocal elements, taken from a paragraph of *Ulysses*. The first stages of the work consisted in simply reading the text, either in its original English version, or in French and Italian translations. After this the readings were done by different voices which were desynchronised more or less, and then the different languages were combined in a single vocal counterpoint which shed light on their multiple correspondences in a way which Joyce would certainly have appreciated. In the final stage the various phonetic materials, vowels and consonants, syllables and English, French and Italian words, and recordings of single or multiple voices were used with the greatest liberty and give birth to a kind of musical "anamorphosis" of the literary text.'

I have quoted this at some length as it is typical of a tendency which has recently become apparent in music of this kind, not only that written for electronic means but for normal instruments too—a partial return to the haphazard. The treatment of the vocal elements here is similar to that in *musique concrète*, and the fact that the words are split up and heard simultaneously in various languages destroys any meaningfulness that the work might have had. It is as if the inventors of electronic music were afraid of pushing their mathematical principles too far, and wished to include some irrational element in their works; this is also evident in certain works written for normal instruments, such as Henri Pousseur's *Mobile* for two pianos, where, in addition to the normal 'fixed' music, the players are permitted to insert extra passages at certain points at their own discretion. In Stockhausen's *Zeitmasse* for wind quintet the players are allowed some liberties in individual *accelerandi* and *ritardandi*, and his *Pièce XI* for piano consists of a number of short fragments which are all printed on one large page; the order in which these are to be played, and to some extent also the dynamic attack for each, are left to the performer, again within certain limits. In addition a certain amount of audience participation in some of these works is apparently envisaged; in his *Gruppen* Stockhausen has three orchestras arranged round different sides of the room. We are told that 'here the public no longer sit as pure spectators in front of a stage which is clearly separated from them, but, surrounded by the orchestras, they are invited to a more active perception, which is perhaps the first stage in a continuously growing co-operation'. I should add that a number of electronic works are definitely meant to be heard stereophonically, with four or five loudspeakers surrounding the audience and each playing a different tape channel; the *Gesang der Jünglinge* provides an example of this.

Electronic music is still in an extremely experimental stage, and one cannot say that its musical results up to now have been very encouraging; but it is clearly a medium with enormous possibilities, and a real composer working in this style can certainly produce good results once he has mastered the technique. Two examples of work by Bruno Maderna heard in Brussels bear this out; the first is a *Continuo* which makes a most imaginative use of electronic sounds, and the second is his *Dimensioni* for flute (played live) and magnetic tape, which again shows considerable musical qualities. If these new media do not get bogged down in theorising and technical considerations they may produce some fruitful results in time.

Bibliography: Pierre Schaeffer: *Vers la recherche d'une musique concrète*. Paris, 1948.

Die Reihe No. 1: *Electronic Music* (Universal Edition).

See also: Karlheinz Stockhausen: *Une experience électronique*;

Maurice Martenot: *Luthérie électronique*;

in: *La Musique et ses problèmes contemporains* (Cahiers de la compagnie Madeleine Renaud-Jean-Louis Barrault. Julliard, Paris, 1954);

and, *passim*, *Gravesaner Blätter*, Ed. Hermann Scherchen, Lugano, Switzerland.

EXPERIMENTAL MEDIA: II

MICRO-INTERVALS

By Maurice Ohana

THE USE of scales in thirds and fourths of a tone is nothing new in the history of music. In the fourth century B.C. Aristoxenus mentions the use of what the Greeks used to call the chromatic modal scale which included two intervals of quarter-tones. It did not last very long and had very much the same effect on musical ears at the time as that of some of the most virulent dodecaphonic theorists' music in the past twenty-five years.

The use of scales in one-third and quarter-tones in our day seems to have originated in Mexico where Gomez Carrillo, a Mexican composer, first had instruments built at the end of the last century to answer the requirements of his conceptions. Although then aged eighty-five, he appeared at the Brussels Exhibition in 1958 at the head of some fifteen pianofortes tuned in thirds, fourths, fifths and sixths of a tone. At the moment easily available instruments include only zithers and guitars, although it is said that horns and trumpets will soon be available also.

The notation is not yet fixed, but for thirds of a tone on the zither, which has a compass of only one octave, from D flat to D flat, the clearest notation would seem to be the following:

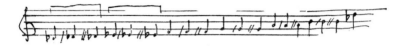

This instrument is therefore tuned in full tones, and each tone is divided into two intervals marked / for the first third, and // for the second. Its only defect at present is that it excludes the semi-tone. Of course any other scale could have been chosen, but I am planning a new instrument ranging from

As it is, each string is divided into two parts by a 'ponticello', so that the upper part of the string gives the octave above, and the lower part the actual sound:

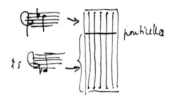

Needless to say, thirds of a tone are playable on the violin or guitar, but these instruments never give a genuinely tempered sound.

The zither in quarter-tones is much larger in size than the one in thirds of a tone but also has a range of only one octave, *plus* the corresponding octave higher played on the upper part of the string. The existing ones give, besides the semi-tone, two quarter-tones, two eighths and four sixteenths. This makes it rather unwieldy since the pitch is indicated in the score by a number corresponding to a string, and in order to play accurately a certain amount of deliberation is required.

There is a difference of tone between the two instruments. The zither in thirds of a tone is much sharper and has a crystalline quality which is lacking in the zither tuned in quarter-tones.

Zither tuned in quarter-tones

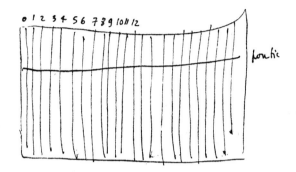

o = C
1 = C + 1/16th.
2 = C + 1/8th.
3 = C + 3/16ths.
4 = C + ¼ etc. . . . Therefore, from C to D there are 16 strings. I find this partition rather excessive, and suggest that C, + ¼, + ½ tone (*C sharp*), *C sharp* + ¼ would be sufficient. Mr Carrillo's achievements seem to be confined to adding a lot of *glissando* passages to scores otherwise written in fair post-Franckist or Wagnerian styles.

I believe myself that in order really to enlarge the scope of a melodic line by the use of these intervals, the ear requires to be carefully trained to a new approach. Monodic music offers vast possibilities for the use of third or quarter-tones. Two-part writing, and three-part, if carefully handled can be very striking, as also certain clusters of tones struck or plucked. The use of these intervals is most striking, however, against a background of tempered instruments tuned in ordinary semi-tones (like the piano). After a short while the ear follows astonishingly well all the subtle changes in between the tones, whether in thirds or quarters. After all, one frequently hears intervals of third and quarter-tones in certain types of popular singing, e.g. the *Cante Jondo*, and although this is due rather to lack of pitch, it sounds quite acceptable to the ear.

So far as I am concerned, my interest in these intervals has always been great since I first began to compose, and I was glad to seize an opportunity to make a decisive experiment two years ago with the new instruments available.

The use of these new intervals seems to me to be a natural step towards the conquest of one more of the harmonics coming next after Debussy's ninths and Ravel's elevenths and thirteenths, etc. The only new thing is that they are deliberately played and thus enlarge the possibilities of melody to an immense extent. Some attempts have been made already to create an aggressive movement based on these discoveries, presenting them as the only possible line of future development for music, and tending to cast anathema on all improper tendencies. But I believe that this will be a dangerous weapon to handle for those who do not feel instinctively the need for this extension of the range of the ear. As in all discoveries (and when I say 'discoveries' I mean the *re*-discovery of means of expression which are at least fifteen centuries old: *Il n'y a rien de nouveau sous le soleil!*), there is a danger that the theoreticians will soon turn it into a hateful 'system' appealing to those who have already worshipped other gods with the same passion and found nothing at the end of their speculations.

NOTE

Readers interested in this subject may like to know that Maurice Ohana has written, with the use of two zithers in thirds and quarters of a tone, or with the zither in thirds of a tone only, the following works:

Incidental music to *Les Hommes et les Autres* (Elio Vittorini).
Music to the film *Goha*.
A *Suite for nine instruments* from *Les Hommes et les Autres*.
A *Christmas Oratorio*, *Récit de l'An Zéro*, on a poem by George Schéhadé.

(*The Editor.*)

PART II

A SURVEY OF CONTEMPORARY MUSIC IN EUROPE, U.S.A. AND LATIN AMERICA

XII

MUSIC IN AUSTRIA AND GERMANY TODAY

By Karl-Heinz Füssl

IN THE COURSE of its development, Western music has continually created new standards, new values. Indeed, in the long period of its prime there was, in fact, nothing else but new music, for the music of previous epochs was never able to compete with the contemporary music of the day. It was not until the present time, which is lacking, or believes itself to be lacking, in values of its own, that a return was made to the glories of the past—glories which have only recently been opened up to us by the work of historians and whose wealth and abundance are almost paralysing for the cultured composer of today.

When art was still the prerogative of the privileged few, the taste of the masses had no significant influence upon the intentions of the composer. Today the masses, encouraged, if not educated, to be consumers of art, are served by a gigantic entertainment industry. Suddenly the 'New Music' appears in contrast to that of the past. This development began in the late nineteenth century. While Beethoven, in 1802, could still write in a letter to the publishers Breitkopf: 'Apart from this it is always others that tell me when I have new ideas, for I never realise it myself', Richard Wagner characterised the altered situation with the famous words: 'Do something new, chaps!' The 'New Music' was born and has ever since been the concern of the élite among composers.

*　　*　　*

Contemporary music in Germany and Austria shows no sign of a new revolution, but rather a multiplicity of individual attempts to synthesise the results of the revolutionary mood of the twenties: for, to revolt, we must believe in what the revolution is to achieve. The optimism of the twenties, based upon humanism and intoxicated with the blind worship of authority, was soon followed by a disillusionment, at the end of which came the Second World War. In both countries this second post-war period of our century was characterised by spiritual as well as material dearth; but the ravages of physical hunger heal quicker than those of scepticism and cynicism. Everyday existence satisfies us today less than it ever did, and those who wish to escape from it do not seek an art that is born of our time. If one believes in anything at all, then it is only in what has been proved a thousand times over. It has already become a permanent article of faith that the art of the past is 'great'—but the present is anything but permanent. Can, therefore, its artistic utterances be expected to inspire? The *Musica Nova* of the fifties plays to empty houses, and revolutions can hardly take place without a public.

Modern man, as consumer of art, clings to the artistic ideals of the past and so cannot be surprised if he is no longer, as formerly, the measure of all things. Indeed, from the point of view of the creative artist, he has long ceased to be so. Now, with the beginning of the atomic age, the individual human being seems to be delivered helplessly into the power of the atom, lost as never before. But the artist, too, has taken refuge in the already known, thus reflecting the general flight. On the one hand, some believe mathematical logic to be more trustworthy than man, who has so often erred, while others seek their justification in the applause of the public.

Schoenberg's twelve-note technique, once regarded as a diabolical heresy, later as the grandiose achievement of a despairing individualism exerting all its powers for a last break-through, has acquired for the former a new meaning: matter, the embodiment of physical law, must be forced to speak, where man, as it appears, has nothing to say. There can be no other explanation for the re-birth of serial composition. The German musicologist, Theodor Adorno, a pupil of Alban Berg, defined the three giants of the Viennese School thus: Schoenberg composes as though there were no tone-rows, Berg bewitches them, and Webern forces them to speak. Is it then surprising if the twelve-note composers of today inscribe, not Berg or Schoenberg, but Webern on their banners?

The other composers, however, preferring to remain nearer to the traditional conception of a musician and distrusting the insidious ideas of musical engineers and philosophers, recall again the great achievements of the past—which is all the easier to do, in that distance not only guarantees greater objectivity but also leads to the recognition that what was once surprisingly and even alarmingly new, in fact grew out of this very past. So they try to take up one of the torn threads, tie it to some tradition and, in general, act as though nothing at all had happened. The 'Romantics' among them return far into the past and fasten on the Baroque or even the Middle Ages, while the less escapist try to imbue orchestral sonority, which in the last century had more and more become an end in itself, with new meaning, continually struggling against the exhaustion of their material and the dulling of their listener's senses.

Adorno calls this, a little unjustly, 'the detestable ideal of the moderately modern', but it should not be forgotten that it is the moderates among the moderns who are seeking to strengthen the weakened link between the public and the creative artist. It is thanks to their mediation that the radicals are now also played outside the confines of a small circle, and that modern music is beginning to gain some small credit with the general public. Slowly but surely they are altering the listening habits of the public and preparing old ground for new seed.

*   *   *

The most important among contemporary composers are of course those who are able to reconcile the old conflict between music as 'sonorously inspired form' and music as 'expression': in Germany today, Boris Blacher, Carl Orff and Werner Egk; in Austria, Gottfried von Einem. A study of their work immediately reveals two common factors: the use, as a means of expression, of a rhythm that moves against the time-signature, and a love of the musical theatre in all its forms. While Orff and Egk write almost exclusively for the theatre, the work of Blacher and Einem shows greater variety. It is true that their popularity springs more from their stage works, as these reach a larger audience—Blacher became known in Germany through his first ballet *Fest im Suden* ('Mediterranean Festival') and his pupil, Einem, attained international recognition through his first opera *Danton's Death*—but both were nevertheless prominent in the field of absolute music.

Blacher (born January 6th, 1903, in New Chwang, China) replaces the more serious, all-pervading symphonic development technique, derived from Beethoven, with a light and graceful interplay of themes and motives: where others would write a development section, he indulges in a fascinating rhythmic game with his material. 'Variable metre', which he has often used to enable rhythmic development alone to carry extended sections, has its origin in the work of Stravinsky, although not exactly in the way Blacher uses it, with a *regularly* varying metre. Despite his elegant counterpoint, Blacher, like Stravinsky, is a melodist. It may be that this gift, which today is something of a rarity, makes its possessors immune to any clique spirit. At any rate, despite all their experiments, neither has let himself be trapped in any tendency or theory, any system or method. Blacher's works include all genres: besides concert and chamber music, ballets and operas, he has written music for films, plays and radio. In expressive content, his work is no less varied. The *Study in Pianissimo*, in the pointillistic manner of Webern, and the *Ornament for Orchestra*, the character of which is implied by its title, are just as personal as, say, the brilliant *Paganini Variations* or the *Concertante Music*. Despite ready comprehensibility—a comprehensibility which results from his sure grasp of form—Blacher's music usually contains an irrational element, leaving behind something inexplicable in the mind of the listener. The contents often express something more, something different from and contradictory to what the always graceful surface would seem to imply. From this aspect Blacher is a little reminiscent of Mozart. In comparison with Einem, his music is far removed from the symphonic heritage of the past. On the other hand, his is the truly historical achievement of teaching German music to dance.

In his popular orchestral works, Einem (born January 24th, 1918, in Berne) recalls the grand gestures of Gustav Mahler, but also, instead of Mahler's strange mixture of intellect and naiveté, the sensuous sonorities of a Richard Strauss—without, of course, that certain *petit bourgeois* element that is familiar in the work of the Bavarian composer. Like the old masters, Einem develops his music out of itself, out of a germinal motif. Every new element is related to something preceding and the form is the result of the organic growth of all the musical elements, never the starting point or blue-print of the work to be created. This implies a classical feeling for texture and balance, which again guarantees a harmoniousness of proportion that is yet free from the schematic. Einem's return to tonality is surprising after the aggressiveness of his early works, but tonality is for him nothing more nor less than another formal element. Even his music for ballet and opera is autonomous, for it never interprets the dramatic action with the expressive techniques of the romantics. For example, just as Franz Kafka makes the reader aware of the many levels of events in the human consciousness by means of a minutely exact description of an everyday, if somewhat dreamlike, reality, so Einem, in basing his second opera, *The Trial*, on Kafka's novel, uses his music to provide, as it were, an analogy. Instead of losing himself in the twilight of impressionistic sound-painting, he allows the music to follow its own laws: indeed, he consciously makes it develop its own, autonomous form in order to provide an equivalent to the clear, matter-of-fact language of Kafka.

Carl Orff (born July 10th, 1895, in Munich) has succumbed entirely to the fascination of the theatre and sees a future for music only within its confines. To go and hear his music in the concert-hall is an absurdity —he has withdrawn his absolute music, all of which he wrote before he was forty. It is difficult to explain his later success as a stage composer in the German speaking countries. Perhaps the most obvious reason is that here is someone who dares to be theatrical in an age and environment when public life absorbs all truly theatrical talent. In addition he dexterously brushes aside old, ingrained prejudices of the German soul, as it were, freeing it, and satisfies the yearning for the 'Origin of all Things', a yearning of the intellectuals as German as is the word *Sehnsucht* itself. Technically speaking, what he has done is radically to simplify and limit his material. He has applied a drastic purge to

German opera, which has all too long been constipated by the symphonic pretensions of its orchestra. Ostinati and the wearisome repetition of simple melodic patterns, which appear primitive in the sober atmosphere of the concert-hall, cast their spell in the magic of the theatre, aided for preference in their work of enchantment by Bavarian dialect, vulgar Latin, middle high German or ancient Greek, quite regardless of intelligibility. Orff's inclination to reduce everything to its primal elements has lead him to resort to the great timeless themes of the past, delving, step by step, ever further into the recesses of antiquity towards Oedipus, the prototype of Western drama, which is the subject of his latest work. As personified wish-fulfilment of the Germans, Orff stands in Germany above all criticism. The serial composers, who in other respects have constituted themselves a dictatorship of the minority in the professional journals, fear to attack, and in him, even East and West meet, for in both parts of Germany he is acclaimed a great master.

Werner Egk (born May 17th, 1901, in Auchsessheim, Bavaria) was long named in the same breath as Orff, but he is, in fact, perhaps the least German of composers. Remarkable is his love of Gallic *esprit*: French literature, especially, seems to inspire and enrich his music. The fact that he has recently written a play is the last consequence of a dual talent. Like Orff, he writes or arranges his own libretti; indeed, the literary element sometimes seems more striking than the musical. Again like Orff, who for many years worked at the introduction of a new method of teaching music to children, and like Einem, who began his career as a *répétiteur* in Berlin and Bayreuth and now helps to devise the programmes of the Salzburg Festival, Egk is a practical musician, having earlier been an opera conductor. As a musician he was self-taught, which may help to explain why his music was never in the least academic. His first opera *Die Zaubergeige* ('The Magic Violin') had a great success, as did his ballets, *Joan von Zarissa* and *Abraxas*, and his latest opera, *Der Revisor* ('The Government Inspector'). Egk's music is difficult to describe—not that it is lacking in personality, but rather because it is without individual technical traits. Characteristic are the cool, crystal-clear harmony (doubtlessly derived from Stravinsky) and the pregnant melodies, which are easy to listen to and remember and illustrate the dramatic situation with Latin concision. His music, too, is far removed from the large symphonic forms.

Among the more individual composers in Germany today, Rudolf Wagner-Regeney (born August 28th, 1903, in Sächsisch-Regen, Siebenbürgen) is the most singular phenomenon. His music avoids all artifice and experiment, all grand gestures and dramatic outbursts: indeed, it is as though it were determined to remain inconspicuous. The composer, a harpsichordist and collector of beautiful antiques, seems hardly to belong to the present century. With the press and public, accustomed as they are to the sensational, he has a difficult time, but those who get to know his music better learn to treasure it. As with the art of Chagall, it has sombre undertones, yet there is something strangely homely about it that recalls long-forgotten memories. Simple without being primitive, clear, almost cool, yet not without mystery, it achieves its effects with the simplest possible means. It is beautiful music; but beautiful without the monotonous surface smoothness of the merely beautiful, and its aphoristic concentration bears witness to a carefully controlling hand. The operas, *Der Günstling* ('The Court Favourite'), *The Burghers of Calais* and *Johanna Balk*, show a convincing return to the old operatic form of separate, set numbers. The style is a little influenced by that of Kurt Weill but, as a whole, less tense and aggressive and without the deep melancholy of Weill's music. Spiritually, the works seem most akin to the music of Janáček—not that they have any of his explosive passion, but rather in the quiet power and flow of their dramatic narration.

Wolfgang Fortner (born October 12th, 1907, in Leipzig) is more strongly possessed by the desire to synthesise all previous trends than any other German composer. His work is influenced by Hindemith and Schoenberg, by Bartók and Stravinsky, by twelve-note methods and dissonant counterpoint, expressionism and neo-classicism, and as he makes use only of the most characteristic elements in the work of the leaders of modern music, it is not surprising that such an amalgam of divergent, rather than convergent, tendencies should sometimes fail to convince. His determination to synthesise leads him to write in all genres. Trained in the contrapuntal school of Grabner, he is also interested in the past as well as the present, especially in the music of the Baroque and even of the Middle Ages. In fact he attempts too much to be able always to remain himself at the same time, and occasionally disappears under his self-imposed burden. He is at his most personal in the smaller forms. In the 'Shakespeare Songs', for example, he even succeeds in bridging the gap between the extremes of Neo-classicism and Expressionism without renouncing his personality. Here he is less earnest without, for that reason, becoming any the less serious, and in this, perhaps his most concentrated work, the magic of the stage lives alongside the more intimate beauties of the song.

The work of Hans Werner Henze (born July 1st, 1926, in Gütersloh, Westfalen) and Giselher Klebe (born June 28th, 1925, in Mannheim) shows a similar variety, even to the point of confusion, but for a very different reason. They are not weighed down by tradition. Klebe is searching for a style, while Henze abruptly changes direction and system for the same motive. Unlike Schoenberg and his circle, they regard 'twelve-note' as a style rather than a method and do not try, like Fortner, to synthesise the multitudinous influences to which they are inevitably exposed. Rather, less resigned to the problem than unworried by it, they change their personalities with their style or system. Klebe was a pupil of Blacher, but in both matter and manner his work is radically different from his teacher's. In comparison with Henze, a pupil of Fortner and Leibowitz, he is the more consistent, the more skilled technically and perhaps also the more personal. Capable of a farcical humour in the spirit of Klee's painting *Die Zwitscher-maschine* ('The Twittering Machine'), he lacks the affected, decadent world-weariness of which both the music and the writings of Henze are so full. For it should be said that Henze is also extremely active as his own biographer and is always pleased to give account of his doings in public. He once spoke, in connection with his own work, of a 'new kind of musical surrealism'. Another quotation seems more instructive: 'In the summer of 1947 I had the idea of a piece for violin and orchestra, with long, tender cantilenas and delicate sonorities—music such as I had often heard at night when I was seventeen.' As poets of the atmospheric, both composers love sound for its own sake. Refined, modern (with Henze often morbid), pregnant with the poetry of adolescence, it is for them an end in itself and with some justice they might be called neo-romantics, if the term had not already been applied to those epigones of the romantic movement of the last century to whom the name 'bourgeois realists' would in fact seem more appropriate.

Another pupil of Boris Blacher, the highly promising Heimo Erbse (born February 27th, 1924, in Rudolstadt) is the very opposite of Henze and Klebe. For him sound is no more than the means necessary to give concrete form to his musical ideas. It is in no sense 'a veil', as Schoenberg used to say, 'behind which the absence of ideas will not be noticed'. On the contrary, it is intended to sound spare, being considered by the composer neither as a thing in itself, nor as a means of decoration. If one adds to this quality the brutal tensions, full of dynamic vitality and based on a rhythm which continually breaks down the basic pulse of the piece, the result is music which is anything else but 'agreeable'. His most personal work is his chamber music. Up to now this has been written for the traditional combinations of instruments, and the fact that Erbse can dispense with unusual combinations, with their 'interesting' sound qualities, is an indication of the strength of his musical thinking which, in conjunction with his temperament, seems to be leading him towards the dynamic development form derived from Beethoven. Occasional colouristic elements are used, as with Bartók but in contradistinction to Henze, not for their own sake, but as contrasting factors in the overall movement of tension and resolution. He selects with care from all the musical panaceas of this century that which accords with his own personality. The strength and vitality of temperament to call in question the new as well as the old are also his. Indeed, he has in him the stuff of a considerable symphonist.

The only established representative of the symphonic tradition in Germany today is Karl Amadeus Hartmann (born August 2nd, 1905, in Munich). Hartmann's music is full of contrasts and he himself is an opponent of every sort of restriction. His numerous symphonies are accordingly not confined to the classical formal scheme. Without in any way renouncing experiment, he likes to make use of all possibilities in his work—as, for example, in his very personal use of Blacher's variable metre—and aesthetic speculation is quite foreign to

F

him. His style is occasionally reminiscent of Bartók, above all in the barbaric, orgiastic quality of the sound, but this springs rather from bear-like energy than from a nervous inner tension, such as is to be found in Bartók's works.

Bartók has, in fact, had fewer followers in Germany and Austria than one would have expected, considering his stature, and least of all in the most essential element of his style—in folk music. It is true that German and Austrian folk-song is still alive, but it is hardly capable of bearing new fruit. The last person to whom it afforded inspiration was Gustav Mahler. In the work of Alban Berg its vestiges are present, but only as a single element used here and there to heighten or contrast. Germany and Austria, with their long cultural tradition, were of course never an exotic paradise like Spain, or those countries which first entered the musical scene in the last century and added a new colour to European music with their national characteristics. Attempts, made more or less systematically in various places today, to draw inspiration from the spirit of folklore end either in a hopeless salon-music style, in such cases where the original song or dance remains stronger than the final product, or in a still more hopeless, decadent philistinism, which in East Germany and the other communist countries is called 'social realism'. Utterly *petit bourgeois* in taste, this pretends to fight against 'formalism', but itself lands in ultra-formalism. The only oasis in the desert of East Germany is the music of Schoenberg's pupil, Hanns Eisler (born July 6th, 1898, in Leipzig), the greatest master of the German Lied since Brahms and Mahler. But his work has undergone no important further development since the end of the Second World War.

*   *   *

A section on electronic music must be devoted to Germany alone, as Austria, or rather the Vienna Academy of Music, will be equipped with a studio for electronic music, such as the Westdeutscher Rundfunk has had for years, only in the near future. It is with intention that the name of Karlheinz Stockhausen (born August 22nd, 1928, in Altenberg near Cologne) is first mentioned here, for his importance in the field of electronic music is up to now considerably greater than in that of instrumental music, and also greater than that of the other composers who are experimenting in this field. It is true that his non-electronic music shows an absolutely novel imagination, but it is not capable of expression, or only inadequately so, through conventional instruments.

'Extravagance in imposing restrictions is still extravagance.' So defined the Viennese composer Hanns Jelinek the problem of the serial 'pre-formation' of the electronic material.[1] In the case of Stockhausen, it would in fact be more precise to call his musical imagination extravagant rather than the restrictions of the serial pre-formation of the material. Already in his first published works (called, for the sake of a slogan, 'post-Webernian') he was thinking in terms, not of conventional musical material, but of sound complexes: complexes which, because their structures are not fully perceptible to the ear, are by their very nature much more autonomous and much less concerned with audibly perceptible, meaningful relationships than, say, the thematic material of Webern. In other words, the detailed structure of this music becomes of less and less consequence, the more pedantically it is worked out. This important, if not altogether surprising, fact is all the more depressing in that it has produced numerous misunderstandings among composers and writers. The listener is no longer in a position to integrate the details into a whole, and if he welcomes this, it is for the doubtful attraction which the uncomprehended and incomprehensible—the two are here inseparable—exercise upon some temperaments.

Not until Stockhausen applied himself consistently to electronic music did these technical methods produce something of novel significance, all clothed in a new complexity of sound which seems suited to his imagination alone. While Gottfried Michael König, Herbert Eimert and even a master such as Ernst Křenek have so far failed to think truly in terms of the new medium, Stockhausen, the former pupil of Messiaen, succeeded *a priori*. A work such as his *Gesang der Jünglinge* ('Song of the Children') gives the effect of a

---

[1]Normal instrumental tones are made up of a number of pure or sinusoidal tones, related to each other in pitch according to the natural harmonic series and sounding simultaneously. Electronic sounds are generally made up of pure tones in the same way but their pitch relationships are dictated, with Stockhausen and most other electronic composers, by an artificial series.

highly unified whole, but also, paradoxical as it may seem, of inspired improvisation. Stockhausen's true significance is in no way indicated by his wearisome philosophising in word and deed—the latter disguised as instrumental music where, continually on the search for new sensations, he 'discovers' old established practices, such as the baroque use of spatially separated groups of instruments or voices. No, the important thing is that, when the 'philosophers' and musical engineers had finally succeeded in de-personalising music, there was someone there who could find a way forward.

*   *   *

Austria is famed as the land of music, but at present it seems to be resting a little from the exertions which such an honour implies. Apart from Schoenberg's circle, which was the leading intellectual group, although never officially recognised as such, many of his contemporaries, flattered by press and public, persisted all too long either, if they were serious, in confusing the idea of form with an empty scheme, or simply and thoughtlessly in pandering to the desire of the broader public to be entertained. Not only did these composers produce nothing new of significance, they also resisted any new ideas that here and there started to spring up. Thus two camps were formed, and those who wanted to live peaceably in the middle were condemned by both, either as too radical or too conservative. Yet Austria is no land of artistic extremes. It is true that Vienna particularly has for too long been the home of euphony, of sweet and sensuous music, and that it was therefore only to be expected that, there above all, a Schoenberg should arise to be its most extreme opponent; but nevertheless it would be more correct to say that the whole range of music, from the most conservative to the most radical, is more readily to be found in Austria than elsewhere.

As to the middle course, in Germany the barren fruits of academic industry have for some considerable time been collectively designated 'Spielmusik', a sort of neo-baroque that is similar in spirit to the simple music for amateurs that was propagated there between the two wars for social, rather than purely musical reasons, but which is now lacking in any justification whatever. In Austria the equivalent is to be found in those epigoni of the post-romantics, who have pursued into the harsh light of the present day the vision of romantic intoxication and sweet soulfulness, but now are fading into a golden sunset. It would be a waste of time to discuss them here, for they neither are, nor wish to be, composers of our time. Some of their pupils have, however, tried desperately to break out of this enchanted garden—not, alas, always with success.

One of those who have succeeded is Theodor Berger (born May 18th, 1905, in Traismauer, Lower Austria). Like most other Austrian composers, he is an individualist; for the Austrians, in contrast to the Germans, rarely form themselves into groups, but prefer to go their own ways alone. Strangely enough it was Furtwängler who, though generally averse to new music, first promoted him through performances of his work. Berger was a pupil of Franz Schmidt, who is very popular in Austria. From him he got his love of rich sonorities, while his bright and variegated musical palette owes something to Impressionism. To this movement he also has a spiritual affinity when he paints pictures of our time. The music here is mainly of two extremes: on the one hand a-rhythmic and shadowy, on the other dynamic, rhythmic and pounding in a way that seems to be derived from the Stravinsky of *Sacre du Printemps*. Such music is naturally vital and full-blooded, but it should not be overlooked that Berger's music mirrors our time rather than penetrating to its core.

The individuality of the Austrian composers is to be seen even among the twelve-note composers who stem directly from Schoenberg's circle. Despite similar methods each of them comes to quite distinct, personal results, unlike the 'post-Webernians' whose works resemble each other as the wares in one branch of a chain-store resemble those in the next. The music of Hans Erich Apostel (born January 22nd, 1901, in Karlsruhe), a pupil of Berg, is above all lyrical. His Lieder, choral and chamber music are restrained in expression. His iridescent harmony is not merely the result of the part-writing, nor yet just a subtle colour effect: each single aspect of the music is considered with care. Such cautious expressionism results in music that seems to be directed inwards rather than outwards. The *Haydn Variations*, one of his few orchestral works and one that quickly became well-known, emphasise both in the choice of theme and in the inventive variation-technique their origin in the method of composition taught by Schoenberg on the model of the Viennese classics.

It should here be mentioned that the Austrian, both as man and as artist, is deeply conservative and attached to his traditions. The music of the Austrian twelve-note composers of today, of whom there are more than can be considered in this article, is also derived from a tradition, and no less immediately so than Schoenberg's: from a tradition which still lives today, even in the form of what is apparently a negation—as atonality is so often called. With Hanns Jelinek (born December 5th, 1901, in Vienna), as with Ernst Křenek, an affinity with the music of the past is to be taken for granted. He exhibits classical tendencies in both symphonic and chamber music, the form and even the very gestures of the music being based on classical models. His consistently solid craftsmanship has made him sought after as a composer of *Gebrauchsmusik*. The care and meticulousness of his work is demonstrable also in this field, without his in any way lowering his own standards. Apart from this, Jelinek is the composer of a (tonal) operetta, and has recently become one of the very few composers in Germany and Austria to contribute successfully to the tradition of art-jazz. His absolutely un-doctrinaire approach to composition increases the range of his work.

It is strange that even the greatest Austrian composers have mostly succeeded in establishing themselves only late in life. Among the contemporary composers, Gottfried von Einem is an exception and it is significant that, although he can be considered a representative Austrian composer, he received his musical training outside Austria. This means that while, on the one hand, he became fully acquainted with the great traditions which Germany and Austria to some extent share in common, on the other hand he remained untouched by the inhibiting local traditions in which Vienna especially is so rich. In contrast to Einem's relatively early prominence, one may cite the case of the aged Josef Matthias Hauer. Born in 1883, Hauer developed a twelve-note method at the same time as Schoenberg. Both arrived at similar results, although their premises were quite different, Hauer having taken tropes as his starting-point. Hauer is a strange, solitary figure with the purest artistic aims. Composition is for him, as for Haydn, an act of worship, and his music has an ethos that is unequalled today. Yet unfortunately he still remains unknown to the general public.

* * *

Except among the professional *avant-garde*, the emphasis in the term 'Modern Music' is shifting more and more towards the word 'Music' In the minds of the twenty-year olds among the composers of both Austria and Germany, the full emphasis is, however, still laid on 'Modern', with all the rather vague magic which the word conjures up. Their doubtless sincere, but nevertheless somewhat unconvincing revolutionary mood has led as yet to few concrete results. Most of them seek novelty for its own sake rather than out of any inner compulsion—although not just out of the desire to be up to date, let alone provocative. On the contrary, they quite honestly suffer from the fashionable illusion that nothing more can be done with our tonal material. Naturally they write serial music: examples create precedents and they thus hold the latest works of Stravinsky to have inaugurated the reign of the serial. But though it was with considerable justice that Stravinsky called the music of the much honoured Webern 'dazzling diamonds', one must insist that the composer of *The Firebird*, of *Noces*, of *Agon* is a full-blooded musician. Theodor Adorno said that, for the normal mortals among composers, dreams of the music of the spheres must end in a rude awakening. What composing 'philosophers' throughout the world like to call the music of the spheres is little more than the bare, unformed material of music, and to believe that the desired sensation is to be found in the material itself, rather than in the fashioning, the mastering of it, is a luxury that only ambitious youth can allow itself.

After some one hundred and eighty years of social emancipation, the creative artist is again seeking patrons, without, however, allowing them to interfere in the 'how' and 'what' of his private affairs—as he is pleased to regard all artistic considerations. He wants to enjoy security and artistic freedom—the very different advantages of the eighteenth and nineteenth centuries—both at the same time and thinks he can simply argue away the resulting disadvantages. The extreme difficulty of reconciling the contradiction inherent in this attitude lies in the fact that the patron, like the entertainment industry, considers art to be so much merchandise—an opinion which no true artist can share. The future course of new music depends very much on whether or not this gap can be bridged. To question its use is, of course, senseless, for in art, as elsewhere, what happens, happens because it must, out of sheer necessity. But it is none the less imperative for us to refrain from excessive adulation, from treating what at first may puzzle us with respectful awe, just because it is puzzling—as though its very existence were a guarantee of a higher dignity.

[Translated from the German by Francis Burt]

XIII

BELGIUM

By Paul Collaer

DURING THE fifteenth and sixteenth centuries the Netherlands poly-
phonist school was famous above all others. The composers who
formed it were all from the southern provinces, that is to say Flanders,
Zeeland, Brabant, Hainaut and the Artois. Flanders had a life and
culture of its own which found expression in the fields of architecture,
painting, sculpture and music. It is scarcely necessary to recall here that
this culture was represented on the highest plane by artists of the calibre
of Memlinc, van Eyck, de Laeyens, Sluter, Josquin des Près, Ockeghem
and Lassus. This culture was known as 'Flemish', because it was in
Flanders that it had flourished most intensively. It should not, however,
be forgotten that all the provinces above mentioned had a share in it,
and that their inhabitants spoke either French in the dialects of Wallonie
and Picardy, or the language of the Netherlands in its Flemish dialects.

After Roland de Lassus had died in 1594 and Claude Lejeune in
1600, there was no one in the Netherlands to succeed them or continue
in their tradition. Lassus was the last musician of a line which had
carried the fame of Netherlands music far and wide, to Italy, Spain,
France, Austria and Germany. Claude Lejeune was the first composer
of another school which broke away from the Flemish polyphonic
tradition, turned towards France, adopted Paris as its cultural centre
and cultivated musical forms which were based on harmony.

In the course of the centuries that followed, Belgian music no longer
occupied a leading place in the development of the arts in Europe.
Belgium produced only composers of secondary importance, isolated
in their *milieu* and deriving their forms and aesthetic principles from
foreign cultural centres. Thus Charles Guillet of Bruges derives from

Claude Lejeune and Du Caurroy; Henri Dumont had affinities with the Louis XIV 'chapelle'; Grétry made his name in French *opéra-comique*, while Loeillet settled in England and was the representative there of the French clavecinists.

The nineteenth century, after Belgium had won her independence and the unity of her people and territory was assured, saw the rise of a separatist movement, dividing the Flemings from the Walloons. The cleavage was most marked in the realm of literature and music. The part played by the Liégeois, César Franck, in the renaissance of French music is well known. Ever since then, the Walloons have continued to look upon Paris as their cultural home. Not so the Flemish musicians.

Thrown back upon themselves, separated from France by their language and from Holland by their religion, the Flemish ideal was to create, or re-create a homogeneous ethnic community. They had no desire to see a division between an intellectual *élite* and the rest of the community. Their artists were concerned with cultivating popular taste, and devoted themselves to the education of the people. At the head of this movement were the novelist Hendrik Conscience and the musician Peter Benoit (1834-1901). The latter wrote vast cantatas on historical or descriptive subjects concerning the life of the country. He did so in a simple, highly lyrical style, and his melodies are unencumbered by harmonic subtleties or contrapuntal meditations. This artistic policy was pursued until the beginning of the twentieth century, its principal exponents being Gustave Huberti (1834-1911) and Jan Blockx (1851-1912) who was instrumental in bringing about the creation of a Flemish Opera in Antwerp.

About this time religious oratorio was enjoying a lasting vogue in Germany, especially among adherents of the Reformed Church. Edgard Tinel (1854-1912) had the happy idea of creating a romantic form of oratorio for the benefit of Catholics. Deriving from Schumann, he composed two oratorios, *Franciscus* and *Godelieve*, which are still performed in Flanders. Tinel's style is more elaborate, and shows more classical influences than that of his contemporaries. His talent and skill are seen at their best in an opera on the subject of the martyrdom of St Catherine, and in a very brilliant *Te Deum*. As is the case with

Benoit and Blockx, Tinel's works are still in the Flemish provincial repertory, despite the profound social and stylistic changes that have come about during the last quarter of a century. There is no doubt that the works of these composers are an expression of the cultural aspirations of the people to whom they belonged and for whom they worked.

Paul Gilson (1865-1942) was primarily a symphonic composer. His best orchestral works are: *La Mer* and the *Variations Symphoniques*. *La Mer* portrays the opalescent reflections on the grey and mighty North Sea and its sturdy, cheerful fishermen. The *Variations* are on a very simple theme, given out by a solo clarinet, which is then subjected to a series of metamorphoses. Gilson also wrote an important cantata, *Françoise de Rimini*, and an opera, *Prinses Zonneschijn*.

Among the composers of this generation the most original is Flors Alpaerts (1876-). Well versed in modern orchestral technique, he is particularly attracted by the truculent and fantastic aspect of the art of Breughel, Bosch and, nearer our own times, Ensor. Truculence is also a feature of the novels of Felix Timmermans. Based on one of the latter's pantheistic novels Alpaerts has composed a very effective orchestral triptych named after the hero of the book, *Pallieter*. He has also written a *Suite James Ensor*, inspired by the paintings of the Ostend master. In a similar vein, the *Tableaux breugheliens* of Michel Brusselmans (1886-) are very pleasing.

There was no musical movement in the Walloon provinces comparable with that which gave to Flemish art its social significance. The renewal of activities on that side was due mainly to artists belonging to a younger generation. As has been said, the Walloons had always looked to France. In succession to César Franck, Charles Bordes and Vincent d'Indy adopted their master's ideas and made them the basis of a teaching opposed to that of the Conservatoire which had become too academic. This new method was taught at the Schola Cantorum. The most gifted among the Walloon musicians went to Paris to receive the heritage of Franck, of whom Eugène and Théo Ysaye were enthusiastic and devoted disciples. Victor Vreuls (1876-1944) himself went to teach at the Schola. Author of an excellent *Sonata for piano and violin*, some chamber music works and an opera, Vreuls' most important work is a long symphonic poem, *Werther*. His art was strongly influenced by

Chausson and d'Indy. The most remarkable Walloon composer of this generation is Joseph Jongen (1873-). Although in the Franckist tradition, he is distinguished by a charming spirit of fantasy which provides a welcome relief to the sometimes excessive severity of that tradition. A prolific composer, Joseph Jongen has written works of merit, notably *Impressions d'Ardennes*, imbued with the peaceful and misty atmosphere of the forests and hills he loved so well. His *Symphonie pour Orgue et orchestre* is on a grand scale, while his charming *Fantaisie sur deux Noëls Wallons* invites comparison with the famous *Airs Angevins* of Guillaume Lekeu.

One cannot fail to be struck by the fact that all the Belgian composers mentioned so far have shown a tendency to be conservative. Not one of them was affected by the new movements which came in with the twentieth century, both in Germany and in France. The fact is all the more strange because musical life in Belgium had already been very intense before 1914. All the latest productions of Mahler, Strauss, Debussy and Ravel could be heard there. The Théâtre de la Monnaie in Brussels, always ready to open its doors to anything new, produced *Pelléas et Mélisande*, *Ariane et Barbe-Bleue*, *Pénélope*, *Fervaal* and *L'Etranger*. Richard Strauss conducted *Salome* and *Elektra* there. And yet the mentality of our composers somehow did not respond to the curiosity and demands of the public in the capital.

The situation changed after 1919. Belgium by then had emerged from the isolation imposed by her neutrality. The acquisition of a European spirit and outlook became a matter of primary concern to the country. In 1920 already there was a welcome for Satie and the 'Six', Schoenberg, Berg and Webern. The lyric theatres mounted works by Milhaud, Honegger, Berg, Prokofiev and Hindemith. Stravinsky entered the repertory. A young generation of composers reacted vigorously to these contacts. At the same time the cleavage between Walloon and Flemish musicians became less marked.

Fernand Quinet (1898-) was at one time greatly impressed by Ravel, Stravinsky and the Schoenberg of *Pierrot Lunaire*. His *Moralités non légendaires*, certain chamber works and the *Trois Pièces pour orchestre* seem as fresh today in their inspiration as when they were first composed. Some works by Albert Huybrechts (1899-1938), whose premature death we deplore, are characterised by their lyric and dramatic qualities, somewhat reminiscent of Milhaud. He wrote a charming *Serenade* for orchestra, a *Divertissement* for brass and percussion, a *Concertino* for violoncello, sonatas and quartets. Francis de Bourguignon, on the other hand (1890-), came under the spell of the rich sonorities of *The Firebird*. Two *Esquisses symphoniques sud-américaines* and an *Eloge de la Folie*, which is a commentary on Erasmus, bear the stamp of a considerable personality.

Finally, a new generation grew up which, although familiar with the thought and language of the masters of contemporary music, yet has escaped their direct influence and preserved its independence. One has the impression that Belgian composers of this generation have succeeded better than their predecessors in putting across their own individual personalities. Marcel Poot (1901-), a gay and care-free temperament and an excellent orchestrator, is well known for his *Ouverture Joyeuse*, a concise and lively work whose youthful spirit is particularly pleasing. An excellent cantata which he wrote for the *Jeunesses Musicales*, *Le Dit de Routier*, deserves to be better known for it reveals its author's most characteristic qualities, notably a sly humour reminiscent of Prokofiev or Chabrier which finds its full expression also in his ballet *Pâris et les Trois Divines*.

Jean Absil (1898-) is fond of rapidly moving melodic lines ornamented with scintillating arabesques. He combines liveliness with strength, and expresses himself in an eloquent and attractive style. A prolific composer, his works include songs, piano pieces, concertos and chamber music. A very moving *Suite* for vocal quartet and orchestra, *Chants du Mort*, is inspired by popular Rumanian poetry. A more capricious side of Absil's character is revealed in some vocal and instrumental fantasies on various subjects, such as *Philatélie*. Mention should also be made of a powerful *Cantique du Port* from the pen of Auguste Baeyens (1895-) on a text by Roger Avermaete.

Of all the Belgian composers of this century, the most independent and the most remarkable is Raymond Chevreuille (1901-). A poet and a visionary, he observes no laws other than those imposed by his own conscience. The influences which have contributed to form his language are immediately amalgamated in a complex whose separate elements can no longer be distinguished. His language, like his thought, is essentially personal. In his hands symphonic forms are perpetually renewed, moulded not in a consciously constructive spirit, but in obedience to an inner vision of what is best fitted to express each musical conception as it arises. The greater part of his considerable output is still unpublished—which explains to some extent why so remarkable a composer is so little known. Chamber music and the orchestra have an equal attraction for Chevreuille. A composition such as his *Evasions*, on poems by Maurice Carême, is literally unique and inimitable. The poems are sung *sotto voce*, forming, as it were, a kind of background to the orchestra, which supplies a commentary. This is dream-music, full of tenderness and intimate happiness. Another suite for baritone and orchestra, *Les Saisons*, is no less interesting than *Evasions*, and the same is true of the *Deuxième Symphonie avec quatuor vocal* and the *Concerto pour trio d'anches et orchestre*.

René Bernier (1905-) is also a poetic interpreter of dreams and the author of several charming and elegant works. Victor Legley (1915-) has also written some instrumental music of high quality. David van de Woestijne (1915-) is the author of a fine and adventurous symphony with a solo voice, *La Belle Cordière*, on some sonnets by Louise Labé, and of a fine sonata for two pianos.

After many years spent in North Africa, Louis de Meester (1904-) has expressed himself completely in a most original work, *La Tentation de Saint Antoine*, on a text by the dramatist Michel de Ghelderode. In this work, once again, the music is inspired by dreams and visions of Jerôme Bosch, a character who seems to be a constant in Flemish art. In this impressive composition de Meester employs a chorus, solo singers, a symphony and a chamber orchestra, jazz and *musique concrète*. Specially designed for broadcasting, this score is one of the most masterly achievements of Belgian music. Both van de Woestijne and de Meester are carrying out researches in the realm of *musique concrète*, while Henri Pousseur (1929-) is mainly concerned with electronic music.

Among the best musicians I have left to the last are André Souris (1899-), Marcel Quinet (1915-), Pierre Froidebise (1914-) and Camille Schmit (1908-).

[*Translated from the French by the Editor.*]

XIV

TRENDS AND TENDENCIES IN
CONTEMPORARY FRENCH MUSIC

By Claude Rostand

SINCE THE last war the French musical scene has exhibited a certain number of new and somewhat unexpected features which have changed the appearance of our music in a way that may seem, at first sight, to run counter to the age-old traditions of our country, but which, on closer inspection, will be seen, after all, to lie well within the bounds of those traditions; I am thinking more especially of the new tendencies exemplified in 'serialism' and the techniques of concrete and electronic music. But this is only one aspect of the situation, and if we wish to obtain a clear picture of the whole, we must glance at certain other aspects typified by some of the other young or not-so-young musicians.

We will begin, then, by taking rapid stock of the situation as regards some of the not-so-young composers, especially those who belonged to what were once known as the 'Group of Six', the 'École d'Arcueil' or the group 'Jeune France'. The case of Darius Milhaud (1892-) is too internationally well known to detain us now, so that we need scarcely pause to consider the production of a master whose age has in no way affected his abundantly fertile output nor, indeed, brought any changes of any kind. The same applies, in the main, to Francis Poulenc (1899-), as can be seen from his latest important work, *Les Dialogues des Carmélites*, which shows, nevertheless, that his art has matured and that he has acquired a sound operatic technique. He takes a lively interest in the researches of the young 'twelve-note' composers, and gives them his moral support, although he has no intention of borrowing anything whatsoever from their technique. Georges Auric

(1899-) on the other hand, has progressed in an interesting way. He has completely abandoned the acid, nervous style of his early youth, and his last works (*Phèdre*, *Le Peintre et son Modèle*, *Chemins de Lumière* and *La Chambre*) represent a complete break-away from the old aesthetic of 'Les Six', and are remarkable rather for their strength and vigour, grandeur and gravity, violence and even tragic intensity. Auric, too, is passionately interested in the researches of the younger school which he follows attentively and encourages.

Of those who once formed the 'École d'Arcueil', only Henri Sauguet (1901-) is still active and in full production. His ballet *La Dame aux Camélias* (first produced at the Berlin Festival in 1957) and his Violin Concerto (*Orphée*) which had its first performance at the Aix Festival in 1955, are proof that, although he shows no desire to adopt the twelve-note technique, it interests him to some extent and may account for the sort of free atonality to be found in some of his works. But even when a 'series' can be discerned, it is not worked out at all in the Viennese manner.

Of the four composers who in 1936 formed the group 'Jeune France' (Messiaen, Jolivet, Lesur and Baudrier) only the first two have contributed anything new. André Jolivet (1905-), who is strongly opposed to the twelve-note school, campaigns against it with often excessive violence; in his own music he makes a most imaginative use of 'modality', especially of an exotic kind. His latest Piano Concerto, for example, situates him in the direct line of the 'orientalisation' of Western music heralded by Bartók and Debussy—a process which, in Jolivet's case, is based on the use of modes no less than on research into problems of timbre and rhythm which he pursues with the greatest ingenuity and refinement.

As regards Olivier Messiaen (1908-), he must be regarded as one of the leading personalities of the contemporary school, both as a teacher whose influence has been enormous and far-reaching, and as a composer. In the former capacity he is at present in charge of a class of analysis, aesthetics and rhythm at the Paris Conservatoire. It is, moreover, thanks to his teaching that the younger generations who have passed through his hands for the last fifteen years have adopted the new, anti-traditional techniques. Messiaen's teaching is quite extraordinary—it covers a vast field, is extremely bold and new, and as far removed from academic or traditional teaching as possible. Thus, while naturally not neglecting the classic masters, it covers in addition Hindu and Balinese music, Schoenberg, Stravinsky, Bartók, etc., whose works are commented on and analysed in masterly fashion. The great quality of Messiaen's teaching is that he does not seek to impose his own theories of composition on his pupils. His aim is merely to arouse in them something more than a desire to achieve the work for which each one of them perhaps feels he was born to create—a desire to find a creative solution to the contemporary problem of ensuring the vital and natural evolution of music, and a desire to enrich and develop the language of music and discover new means of expression. This teaching is unique, and characterised by its honesty, frankness, courage and widely humanistic spirit, its whole aim being to stimulate the curiosity and increase the knowledge of his pupils without *parti-pris* or exclusiveness of any kind. The great merit of Messiaen's method is that it has aroused an intense curiosity among young people with regard to everything that has authentic value outside the narrow limits of academic training, and all 'new ways of listening' capable of enlarging the domain of contemporary music.

As a composer, Olivier Messiaen has not modified appreciably the aesthetic theories he held before the war. He remains, and wishes to remain, a 'catholic' and 'theologic' musician (and not a 'mystic' as he has so often been wrongly described). As in the past, he continues to use ancient modes. But at present he is chiefly concerned with Hindu modes and rhythms and with the modes and rhythms of bird-song which he combines with certain procedures borrowed from serial music treated very freely. In this sphere his master-work is the *Quatre Etudes de Rythmes* for piano solo which made such a profound impression on young composers of all nationalities when it was first performed at a recent Festival at Darmstadt. This work constitutes one of the most complete syntheses of musical means of expression in existence, and is one of the most advanced examples of Messiaen's technique. The most significant of the *Four Studies* is the one entitled 'Modes de valeurs et d'intensités'; it applies the system of full chromaticism to sound elements other than pitch in the strict sense of the word, especially to duration and intensity. For example, it makes use of a chromatic duration-mode ranging from a demi-semi-quaver to a dotted crotchet, passing through all the intermediate values obtained by adding to each the value of a demi-semi-quaver. In this way one arrives at a series of twelve values separated by what could be described as the 'chromatic interval' of a demi-semi-quaver. The same process can be applied to the other sound elements with the result that music is now tending towards the idea of an 'absolute continuum'—an idea which has been taken up by the electronic musicians.

The *Four Studies*, while calling for a high degree of pianistic virtuosity, are nevertheless in the main *abstract* and experimental in character, whereas Messiaen's most recent compositions are, to borrow an expression applied to painting, *figurative*, or *representational*. This is true of the *Messe de Pentecôte* for organ in which Greek and Hindu rhythms are used contrapuntally, as well as plain-chant *neumes*, birdsong and serial combinations of *timbres*, pitch and intensity. Furthermore, under the counter-influence, no doubt, of his own pupils and the tendencies of the younger generation, Messiaen's art, in the *Messe de Pentecôte*, is more austere, and has lost that over-lush and voluptuous, almost 'sugary' flavour that characterised some of his earlier works. His *Livre d'Orgue* marks a further step along the road to a more sober style. Like the *Messe*, it is a religious work which can also be described as 'figurative', since it illustrates in sound texts from the Bible. Its seven parts are almost all ornamented by bird-song freely and imaginatively treated, but the whole thing is supported on a solid contrapuntal and serial structure—especially the last section which contains sixty-four chromatic time-values of from one to sixty-four demi-semi-quavers, grouped in fours, with the extremes in the middle, played alternately in straight and retrograde movement, and treated in retrograde canon.

The three latest works of Messiaen are again of a rather special nature, and are based entirely on bird-song taken down from nature and noted with the most meticulous rhythmic and melodic exactitude. They are *Le Reveil des Oiseaux* (Concerto for Piano and Orchestra) *Oiseaux exotiques* (for solo piano and small wind and percussion ensemble) and *Catalogue d'Oiseaux* (Bird Portraits, for piano solo). These three scores, which are based exclusively on bird-song transposed in terms of human musical instruments and organised according to human musical methods, may be considered as the modern equivalents of the romantic 'symphonic poem' and the suggestive evocations of the Impressionists. Whether or not one is in sympathy with Olivier Messiaen's aesthetic, it is obvious that his theories of composition are the fruit of a genuine musical humanism.

Among the younger generation, aged between twenty and forty, two main currents can be distinguished: on the one hand the composers who have remained faithful to the diatonic musical tradition and who yet seek to bring the language of music up to date; and on the other hand, those who adhere more or less strictly to the cult of serial music. In the first of these categories the outstanding figure is Henri Dutilleux (1916-). He is a genuine independent, who conforms to no system or school or doctrine. Classical in his attachment to musical architecture and counterpoint, his harmonic language proclaims him a modern. He has certain affinities with the previous generation, notably Fauré and Ravel, but his language from the first has always been very personal and reveals a sort of un-organised atonal instinct. His most important works are a piano sonata and a symphony which is already well known internationally.

In somewhat the same category as Dutilleux is Marcel Landowski (1915-), whose tendencies are romantic rather than classical, and even tinged with a kind of romanticism *à la* Honegger. His language, though solidly anchored in tonality, nevertheless makes use of the most recent means of expression made available by modern techniques; but, unlike Dutilleux, he is not precisely a devotee of 'pure music', and all his scores have an ideological, poetic or dramatic substratum (e.g. the symphony *Jean de la Peur*, *Rythmes du Monde*, *Le Fou*, etc.).

1947 saw the formation in Paris of a group of five young composers known as 'The Zodiac'. This group is now more or less dispersed, except for one outstanding personality who claims our attention— Maurice Ohana (1914-), a Gibraltar-born Spaniard domiciled in Paris. In opposition to the neo-romanticism of 'La Jeune France', he aims at restoring to Western music its Mediterranean spirit and normal evolution, combating Central European intellectualism and reverting to the medieval and pre-classical tradition. His language is free and could be described as a synthesis of various contemporary elements including tonality, atonality, polytonality, modality, polymodality and even dodecaphony. His most important and characteristic works are perhaps the setting of Lorca's *Llanto por Ignacio Sanchez Mejiaz* (the famous torero), the *Cantigas* and music for *Don Quixote*.

Of the same generation it is unnecessary to do more than mention Jean Françaix (1912-) and others of his kind, although he has an international reputation. He has forged for himself since early youth a stereotyped style, agreeable but invariably the same in all circumstances. He repeats himself with talent.

On the other hand it would be a mistake not to mention the young school of organist-composers—Maurice Duruflé (1903-), Jean Langlais (1907-), Gaston Litaize (1909-) and Jean-Jacques Grünenwald (1911-). It is to them that we owe the renaissance of French organ music in reaction against the post-Franckian deviations at the end of the nineteenth and beginning of the twentieth centuries. They make an extensive use of the ancient modes, and their work is inspired by an extremely lively and fertile form of neo-Gregorianism.

This brings us now to the second category of the younger musicians, for the most part pupils of Olivier Messiaen, who have adopted either partially or completely the serial method of composition. It should be remembered here that, as I said before, Messiaen did not systematically direct them to twelve-note music; he made them acquainted with all the modern techniques, and if some of them have gone over to dodecaphony, they have done so freely and spontaneously.

In this group by far the most outstanding personality is that of Pierre Boulez (1925-). He has not confined himself in practice to the strictly classical serial method, but is one of the three or four living composers who have enriched this method with the boldest and most far-reaching amplifications. Thus, although remaining faithful to the basic principle of the serial idea, he has extended its consequences, even further than Messiaen, in every direction—not only to melody and *timbre* (where he follows Webern and his musical 'Mallarméisme'), but also to rhythm and structure. In his music the subtleties of a Debussy or a Messiaen are made to serve the purposes of a temperament at once unyielding and inclined to dramatise itself. Contrary to what might seem, at first sight, to be the case (and as conservative critics are always contending), Boulez has in no way broken away from the French traditions. It is equally incorrect to say (as these same critics maintain) that he has introduced a 'foreign technique' into France. The art of Boulez is, on the contrary, stamped with the permanent characteristics of our music: a taste for well-balanced structure, clarity in writing and even that kind of 'impressionism' in sound that has flavoured almost the whole of French music since the fifteenth century. By capping the suggestions of the Viennese school with an essentially French solution Boulez is building a new world of sound and a new, extremely rich and vital art. It is worth noting incidentally that he has now begun to work in the electronic field after having toyed for a short time with concrete music which he soon abandoned.

Along with Boulez should be mentioned Jean-Louis Martinet (1914-), Serge Nigg (1924-), Maurice Le Roux (1923-), Yannis Xenakis and the youthful Magda Lovano and Gilbert Amy.

The two first-named are rather special cases. J. L. Martinet, a late convert to atonality, had previously undergone the influence of Debussy, Stravinsky, Bartók and Messiaen (*Orphée, La Trilogie des Promethées, Sept Poèmes de René Char*). He then made his debut in twelve-note music with some remarkable pieces for string quartet which attracted a lot of attention. Here he seemed to have found himself more effectively than ever before. Then suddenly, in the course of the last two years, he turned to the kind of music derived from the so-called 'progressist' aesthetic recommended by the official Soviet theoreticians—that is to say, 'music that can be easily understood by the masses'. The case of Serge Nigg is analogous. He showed every promise of being one of the most brilliant of his generation, and one of the most intelligent and highly cultured from the musical point of view. After passing through a phase of exoticism, he took up twelve-note technique, seeing very clearly the place it occupied in the normal and natural evolution of music, and made his mark in that field. Then suddenly his political beliefs led him to frequent Communist circles, with the result that he burnt what he had adored and embraced the doctrines of the 'progressist' school.

As regards Le Roux, Xenakis, Magda Lovano and Gilbert Amy,

they have not as yet produced very much and it is difficult to form an opinion on them at this stage. Xenakis seems very promising and exceptionally gifted; he has studied both music and architecture, and composed an electronic score for the pavilion built by Le Corbusier at the Brussels Exhibition. Gilbert Amy is still under the influence of Boulez, but what one knows of his work gives promise of original and interesting things to come.

In the sphere of electronics, French composers are for the most part far behind their German or Italian colleagues. The fact is, electronic equipment in France is quite inadequate for any serious work to be accomplished. As for concrete music, after originating in France and making considerable progress after the war, it is now rather on the down-grade, which is not surprising since it is based on a number of misunderstandings and has, in any case, been supplanted, as regards the future, by electronic music.

In the presence of all these tendencies, what is the public's reaction? The public in general reacts, on the whole, badly; or rather it would be more correct to say it does not react at all. And that again is not surprising, because it was ever thus all over the world. Yet a certain élite has sprung up which takes an interest in all these movements. In this connection, it is noteworthy that up to four years ago France did not possess a single society for contemporary music. The radio alone contributed something, but not enough, to the cause of new music. Then came the microsillon disk which gradually accomplished something in this sphere, and finally Pierre Boulez, with the active support of Jean-Louis Barrault and Madeleine Renaud, founded his society under the title of *Domaine Musical*. At first these concerts attracted two or three hundred people to the Petit Marigny theatre. Soon afterwards, when his venture had proved successful, Boulez had to give his concerts in a larger hall, the Salle Gaveau, seating about one thousand. This was regularly filled, and last year it became necessary to give the concerts in a still bigger hall, the Odéon Theatre. There can therefore be no doubt that the revelation of contemporary music has created a public. The efforts of the conservative critics will perhaps succeed in delaying its growth, as happened before in the case of painting, but it is very unlikely that they will be able to prevent it from increasing, provided it is presented with works of real value. Life must go on. And even if contemporary music has produced some still-born failures, it is nevertheless very much alive itself and full of vigour.

[*Translated from the French by the Editor*]

XV

ITALIAN MUSIC TODAY

By Roman Vlad

THE MOST significant trends in Italian music since the war have been the substantial weakening of the tendencies that shaped its development between the wars and the introduction and gradual spread of dodecaphony. The last of the more or less traditional opera-composers—Mascagni, Franchetti, Giordano, Zandonai, Wolf-Ferrari, Cilea—all died in the years around the last war. But the decline of the old tradition certainly cannot be attributed to this fact alone, since the evolution of Italian music between 1920 and 1940 was not decisively influenced by these composers, who all wrote in a style that was out-of-date before they died. Moreover, the important composers born around 1880—Alfredo Casella, Gian-Francesco Malipiero, Ildebrando Pizzetti, Franco Alfano, Vincenzo Tommasini—who must in varying degree claim the credit for the recent reform of Italian music, were still in this period at the height of their powers (Ottorino Respighi, who, however, was not one of the progressive composers of this generation, was dead by 1936).

But although these composers continued to write works of undeniable intrinsic worth the historical mission they had undertaken seemed to have been completed. Their mission was historically necessary for two reasons: they had first of all to take up the threads of the instrumental tradition that the nineteenth-century opera-composers had neglected; and secondly they had to bring Italian music into line with the latest developments in European music as a whole, from which the opera-composers (with few, but notable, exceptions) had become isolated.

The first of these tasks introduced into modern Italian music (at least in the early stages of its development) a self-conscious archaism, deriving from the adoption of pre-classical models. The second meant that the technical features of French impressionism, central European chromaticism, the new Russian school and the various kinds of diatonic writing of the other national schools of the day were gradually absorbed into Italian music.

Casella and Malipiero, the two most forward-looking composers of the 1880 generation, had approached so close before 1920 to the expressionist chromatic writing of the Viennese school as to make it seem surprising when, instead of following the example of Schoenberg and continuing beyond this date to adopt his formal innovations, they accentuated the diatonic (or neoclassic) and modal (or nationalist) aspects of their music. The same tendency is indeed noticeable in the logical evolution of modern Italian music as a whole.

The successive stages in the development of the music I have been discussing could not provide a sense of continuity. Before reaching the threshold of dodecaphony Italian composers had to go exhaustively through all the earlier phases I have mentioned. And it certainly cannot be said that in the works they wrote before 1920 they had fully rediscovered the Italian preclassical tradition or absorbed nationalist folk elements into their music. The grafting of dodecaphony on to Italian music would have been premature before the neoclassical and nationalist phases had been completed. The works that Casella wrote between the wars were fundamental contributions to the flowering and decline of these phases. But although for the reasons I have given Casella shied away from Schoenberg's example, he never denied its validity for the general development of European music.

The work of Casella himself would eventually have taken us to the moment when the rapprochement with dodecaphony became an actual fact. An indication of this is found in his last large-scale work, the *Missa Solemnis 'Pro Pace'*, composed in 1944. The *Crucifixus* of this mass is conceived as a *passacaglia*, whose *basso ostinato* is a note-row. The final invocation, 'Pacem, pacem', is founded on the same series, but the work is not on the whole invested with twelve-note characteristics. Serious illness and premature death (in 1947) cut short Casella's activity and prevented his following up this first approach to twelve-note technique.

None of the other composers of Casella's generation was able to undertake the task of establishing dodecaphony in Italy, which would have completed the process I have described of making Italian music more 'contemporary'—not even Malipiero, who, however, in some of his recent works, such as the *Fantasie concertanti* (1954), has begun to profit from twelve-note procedures. But we are dealing here only with a partial approach to dodecaphony, whose influence can be seen, by reflection as it were, in so far as its methods, which by now are firmly established, can be reconciled with Italian musical practice. Casella's other contemporaries did not abandon their increasingly conservative positions. Of these men only Pizzetti is still composing. No one would deny the intrinsic value of his latest works, particularly *La Figlia di Jorio* (to a libretto from D'Annunzio's play of the same name) and *L'Assassinio nella Cattedrale* (1958, based on T. S. Eliot's *Murder in the Cathedral*): but they add nothing to the general picture of his art, the salient features of which have been clearly formed for nearly half a century.

A leader of the Italian twelve-note *avant-garde* did not even appear among the composers belonging to the generation born around 1890, in spite of the fact that, though some of them (like Guido Guerrini, a pupil of Busoni) remained conservatives, others eventually adopted the twelve-note system, either sporadically, like Giorgio Fedérico Ghedini (1892-) in his *Canoni* for violin and 'cello and Piano Concerto (both 1946), or more logically, as Carlo Jacchino (1889-) and Antonio Veretti (1900-) have done for some years past. The name of Luigi Cortese (1889-) also comes to mind in connection with this group, since he has used serial techniques, notably in his *Cinque momenti musicali*, op. 19, and in his *Psalm VIII*, op. 21.

All these composers had started out by using an archaic, modal-diatonic style. Much the same may be said of the principal composers born in the first years of the present century, who can claim the lion's share in shaping the present face of Italian music. Even Luigi Dalla-piccola (1904-), who was the first and most assiduous exponent of serial technique in Italy, is no exception: indeed, the two fundamental elements which, as I have said, determined the stylistic development of modern Italian music are still operative not only for him but even for much younger composers. Although I am anticipating the conclusion of my essay, I ought to say here that the rebirth and exuberant vitality of this music are due to the very fact that, while remaining true to traditional features in the Italian musical genius, modern Italian composers have been in a position, in every stage of its development, to assimilate the mature technical products of other parts of the Continent and then to contribute in return to European music a series of completely individual works. And especially in the case of the composers most deeply committed to dodecaphonic writing the balance, on the one hand, of the ingrained traditional qualities of the Italian musical genius and, on the other, of the more complex technical procedures that had grown to maturity in the Viennese school played an important part in freeing dodecaphony from the shackles of arid experimentalism. The particular niche that Dallapiccola occupies in the general picture of twelve-note music has been determined by the point of departure that he shared with other Italian composers of today. His earliest works (up to about the *Sei Cori di Michelangelo Buonarroti il Giovane*, written during the years 1933-36) are characterised by severe modal-diatonic writing of preclassical derivation, though without neoclassical or baroque qualities; in his next period, as he wrote more and more music, he introduced into the tonal web of his works chromatic strands which eventually elbowed out the remaining diatonic elements and, in his third period (from the *Liriche greche*, 1942-45, onwards), have been governed exclusively by the laws of serial technique.

However, in three of the main works of his first maturity—the *Tre Laudi* (1936-37) for voice and chamber orchestra, the one-act opera *Volo di Notte* (after Saint-Exupéry, 1937-39) and the *Canti di Prigionia* (1938-41)—written before chromaticism swallowed up the diatonic element in his style, Dallapiccola was able to achieve a truly remarkable synthesis out of these virtually irreconcilable elements. Notably in the *Canti di Prigionia*, based on a true structural 'counterpoint' between a twelve-note series and a Gregorian melody (the *Dies Irae*), the composer achieves the most intimate fusion of all the elements he had used hitherto and succeeds in conferring the utmost expressive power upon them. The lyrical inspiration, the extraordinary emotional intensity and the dramatic truth of these songs are indeed remarkable and make them one of the outstanding and most original works in the whole of contemporary music. One can say of this work, as one can of few others, that it attains the ideal of belonging wholly to our time. And this is not because it refers more or less allusively to incidental events but because one can see that its emotional premisses could be realised within the artist only through vivid personal experience of dramatic events of a kind that human beings have always experienced. Massimo Mila rightly declares that 'only very few musicians understand with such intensity, reinforced by intelligence, the terrible tragedy of our time, the religious struggle fought out to the last drop of blood between the ideals of the spirit and of liberty and the inexorable materialistic onslaught of brutal tyranny'.

The dialectically connected impulses, deriving on the one hand from the deepest obligation to living things and on the other from a need to lift all earthly considerations on to a purely spiritual plane, inform, in differing degree and with a variety of nuances, the expressive and imaginative materials of one after another of Dallapiccola's major works. After appearing in a tragic light in the one-act opera *Il Prigioniero* (1944-47) and in the guise of tormenting doubt in the one-act 'sacra rappresentazione', *Job* (1950), these impulses seem to find their catharsis in the *Canti di Liberazione*, completed, significantly enough, on the tenth anniversary of the liberation of Italy.

Goffredo Petrassi (also born in 1904) approached dodecaphony more gradually than did Dallapiccola. At one time the respective positions of these two composers in the Italian musical scene seemed comparable to those that Schoenberg and Stravinsky occupied for so long in the wider scene of contemporary music as a whole. Petrassi at first developed along a path parallel to those followed by older composers like Casella, Hindemith and Stravinsky, characterised by various kinds of diatonic writing and with rhythmic interest predominant; he managed very soon to forge for himself a personal style which found its consummation in the *Coro di Morti* (1940-41), a work which is in my opinion one of the incontestable masterpieces of modern music. The

Coro di Morti, along with two other big choral works which immediately preceded it—*Psalm IX* and the *Magnificat*—deservedly put Petrassi in the forefront of contemporary Italian composers. He was at that time the leading figure among the new Italian exponents of 'polydiatonic' tendencies. But during the last few years of Stravinsky's neoclassic period (before his much-publicised turn to dodecaphony) Petrassi began that slow and gradual approach to dodecaphony which, especially in the orchestral concertos he has composed during the last five years, has enabled him to assimilate its most valid products for his own ends.

It is true to say that none of those who really count among the Italian composers contemporary with, or younger than, Dallapiccola and Petrassi has remained impervious to the influence of serial technique.[1] Some of them have used it logically within the limits of what we now regard as the classical method of Schoenberg. This is true of Riccardo Malipiero (1914-). Others, like Riccardo Nielsen (1908-) and Gino Contilli (1907-), have tried above all to make serial writing appropriate to a discursive style of the utmost simplicity. Mario Peragallo (1910-) established his reputation before the war with several works conceived in the spirit of traditional stage music, but he is now an adherent of dodecaphony, from which he has attempted to derive more elastic methods through a personal way of integrating note-rows harmonically. The formal means which he has thus forged for himself have enabled him to achieve notable results in two fields: the concerto (in 1954 his Violin Concerto won first prize in the competition 'Opera del XX secolo'), and stage music (after a stormy *première* at La Scala *La Gita in Campagna*, a one-act opera to a text by Alberto Moravia, is now gaining an international reputation). The present writer has extended serial technique to other sound-dimensions (mainly rhythm and tone-colour, but stopping short of abstract

1 Only certain composers of the schools of Pizzetti—for instance, Virgilio Mortari (1902-) and Nino Rota (1911-)—and of Respighi—for instance, Carlo Pizzini (1905-), Renzo Rossellini (1908-) and Lino Libiabella (1906-)—have shown themselves completely unsympathetic to dodecaphony. Among pupils of Respighi, Mario Labroca (1896-) has a more contemporary outlook, but his administrative duties have diverted him from creative activity. Of those isolated in mainly conservative positions one should mention Adriano Lualdi (1887-), Vito Frazzi (1898-) and Ludovico Rocca (1895-); the last-named above all has enjoyed considerable success, thanks in particular to his opera *Il Dibuk*.

pointillisme) and has also extended it by permutational procedures and even on occasion by recourse to quarter-tones.

Other composers, though following different paths, make occasional use of the twelve-note system. Among them are Adone Zecchi (1904), Valentino Bucchi (1916-, a pupil of Dallapiccola), Gino Negri (1919-) and Guido Turchi (1916-). The last-named, although not very prolific, is one of the most admired composers of his generation. He first of all followed the example of Hindemith and Bartók and used twelve-note techniques for the first time in his as yet unperformed opera *L'Ingenuo* (from *The Adventures of the Good Soldier Schweik* by Jaroslav Hašek). Although they do so more sporadically, even composers of more conservative stamp have not hesitated to introduce serial elements into their music: two such composers are Ennio Porrino (1910-), who writes in a nationalistic idiom influenced by folk music, and Mario Zafred (1922-), who was for a time the most enthusiastic Italian representative of the so-called 'neo-realism' advocated in the musical field by the theorists of the extreme left, but indistinguishable in the aesthetic.field from the standpoint of right-wing reactionaries.

The younger Italian composers can be divided into two groups. The leading figures in the first group are three who live in Rome and are disciples of Petrassi—Aldo Clementi (1925-), Domenico Guaccero (1927-) and Ennio Morricone (1928-)—and three who live in Milan —the Dallapiccola pupil Carlo Prosperi (1921-), Vittorio Fellegara (1927-) and Nicolò Castiglioni (1932-); while not renouncing the example of Webern they stop short of extending serial organisation to all the dimensions, to the entire organisation, of a given work. Thoroughgoing serialism, on the other hand, is advanced by the second group, the *avant-garde* composers animàted by a spirit similar to that of the post-Webern composers associated with the Kranichstein Institute at Darmstadt. Of these composers Camillo Togni (1922-), although aiming at the strictest serial treatment of the smallest details of his works, generally stops short of completely abstract *pointillisme* and remains substantially in contact with Schoenbergian expressionism. The most radical tendency towards *pointillisme* appears in the work of Bruno Maderna (1925-), Luciano Berio (1925) and Luigi Nono (1926-). The case of Nono is particularly odd: while he is scarcely known or is almost completely ignored in Italy, by critics and public alike, several foreign critics, especially German ones, consider him 'the most well-defined personality among the young generation in Italy'.[1] And so far it is mainly in Germany that he has made his mark.

Berio and Maderna are also known as the most active exponents of electronic music, the equipment for which Radio Italiana has put at their disposal at the Studio di Fonologia in Milan. But although these young men function right in the front of the *avant-garde* and allow themselves at times to be sidetracked into controversy they generally manage to avoid the pitfalls of extreme dogmatism and temper their outlook with that regard for tradition and that instinctive musicality which are qualities peculiar to the Italian character. Even these composers may be included in the generalisation I made above—that, in spite of certain deceptive appearances to the contrary, the great majority of Italian composers remain true to the Italian musical character and to the specific premises of their country's musical situation. It is precisely because of this that the mutual relations existing today between European music as a whole and Italian music are so healthy. In this connection Karl H. Wörner, one of the most authoritative German writers on modern music, speaking of Verdi's concern for the future of Italian music, has affirmed as a fact that the grand old man 'certainly could not have foreseen' that 'Italy, dominant in the nineteenth century as a land of opera, would recover in the twentieth a leading European position in the quest for new and valid forms and means of expression in the field of instrumental music'.[2]

[*Translated from the Italian by Nigel Fortune.*]

POST-SCRIPT

By The Editor

No account of the present state of music in Italy would be complete that failed to include the name of the writer of the foregoing pages, who is himself a distinguished Italian composer. Roman Vlad was born

[1] Cf. Karl H. Worner, *Neue Musik in der Entscheidung* (Mainz, 1954), p. 155.
[2] Cf. ibid., p. 148.

in 1919 at Czernowitz in Bukovina, and for the last twenty years has lived and worked in Rome, adopting Italian nationality in 1950. Among his most important works are the following: A ballet, *La Dame aux Camélias* (Rome Opera, 1948); a one-act opera, *Storia di una mamma* (Venice, 1951); a symphony (Venice, 1948); *De Profundis*, for soloists, chorus and orchestra (Paris, 1947); *Variazioni concertanti* for piano and orchestra (Venice, 1955); *Le Ciel est Vide*, a cantata for chorus and orchestra, (Turin, 1954) and *Musica concertata* for harp and orchestra (Turin, 1958). He is also well known as a critic and writer on music and, besides contributing to various musical periodicals at home and abroad, is the author of *Musica e tradizione nella musica contemporanea*, a study of *Dallapiccola* (1957), a history of the twelve-note technique (*Dodecafonia*, 1958), and a recently published volume on *Stravinsky*.

XVI

IANUS GEMINUS:
MUSIC IN SCANDINAVIA

By Robert Simpson

THE LATE flowering of the arts and humanities in the North is a
phenomenon of more than local significance. To put it simply: human
culture began in the sun, and its subsequent growth in regions where
conditions are less favourable is the result of modern technology.
Were it not for a general human advance in scientific and technical
knowledge, civilised life in harsh climates would not be possible. The
significance of modern Nordic culture is therefore human in a general
sense—especially for the future. The present state of things in Scandinavia (including, for the purposes of this chapter, Finland) exerts,
however, a dual fascination. It must not be forgotten that Scandinavian
civilisation as we know it now is scarcely more than a century and a
half old. This means that the tremendously long, stern past is still
barely hidden beneath the new soil; occasionally in the arts, and in the
individual characters of people, one can suddenly become intensely
aware of outcroppings of hard, sharp rock, jutting obstinately from
the carefully tended surface. This grim past, that still lies in the thews
and brains of the people, and the modern constructive attitude towards
the future that dominates the Scandinavian mind, provide this dual
fascination for the onlooker. In this region, more noticeably than elsewhere in Europe, perhaps, arts and attitudes express a remarkable blend
of the instinctive and primitive on the one hand and the civilised man's
conscious awareness on the other.

It is significant, too, that both in spite of and because of the long
crepuscular past of Scandinavia, its modern existence has taken stock

of both achievements and failures of its Southern precursors. All the accumulated humane and technological discoveries of older cultures have been freely available to the Scandinavians who have, in building freshly, made use of them in their own ways. So we find the Nordic cities are municipally and technically highly organised and equipped; Northern laws are at once more humane and more logical than those of, say, the Mediterranean countries. All this is basically the result of modern science, for the climate is no kinder than it ever was. The crux of the matter, in terms of general human development, is that it is now possible for the higher types of culture to flourish in climates that were previously hostile to them. The Scandinavian peoples, after millennia of struggles against intractable conditions, have only comparatively recently found themselves in possession of the means to a new life. This enthralling change is still fairly new; whether, as some critics aver, it is too sudden and is causing softness and complacency in the people, still remains to be proved. All the Scandinavian arts are at present reflecting the same conflicts that now increasingly obsess humanity at large, and it is not impossible that the resilience and realism expressed by the best of these arts may be a kind of salutary repayment to the South for all that the North has learned from it.

Any consideration of Scandinavian music must take into account all these facts. Music is always the last, the crowning artistic manifestation of civilisation (provided, of course, that it is a society where musicality is reasonably common). The arts of literature, painting, sculpture, architecture, always precede it in high development, and music, being less concerned with the explicit representation of literal ideas, bides its time before reflecting trends that the other arts have already explored. The so-called 'baroque' period in architecture, for example, was almost at its end when what is loosely known as 'baroque' music began to flourish; 'romanticism' as a conscious cult took place in music some fifty years after it characterised the literary and visual arts. In Norway Ibsen was creating a new world in the theatre while Grieg (fifteen years younger) was content to write charming 'romantic' drawing-room music, unable or unwilling to emerge from the snug cocoon of domesticity into the real Norwegian world outside, the existence of which is nevertheless timidly reflected in his music. It was left to

Sibelius and Nielsen, some forty years later, to do for Scandnavian music what Björnsson and Ibsen did for the drama. The situation of music is prepared and consolidated by the other arts; it is as if Orpheus, watching from the Elysian fields, waits for the apt moment to fill the air with sound, expressing his feelings about the state of mind that Man has got himself into.

Jan Sibelius and Carl Nielsen, who were both born in 1865, represent to perfection the two sides of the dual nature of the Nordic consciousness. In listening to the music of Sibelius, one seems to become part of the dim and savage past; there is a corner of Sibelius's mind that is deeply and thrillingly barbarian. It is no apparent effort for him to think as Lemminkäinen might have felt. Although Sibelius was of partly Swedish descent (a fact that gives him an urbane side) his music belongs essentially to the Finnish past, as if centuries of pent-up instincts had at last found a mighty voice. Nielsen, on the other hand, looks forward. While there is in him the toughness of the old Viking, his heart and his intelligence are applied vigorously to the potentialities of the modern world. Coming on the scene when the North had definitely achieved its new and refreshing civilisation, and after artists in other fields had fertilised the new soil for music, he was able to give vent to new hopes, not unmixed with severe conflicts. It was impossible that these two masters should fail to know each other's work, though whether they each realised the full significance of the other is doubtful. Two sides of the same coin must of necessity face in opposite directions. So far as can be discovered, Nielsen never wrote down his opinion of Sibelius (though he expressed admiration and respect for him on many occasions); Sibelius, however, sent a message to the Copenhagen Nielsen Festival of 1953, and it is worth quoting, since it illuminates the differences as well as the points of contact between the two:

'Carl Nielsen, Denmark's great son, was a born composer of symphonies, although his work embraced all forms of music. Through his great intelligence he developed his genius, in order to attain the aims which were—as I see it—clear to him from the beginning. Through his strong personality he founded a school and greatly influenced composers in many countries. One speaks of head and heart; Carl Nielsen had both in the highest degree. The principles he followed, such as the reaction against romanticism, are actual at this moment. Therefore his music exercises a strong appeal in our day.'

The honesty and dignity with which this tribute is expressed reveal not only Sibelius's genuine admiration for the Danish musician but also certain radical points of difference. Sibelius is careful not to say whether or no he approves of Nielsen's 'reaction against romanticism'. It is clear that this is a matter on which he reserves judgment, since his own natural tendencies lay originally in the reverse direction. In his magical conjuring of the ancient Nordic spirit, Sibelius is the finest type of 'romantic' artist, the type for whom the artist's individuality is both subordinated to and strengthened by a vast, impersonal imagination that explores remote racial instincts within itself. This was not achieved at once. The early Sibelius can be dangerously 'romantic' in the bad, unreal sense. The loosest, most overblown music of Strauss scarcely outdoes the *Kullervo Symphony* of 1892 either in length, diffuseness, or (sometimes) banality. The greatness of Sibelius's achievement lies in his enormous and progressively powerful self-discipline. A comparison of his *First Symphony* with his *Sixth* or *Seventh* reveals a startling transition from opulent sensuousness to rigorous, refined concentration. That he was always conscious of his Finnishness is certain; long before he had attained anything as a composer he had searched the heart of the ancient Finnish epic, *Kalevala*, and it is important to notice that most of the works based on the *Kalevala* are early. Such poetry is itself a temptation to a composer to superimpose upon it richly colourful, vigorously sensuous music— and why not? But Sibelius's insight into his own racial heritage was deeper; he seems to have known that in order to equal in power the *Kalevala*, his music must be no mere decorative fresco based upon it, but must exist in equal independence. The splendid legendary clothing was gradually dropped and put away, naïvely illustrative impulses were stiffly resisted, until the naked form of the truth emerged in all its perfection. Sibelius's music is far more Finnish when it is its fully matured self than when it is pre-occupied with illustrating the *Kalevala*. In it the past somehow concentrates itself, rising through the consciousness of a man whose critical intelligence is produced by modern civilisation.

As Sibelius looks back to a reality that has formed him, Nielsen contemplates a reality he is helping to form. It is wrong to describe Nielsen as an 'anti-romantic'. He is simply not 'a romantic'. As a straightforward, richly imaginative realist, he was never compelled to resist the sort of temptations that might have led a different temperament astray. Nielsen was never in danger of romantic exaggeration; whatever he expressed, even in his immature works, was the unvarnished truth about himself and about the world as he saw it. He appeared late enough to be able to sum up the aspirations of his own time, and early enough to show confidence in a future. What his greatest music expresses (the *Fourth* and *Fifth Symphonies*, for instance, or *Commotio*) is still immensely relevant to the problems of today, for it reflects the forces that are still in opposition in modern society. Basically, Nielsen is a powerful optimist; but he is acutely aware of the obstacles and traps that lie in wait for his hopes, and is realistic enough to postulate convincing ways of overcoming them. Where Sibelius creates compelling visions of an essentially static nature, Nielsen lets out a dynamic urge.

Analysis of the music of these two peers confirms the foregoing comparison in terms of internal evidence. Their attitudes to tonality, for example, illustrate the point perfectly. Sibelius's treatment of this prime element is deeply contemplative and conservative; each of his symphonies lies embedded firmly in its chosen tonality, upon which it broods; each is fixed upon an immovable tonal rock. Even when the music modulates, the final return to the tonic leaves the impression that nothing has been disturbed or altered. Such passages as are tonally ambiguous or openly chaotic serve only to confirm the basic proposition by throwing it into relief. If Sibelius moves into a mass of shifting, contradictory tonalities, as in the *finale* of the *Third Symphony*, he reacts to this by asserting the tonic with persistent, forging hammerblows which eventually rise above the unruly tide with such certainty that no further argument is possible. Even the wonderful opposition of keys a tritone apart, A and E flat, in the *Fourth Symphony* cannot disturb the mysterious, inexorable control of A minor. *Tapiola*, one of his vastest conceptions, never leaves the key of B minor, and the magnificent *Seventh Symphony* uses the tonality of C as if it were material from which to construct mighty buttresses.

Tonality in Nielsen serves a totally different purpose. The Dane uses it with complete fluidity, and often almost symbolically. For him, a tonality is usually the starting-point for an adventure towards another tonal country. The intention is entirely dynamic. He was always insistent that music should have a 'current', without which it was as nothing. When, in his *Third Symphony*, he uses the same pair of opposite keys (A and E flat) as does Sibelius in his No. 4, he means to create the impression of a journey into remote territory; in Sibelius the effect is of crosswinds disturbing a dark, still surface. The *Fourth Symphony* of Sibelius leaves a sense of quiescent tragedy when the crosswinds cease to blow; the tragedy in the first movement of Nielsen's *Sixth Symphony* results from a wonderfully suggested fruitless search for the childlike happiness of the opening G major, which never returns. Nielsen's dynamic or progressive treatment of tonalities is one of the subtlest phenomena in music, and one of the most deeply original. In his use of the orchestra he is more dramatic and less homogeneous than Sibelius. Again the static nature of the Finnish composer's conceptions demands a more closely circumscribed, consistent treatment of colours and sonorities, together with a set of personal, easily identifiable characteristics that do not offend because they are as needfully recurrent as the leaves upon a tree (others who have imitated these habits fail, not because they cannot score or invent themes or textures like Sibelius, but because they miss utterly the static depths from which Sibelius's larger forms originate). Nielsen's approach to the orchestra is equally indicative of his side of the Nordic coin; although influenced in his early work by Brahms and Dvořák, he achieved an absolutely personal clarity and vividness of sound, free from inhibiting mannerisms, enormously powerful, sonorous and dramatic. The orchestral colours are used unerringly to illuminate and enliven the tonal current of the music. No one has ever before dared to allow a side-drummer to improvise disruptively against a great symphonic development, as Nielsen does in the *Fifth Symphony*; no one is likely to risk it again. It is one of those wonderful, unique strokes that can succeed only once, and this is but one respect in which this work is without parallel. Nielsen's willingness, even eagerness, to take almighty risks is nearly always justified by his imagination, and it often gives his music a peculiar radiance of its own, by which it becomes a source of positive encouragement to younger composers.

The comparison of Nielsen and Sibelius as the two faces of the Nordic Janus is an inexhaustible subject and need never result in the detriment of either. Although the surface of this subject can barely be scratched here, it has been necessary to discuss it at some length in order to clarify the whole Scandinavian situation. The two giants are still prime sources of influence and, often, causes of reaction. Perhaps understandably, the liveliest musical activity is to be found in Denmark, where Nielsen's music has been a strong stimulant. Sibelius is not quite correct in saying that Nielsen founded a 'school'; a school consists usually of imitators, and Nielsen is inimitable. In Denmark composers have been helped by his example to find themselves; what they have thereby discovered has not, however, always been necessarily valuable, and each of the Scandinavian countries has its small group of fearful intellectuals lurking behind tone-rows, its coterie of twelve-notery, doing its obeisances to edicts it imagines to emanate from older and wise civilisations, but following only the witch-doctor-like mumbo-jumbo of self-tormented intellects bereft of hope. Sweden has proved rather more prone to decadent influences than the other countries. It is all too easy to mistake the rotting remnants of a bed of flowers for something new simply because the smell is different, and the malodorous remains of nineteenth-century romantic decay, arranged into ingenious patterns by various sorts of industrious musical *Leichen-begleiter*, may be sniffed even in the far North. But there are, fortunately, healthier elements to be considered.

Perhaps the strongest composer now living in Scandinavia is Vagn Holmboe (1909-). This Jutland musician, with his eight symphonies, four string quartets, dozen chamber concertos, is predominantly an instrumental composer. His mind is of genuinely symphonic cast and he is more able than any of his contemporary fellow-northerners to think and feel in large spans, and to invent music strong and natural enough to generate energy for his chosen task. The clarity of his lines is typically Danish and stems from Nielsen; he has also achieved a successful synthesis of two apparently irreconcilable styles. At one time he was much influenced by Bartók, whose angular manner and percussively balletic use of rhythm do not easily lend themselves to the building of the long processes necessary to create large-scale harmonic tensions such as are typical of the best modern symphonic writing. Holmboe, in maturing, has somehow contrived to have the best of both worlds, and (although his musical personality is not so strong as either Bartók's or Nielsen's) is free to move suddenly from a Nielsen-like continuity of contrapuntal texture to a Bartók-like abrupt percussive astringency without damaging the cogency of his thought. His music has individuality without self-consciousness; it is spontaneous but he disciplines what flows out of him with great severity, so that the effect is often somewhat austere. Especially impressive are his *Fifth* and *Seventh Symphonies* and his *Third String Quartet*.

In Norway, the dominant figure is Harald Saeverud (1897-). Though of less stature, he is as Norwegian as Sibelius is Finnish, and in a similar sense. The best of his music seems to express the spirit of his country's past, strange, mysterious, vigorous, the harshness and drama of its scenery, and its intemperate climate. This music is not concerned with polite conversation; roughness is frequent and a tough core of hard-headed obstinacy may be felt. Yet he is a sensitive, civilised composer, with a rich and salty sense of humour that often warms his asperities. His *Piano Concerto* is a striking work, full of subtle poetry and sharp contrasts, and his *Peer Gynt* music achieves exactly what Grieg's failed to do; music is again half a century in arrears! As a symphonist Saeverud shows strong character but less certainty of structure; a blend of his imagination and Holmboe's concentration would make a remarkable composer indeed.

So far the Swedes have not produced a musician capable of expressing what Sibelius does for Finland, to say nothing of Saeverud's function for Norway. Hilding Rosenberg (1892-) has the biggest reputation, but not the most natural talent, which belongs to Dag Wirén (1905-), whose cultivated art, though it plumbs no depths, is always polished and fresh. Sweden possesses perhaps the least characterful of the Scandinavian mentalities and the strongest ties with German cultures. Those Swedish composers who, like Karl Birger-Blomdahl (1916-)

and Ingvar Lidholm (1921-), are content to accept the anonymity of style imposed upon them by 'advanced' Central European influences, mislay something of value in themselves. The rest, most of them, settle for a pleasant urbanity which rarely rises above the level of the tasteful interior decorator; such prominences above this mark as there are seem to be almost a monopoly of Dag Wirén. Rosenberg stands somewhat apart; there is in his best moments a certain Old Testament dignity that is impressive when it does not overblow itself, as it does in his symphony *The Four Ages of Man*. He is, in some ways, a composer of the calibre of Frank Martin, who shares with him an exquisite feeling for pale textures and a frequent cultured poise, but who also fails on a large scale.

Apart from that fine and grievously neglected song composer Yrjö Kilpinen (1892-), Finland has produced no really striking figure since Sibelius, who has proved to be one of the world's most dangerous models for imitators. If the latter stages of this chapter do not produce a large and brave catalogue of noteworthy composers, it should be remembered that the populations of the Scandinavian countries are small, that their contributions to the arts and sciences are already far beyond reasonable expectations. Two others should be mentioned, perhaps, Fartein Valen (1887-1952) and the mercurial Dane Niels Viggo Bentzon (1919-); the latter's extreme facility and (one might almost say) musical incontinence place him in danger of becoming a Danish Milhaud or Britten. His style is mannered and brittle, often of great technical brilliance, but very frequently without depth, and he swims with such directionless enjoyment that he sometimes finds himself almost inextricably caught in the weeds. Much of his work, however, is identifiably Scandinavian, even Danish, despite its affectation of cosmopolitanism. Such character cannot be claimed for the Norwegian Valen, whose wilting atonalism has attracted some recent attention. Music such as his is less aware of the real world than was Grieg's; wan, invertebrate, undeniably imaginative at times, it stands nearer to the last twitchings of Grieg's more sentimental impulses than it does to the potent, active forces that may either shape or smash the modern world.

In a chapter of this length it is not possible to discuss in detail all the composers now working in Scandinavia, nor would some of them wish it could they foresee what account might be given of them. Despite many conflicting purposes, confusions of aims, and varieties of mind, however, the basic fact remains that there is now more vital and intelligent activity in the North than at any other time in history. So far, it is the sunny countries that have contributed the most towards the growth of human culture. In the race of the centuries they have, so to speak, been on the inside of the bend. Now that man is achieving ways of living in social security in less friendly environs, and the pursuit of art and learning no longer depends on favourable weather, we are reaching the straight. All civilised people have an equal chance—and more peoples are having the chance to be civilised. Whichever way one looks at it, this is an important point in history; so far as music is concerned we can, if we fully comprehend the twin, opposite, complementary voices of Nielsen and Sibelius, discover just how important it is.

XVII

NEW MUSIC IN SPAIN

By 'Musicus'

SPANISH MUSIC today seems to have entered a period of stagnation. The traditional currents which have kept it alive seem to be lacking in vitality and to have lost their renovating force, while the musicians who cultivated this tradition are now plunged in an almost unbroken silence which invites speculation as to a possible change of direction.

The older composers of various tendencies belonging to the generation of those born between 1880 and 1920 have witnessed a sudden change in the musical scene during the last post-war period. The musical life of Spain had been dominated by the key-figure of Manuel de Falla (1876-1946). His adoption of the impressionist technique—e.g. *Nights in the Gardens of Spain*—had earned him a wide following, especially in the Levant where the prevailing aesthetic is still based on those principles. The far-reaching effects of the Andalucian composer's conquests are reflected in the works of Manuel Blancafort (La Garriga, Barcelona, 1897), Manuel Palau (Alfara del Patriarca, Valencia, 1893), Joaquín Nin-Culmell (Berlin, 1908), Federico Mompou (Barcelona, 1893), Xavier de Monsalvatge (Gerona, 1912), Rafael Rodríguez Albert (Alicante, 1902), Miguel Asins Arbó (Barcelona, 1916), Eduardo Toldrá (Villanueva y Geltru, 1895) and Oscar Esplá (Alicante, 1889). Naturally the movement did not stop here, and Falla's example was sufficiently powerful to inspire a number of personalities of different, and even conflicting tendencies, who were to arrive at results which were sometimes diametrically opposed. To illustrate this one has only to compare the cases of Esplá and Mompou. Esplá is mainly concerned with technique, having an essentially 'Latin' quality; his music is serious and deeply intellectual, his idiom clearly defined and resting on a firm basis. Mompou's music is in the nature of an intimate confession depending on slender and subtle elements—sensitive intuition and miniature form. The results are widely different, although proceeding from the same premisses.

Falla, however, as was only logical, did not stand still. By following a path that led to a neo-classic revival (e.g. *El Retablo*, the *Concerto*) he once more provided Spanish music with a link with the past and opened up an inexhaustible field for the younger generation of composers. Among these must be counted Salvador Bacarisse (Madrid, 1898), Esplá himself to a certain extent, Joaquín Rodrigo (Sagunto, Valencia, 1902), Gerardo Gombau (Salamanca, 1906), Ernesto and Rodolfo Halffter (Madrid, 1905, 1900), Gustavo Pittaluga (Madrid, 1906), José Munoz Molleda (La Línea, Cádiz, 1905), and (as regards some of his works) Julio Gómez (Madrid, 1886).

A little outside the direct influence of Falla, but undoubtedly owing much to his master, Felipe Pedrell, must be reckoned the Basque school of composers represented notably by that faithful upholder of Pedrell's teaching, Jesús Guridi (Vitoria, 1886). His output includes operas, symphonic poems, quartets and organ works, and follows an independent line which reflects the lingering influence of the doctrine of musical nationalism. Almost every student of music from Madrid or the North of Spain has at one time or another passed through the hands of this venerable musician.

A composer of similar tendencies is Francisco Escudero (San Sebastian, 1913), whose ambition it is to 'found a school of Basque music'. His works, which include an oratorio *Illeta*, a symphonic poem *Aránzazu*, a *Basque Concerto* for piano and orchestra and a quartet, are all designed to serve this purpose.

A very different figure is Fernando Remacha (Tudela, Navarre, 1898) for the fact that he belonged to the early school of Falla enabled him to develop independently of any 'standard' conception of Spanish music on lines which are very similar to the general trend of genuinely European music. His *Piano Quartet* and *String Quartet* and the oratorio *Vísperas* are proof of this, and although for some time, owing to certain circumstances, he wrote nothing at all, his situation appears now to have changed since he was appointed Director of the recently established Conservatoire at Pamplona, the liveliest and most advanced in Spain. Nevertheless the fact remains that Falla for the last twenty years of his life (1926-1946) did no creative work at all, and not even the promise of *L'Atlantide* can lessen the significance of this fact. Was it due to an insufficiency of vocabulary?—or to his awareness of the passage of time which makes it compulsory to keep up a steady and active progress? In any case, the composers who followed in this tradition assessed the situation correctly and, to take as an example two of the most representative, Rodrigo and Esplá, have made quite clear the position today of the generation that has now reached maturity.

Joaquín Rodrigo derives, as we have seen, from late Falla. Thus the centre of gravity of Spanish music has moved from the purest form of folk-lore to the purest form of historico-racialism. Rodrigo's quest is directed towards (the expression is his own) 'a new purity' rather than neo-classicism—(Is there such a thing as classicism in music? he often asks). But Rodrigo himself found it necessary to transcend the immediate claims of racialism in order to forge a sort of objective language with the help of existing elements. His most significant work, from this point of view, is possibly the unjustly neglected and little known *Música para un Códice Salmantino* (1952). In this he has succeeded in separating almost completely the picturesque from other elements in his style which hitherto had represented a compromise. But Rodrigo was not yet satisfied, and today, apart from various episodical works in which, like any other composer, he tends to repeat himself, he appears to be preparing in studious silence a radical change of direction which will alter his whole position, although his general aesthetic outlook remains, of course, unchanged.

Esplá's case is more complex. More than anyone he was conscious of the absence of any Spanish musical tradition. And, together with Falla, and working with the material discovered so amazingly by the latter, he succeeded in revising his own personal approach and asserted his right to use a clearly defined and 'traditional' technical language. As the leading intellectual among Spanish musicians he was both widely cultured and acutely and objectively aware of the situation and requirements of Spanish music in his day. It may well be that the principal aim of his most ambitious work, the *Sonata del Sur* (1945), was to create in Spain a tradition of good craftsmanship in music in the same way that this already exists in painting. At the same time, his hostile attitude to anything approaching atonality has estranged him from some sections of the younger school and given him the reputation of being opposed to a great deal of European music today. Nevertheless, and despite the inevitable passage of time, the figure of Oscar Esplá, possibly quite unintentionally on his part, represents in the eyes of the younger generation the 'master'; and although this may be a purely formal acknowledgment of his position, there could be no better proof of his sincerity and the successfulness of his career.

But tradition seems to stop here. In the opinion of many composers, including Rodrigo, music throughout the world is now developing on lines which exclude what has hitherto been considered as the 'typically Spanish idiom'. It is therefore not surprising that (*a*) most of the older composers are now more or less silent, and (*b*) the young men are abandoning what is usually known as 'Spanish music'. It is no less inhuman to ask of men of mature age that they should change their beliefs in the presence of ideas to which they cannot subscribe than it is to expect the younger men to submit blindly to the past; it would be more reasonable to recognise, as Falla did, that it is only logical that they should go out to seek, when necessary, a 'mentor' outside their own frontiers.

These young men for the most part are centred round Madrid or Barcelona. In Madrid there is the recently formed group, *Nueva Musica*, consisting of its founder Ramón Barce and the composers Cristóbal Halffter, Luis de Pablo, Alberto Blancafort, Antón García Abril, Manuel Moreno Buendía and Fernando Ember. All these are inspired by a common aim: to incorporate Spanish music into the main European stream.

Ramón Barce was born in Madrid in 1928. The education he received at the University (Philosophy and Literature) was broader and possibly more solid than his musical training, inasmuch as his language is somewhat hesitant and confused. His principal ideal is the restoration of melody and the search for a linear, atonal idiom which has the same expressive power as the traditional tonal one. The result, based on intuition more than anything else, is a rather confused and at times contradictory sort of music, since up till now the composer has been unable to clarify his language sufficiently. This is because, it would seem, he is not interested in the technical 'thinning out' which every work requires, relying almost entirely on the theoretical content of his creations. His works, which include eleven Preludes for piano, *Canciones de Soledad* for soprano and piano, a string quartet, a piano sonata, a Piece for flute and piano, are evidence of the truth of this.

Cristóbal Halffter (Madrid, 1930) is another quite different case. The first impression his works convey is that of an extremely gifted composer. His musicianship is of a high order; his essential characteristics would seem to be his technical facility and the pleasure he takes in his work. A cousin of the two composers Ernesto and Rodolfo Halffter, he seems to have inherited his own special temperament. And yet apart from these qualities, his music reflects a certain unsureness of judgment. His atonal and at times dodecaphonic affiliation is obvious, but it is possible he has not yet fully realised the consequences, especially as regards form and timbre, which such a revolution implies. His excellent *Introduction, Fugue and Finale* for piano solo shows this clearly. Equipped with a sound and impeccable technique, he allows himself, it would seem, to be guided by a sense of complacency rather than by a genuine spirit of self-criticism. The *Misa Ducal*, the Antífona *Regina Coeli*, the *Concerto for piano and orchestra*, the *Movimientos* for string orchestra and kettledrums, the *Three Pieces for string quartet* are his most representative works. Despite his youth it is already possible to speak of an evolution starting from the Falla of *El Retablo* (*Antífonia*, *Sonata*) and proceeding towards the Viennese school and Bartók (*Movemientos*) *via* Stravinsky, whose influence can be seen in the *Misa Ducal*. All this we find combined with a very definite personality and a combative spirit, determined to tackle the problem of the 'Hispanisation' of existing schools, but from the point of view of temperament rather than of actual substance. Arriaga, Victoria and Diego Ortiz were all Spanish musicians, yet none of them are 'typical' in the strict sense of the word; all that can be said is that their music conveys a quite general impression of nationality.

Luis de Pablo (Bilbao, 1930) is mainly concerned with perfecting a solid technical language capable of meeting all requirements. He seeks an efficient medium of expression. Labelled by the critics as the 'intellectual' member of the group, he endeavours to live up to this description by striving continually to make his musical and human personality as complete as possible. Apparently his chosen path lies between the lyrical synthesis of Webern and the asceticism of late Falla (the Concerto), and he has now adopted wholeheartedly the twelve-note technique in a form which is strict and yet at the same time free, with a full awareness of its consequences. He himself declares that he looks upon this technique as a starting-point, and not as an end; and in certain of his works he enlarges its boundaries if he thinks it necessary. He considers it of primary importance to establish on sound foundations a musical language on which to build a new 'classicism' and a new unity. A common culture and a common language. While, like Halffter, he already seems to have made some slight progress on a level, in view of his age, with that shown by his colleagues, it would be foolish to speak of definite results. Although his early works showed the influence of Mompou's 'intimate' style, or were concerned with experiments in *timbre*, he proceeded towards the clarification and effective 'systematisation' of the contemporary idiom derived from Webern and in synthesis with the rhythmic theories of Messiaen whose works he has studied attentively (cf. *Invenciones*, *Sonata* for flute and piano, *Piano Sonata*, *Coral Eucaristico*) after coming under the influence of Bartók, clearly discernible in the *Quartet*, and writing his Mass, *Pax Humilium*, in a style which is simplified and austere without being dodecaphonic.

Alberto Blancafort (La Garriga, Barcelona, 1928) poses the problem on a definite basis. Widely cultured, travelled, endowed with a keen and sarcastic mind and a mordant irony, he believes the immense majority of present-day experiments are worthless and, bound by a tradition which links him with the general trend of the Catalan school—his father is Manuel Blancafort, one of Catalonia's most distinguished composers—he allows himself to be carried away by what he describes as 'a gourmet's taste for harmony'. In his view, what is important is not the collective effort, but the individual—whatever makes a personal appeal. Having experimented in all sorts of ways, the only valid criteria, he maintains, are what is pleasing or not pleasing. But granted these premisses, he imposes on himself a strict discipline and is rigorously self-critical. His *Piano Sonata*, his *Canciones*, his *Divertimento* for sextet (these represent his entire output since he produces little and is a most meticulous worker) are examples of a maximum of perfection within the limits of a style which could be said to be a sublimation of the French tradition incorporated with that of Spain. Blancafort was for a long time a pupil of Milhaud. Within this tradition he has succeeded so well in lightening and reducing his form to bare essentials that his works always bear the stamp of an extreme precision. His harmonic language is exquisitely refined, but strictly tonal.

Similar characteristics are to be found in Antón García Abril (Teruel, 1933). But what in Blancafort is the result of a definite and conscious attitude, with García Abril is still only a sign of immaturity. A composer of great musical distinction, wholly devoted to his calling, he nevertheless would seem to be guided by an old-fashioned taste, possibly owing to a lack of extra-musical experience. And yet, being completely aware of the exigencies of modern times and of the inadequacy of his vocabulary judged by present-day standards, he has now rejected all his earlier works (*Songs of Childhood*, a *Sonatina*, a *Sonata* for violin and piano, a *Piano Concerto*) and is now preparing to revise his early style and theories. Apparently the system he is likely to adopt is what Oscar Esplá has called 'the amplification of tonality', i.e. a firm tonal basis on which can be built any kind of superstructure. But everything is envisaged from the point of view of tonality without which, in his opinion, there can be no solid musical construction.

A very similar case is that of Manuel Moreno Buendía (Murcia, 1932). His musical ideas, after a period during which he came under the influence of the Rodrigo/Ernesto Halffter school, have varied widely and at the present moment, confronted with the problem of bringing his music into line with modern theories, he seems to have decided on a form of composition based on rhythmic cells which seems to be very similar to that of Stravinsky's second period, although the only theory as such in which he seems to be interested is the twelve-note technique. His works—a *Piano Quartet*, *Concerted Music for Chamber Orchestra*, a *Piano Sonata*—although preserved by their author as being typical of the tendency they represent, belong to his early manner which he himself is the first to disown.

Fernando Ember (Madrid, 1931) is an example of a dilettante who might well become a composer of distinction. As the son of a celebrated pianist, he has been accustomed since a child to the world of music. It would be more accurate to describe him as a splendidly equipped amateur rather than as a professional musician in the strict sense of the term. Nevertheless his studies with Ernesto Halffter, his gay and spontaneous temperament suggests that one day he may well produce more serious works. For the moment his works are in the neo-classic tradition which reigned supreme in bygone years. His only compositions—a *Serranilla* for chorus and soloists and a *Burlesque* for piano—belong to this category. Apart from this, he has been, and is, an indefatigable worker, organising concerts, lectures and courses.

Apart from the 'New Music' group, but affiliated with it to some extent, are a number of composers belonging to the same generation as those mentioned above. Their attitude *vis-à-vis* the group is rather that of 'wait and see', and it is quite possible that, in view of the purpose for which the group was founded, they may soon amalgamate. I am referring to the composers Manuel Angulo and Carmelo Alonso Bernaola.

Manuel Angulo (Campo de Criptana, Ciudad Real, 1930) belongs to the 'intimate', lyrical school, with definite neo-classical-impressionist tendencies. His case is very similar to that of Moreno Buendía and García Abril whose fellow-student he was in the composition class of Julio Gomez—that is to say, he is beginning to develop a definite aesthetic, after serving a sound and practical apprenticeship. His works —*Lyrical Poem* for soprano and orchestra on a text of Juana de Ibarbourou, a *Suite for piano*, a *Quartet*, a *Trio* and some choral pieces— are for the most part in the author's early manner.

A similar case is that of Carmelo Alonso Bernaola (Ochandiano, Vizcaya, 1929). With him the lyrical vein is subordinate to a certain rigorous 'constructivist' spirit which brings him nearer to the contemporary approach, although he is conscious of the same dilemma that confronts all the younger men who are hesitating between what can be learnt and what can be experienced. The fact that his works are very rarely performed (they include a *Wind Quintet*, a *Duo* for flute and trumpet and a *Divertimento* for chamber orchestra) makes it very difficult to form an objective opinion on his output.

In Barcelona musical life is more restless and intense. There is a tradition and 'way of doing things' in that city that sometimes tend to stifle the young composer and impose *clichés* upon him from which he has to break away. Nevertheless, the young Catalan school is much more intransigent and bolder than their contemporaries in Madrid. It may be that owing to better means of communication and a more concentrated atmosphere (Barcelona is the second Wagnerian city in the world!) these young men feel themselves to be more 'European' than their colleagues in Madrid and, for that reason, their reaction has been more violent.

The group 'Manuel de Falla', with José Cercós as their leader, had maintained an extreme *avant-garde* position. Today, now that this group has almost ceased to exist, the work of each of its members remains. José Cercós (Barcelona, 1925) represents the most furious reaction in favour of the strictest and most rigorous form of twelve-note technique. A fervent supporter of jazz, in so far as it represents adventure and live experience, the very titles of his works are sufficient indication of his trend of thought: *Perpendicular Variations on a theme of Webern*, *Triple String Quartet*, *Concerto for thirteen instruments on a theme from A Midsummer Night's Dream* in serial form. With regard to the latter, Barcelona has the advantage over Madrid in that it is the home of Joaquín Homs, the oldest serial composer in Spain. Although music is not his profession—he is an engineer—he has attained, thanks to his convictions and his temperament, a mastery of and a commanding position in what might be called 'Mediterranean serialism'.

Xavier Berenguel Godó (Barcelona, 1931) and Narciso Bonet (Barcelona, 1933) have been hailed by the critics as the most promising of the young generation of Catalan composers. Both belong to the well-established Stravinsky-Parisian tradition, and both have assimilated the Stravinskian technique as the basis of their creative work. This does not mean, however, that they have abandoned that lyrical tradition, so far removed from any deliberate desire for innovation, which is the mainspring of Catalan music. In other words, their music continues the old tradition, but in a rejuvenated form. Of Berenguel's works the most representative are his *Concerto* for piano and string orchestra, his *Movements* for orchestra and the *Sonata*. Bonet's works include a *Sonata* for viola and piano, the *Suite Trufaldi* for two clarinets and bassoon and the *Ocathedron* with piano.

Manuel Valls (Barcelona, 1928) is in the purest Parisian tradition which we have seen exemplified, in some respects, in Blancafort. His religious music, notably the *Penitential Psalm*, follows the tradition initiated by Poulenc in his mystical works. Mention should also be made of his *Variaciones radiofónicas*, the Overture *Antigone* and the *Songs of the Wheel of Time*.

From Seville, geographically remote but in feeling very similar, comes Manuel Castillo (1931-). A precocious musician, he started in the Turina-Halffter tradition (cf. the Sonata) but is steadily evolving an intimate kind of idiom, purged of any excesses, unpretentious, simple and effective, showing a certain affinity with the somewhat austere traditions of the classical Spanish school. He appears to be enlarging his conception of tonality very freely, altering its function so that in the place of tonality, in the strict sense, we find a centre of polarity, as it were, to which groups and centres of equilibrium are attracted. This procedure, moreover, is eminently suited to small-scale works, a sphere in which Castillo is most at home. His most important works are as follows: *Divertimento* for oboe, clarinet and bassoon, a *Wind Quintet*, a *Missa Brevis* and *Movement* for two pianos.

With some exceptions it will be seen that there has been a subtle break in the main current of Spanish music. The assimilation of new techniques has led some musicians to think that the Spanish musical tradition ought to be relegated to a position of secondary importance. This is not to be understood in the strictest sense, although it is true that this assimilation does involve a risk. It is a fact that the conquest of new techniques and methods cannot be ignored, and for that reason the split between the most European-minded and the most consciously Spanish generations has produced a feeling of deprivation of ancestry, the only escape from which is to be found in the very human attitude of solitude and renunciation adopted by a Falla.

For their part, the older generation of composers are either conscious of their obligation to evolve, or are hostile to the idea, although an attitude of understanding and sympathy is more common, if not one of sarcastic curiosity *vis-à-vis* the anxiety displayed by the younger men. Most difficult of all would seem to be a synthesis of both these tendencies, since some sort of effective Spanish contribution to present-day European culture is indispensable. And the young generation is particularly conscious of this obligation.

[*Translated from the Spanish by the Editor.*]

POSTSCRIPT

By the Editor

As the above article refers only to Spanish composers domiciled in Spain (with one exception), I think it only right to add a note on two distinguished contributors to this book, both Spaniards, but both living outside Spain, who are also well-known composers and, as such, deserve a special mention here: I refer to Roberto Gerhard and Maurice Ohana.

Roberto Gerhard, Catalan, was born at Valls, near Barcelona, in 1896. Though a pupil of Granados in early youth, his first important published work, the Piano Trio (1918), showed French influences. Four years later, however, he took the decisive step of travelling to Vienna to study with Arnold Schoenberg, with whom he remained for five years. This encounter had a profound influence on his formation, and to it can be traced Gerhard's present preoccupation with serial twelve-note technique. After the civil war he left Spain and came to live in Cambridge, England, where he has been active ever since and now enjoys a European reputation. His works include: two Symphonies (1953, 1959), a Concerto for violin and orchestra, two ballets, *Don Quixote* (1940-41) and *Pandora* (1944-5), an opera, *The Duenna* (1945-7), a String Quartet (1955), *Cancionero de Pedrell*, for soprano and chamber orchestra (1941), Piano pieces and songs including *Fourteen Cancons Populars Catalanes*.

Maurice Ohana was born in Casablanca, of Gibraltarian parents in

1914. He makes no secret of the fact that his musical education, to quote his own words, 'owes more to Andalucian folk music which I heard since the cradle, and to African and Berber music than to Bach, Beethoven or Brahms'. Having started his career as a pianist at the age of about fourteen, he had just decided to devote himself to composition when the Second World War broke out and for the next five and a half years he saw service in the British army. He then returned to Paris, where he now lives and works. He studied the piano with Frank Marshall, Lazare Lévy and Alfred Casella, and counterpoint and fugue with Daniel Lesur. One of his earliest and best-known works is the setting of Federico Garcia Lorca's poem on the death of a famous bull-fighter, *Llanto por Ignacio Sanchez Mejias* (1950). He has also written two ballets, a lyric mimodrama on a text of his own, *Titeres de la Heroina Fiel* (1954), *Cantigas* (on Spanish poems of the twelfth and thirteenth centuries), *Images de Don Quichotte* (1955) and the music for films in thirds of a tone mentioned in his article on this subject (see page 110). In preparation: *Mayas* for two pianos and orchestra. All the works mentioned have been performed or broadcast in Paris, Hamburg or London.

XVIII

(1) MUSIC IN GREAT BRITAIN AFTER 1945

By Dyneley Hussey

THE END of the Second World War was also the end of a hiatus in the musical life of Great Britain. In the six years since 1939 a new generation of composers had grown up who, though they had had occasional opportunities of displaying their capabilities, only now were able to devote themselves entirely to their art. Of the older composers, Vaughan Williams (1872-1958) had continued on his individual course, producing at the age of seventy, and in the year (1943) of supreme crisis, the serene *Fifth Symphony in D*. In the period after the war he produced four more symphonies, the *Sixth in E minor* (1947) being the most original and powerful, and a number of choral works. Arnold Bax (1883-1953), on the other hand, produced little, apart from the occasional works that his office as Master of Music to the sovereign demanded, while Arthur Bliss (1891-), his successor in that office, found an outlet for his dramatic gifts in ballet. During the war William Walton added only some music for films and ballet and some short orchestral works to his catalogue.

Looking back on the interval since the end of the war one perceives three main trends or influences at work. One may be called traditional or academic (in no bad sense of the word); the second reflects the reaction of British composers to what their immediate predecessors and contemporaries in other parts of the world had done and were doing; and the third was the outcome of a newly aroused interest in opera, partly stimulated by the experience of troops stationed in Italy.

The traditional influence (if we leave aside the conventions acquired during the normal study of technique in composition) derives partly from folk-song with its modal melodies and from early (pre-seventeenth century) music in which modal scales were freely employed, and partly from later English masters, notably Purcell. English folk-song has exercised a potent influence on such composers as Vaughan Williams, who (like Bartók in Hungary) completely absorbed the native idiom into his own musical personality and created out of it an individual style of his own, E. J. Moeran and, to some extent, Benjamin Britten.

It is, however, to Purcell's 'peculiar genius to express the energy of English words' that Britten looks back in the vocal music which represents the greater and most important part of his output. And the same influence appears also in Gerald Finzi, who also owed a debt to Parry and Vaughan Williams, in Michael Tippett and, to some extent, in Lennox Berkeley's settings of poetry, despite his French affinities.

Berkeley (1903-) studied with Nadia Boulanger, one of the great teachers of our time, who has, however, never sought to impose any one style or system upon her pupils. True to type, Berkeley has, in his mature music—the *Symphony* of 1940, the beautiful settings of poems by St Theresa of Avila and a *Stabat Mater* for six solo voices and twelve instruments—emancipated himself from Parisian smartness.

A wider and deeper influence has been exercised by the theories of Arnold Schoenberg and his disciples, partly through the presence in England of musicians who sought asylum from Germany and Austria during the Nazi régime. But the principles governing Schoenberg's creative practice have not been strictly or pedantically applied by his English followers. Among them, Humphrey Searle (1915-), who tempers an admiration for his master with a passionate devotion to Liszt, and Peter Racine Fricker (1920-) are the most important. Searle, who studied with Anton Webern, is a romantic at heart, and his Pianoforte Sonata in one movement (1951) shows how successfully Schoenberg's principles could be applied to a Lisztian musical structure. A Symphony followed in 1953, a powerful and concentrated piece of musical thinking, likewise in one movement. Searle has also turned his attention to the problem, which also exercised Schoenberg, of combining speech with music. His first essay in the form, *Gold Coast Customs* (poem by Edith Sitwell), for speakers, chorus and orchestra

(1949) was followed by *The Riverrun* (James Joyce) and *The Shadow of Cain* (Sitwell) in 1951 and 1952 respectively. This powerful trilogy in which the music succeeds in communicating the emotions expressed in the somewhat obscure texts, together with a *Second Symphony* (1958) constitute Searle's most remarkable achievements to date, and the last two works exhibit his newly acquired mastery over large musical forms. He is at present engaged on *Symphony No. 3*. An opera, *The Diary of a Madman*, after Gogol, was produced at the Berlin Festival in 1958. Fricker, a descendant of Jean Racine, is a more austere composer who makes little concession to sensuous aural effect, for all that he is a pupil of Matyas Seiber, the most sensitive and lyrical of the composers who sought refuge in England from Hitler.

Matyas Seiber (1904-), a Hungarian, had absorbed Bartók's new tonal discoveries and mastered the intricacies of twelve-note (serial) composition before he left Central Europe. His keen intellectual interest in technical procedure is balanced by an exceptional poetic imagination, and he has acquired in the country of his adoption a remarkable command of English idioms. His cantata, *Ulysses*, with a text taken from James Joyce's novel, exhibits his mastery in the setting of words—and, on a superficial view, very intractable words—to music that illuminates them. As a composer, he contrives successfully to combine twelve-note technique with more conventional methods of construction, such as the passacaglia, and with vocal writing that has affinities with eighteenth-century models. Among his other works, his *Third Quartet*, completed in 1951, is of outstanding importance.

One characteristic of the English genius is its capacity to absorb foreign influences, whether artistic or political, into its own system and to convert foreign settlers into Englishmen. Handel is the classic instance in music. Delius is another and the names of Holst and Finzi, the second English to the core, indicate how, after a generation or two, alien blood has been absorbed. The same process is evident not only in the case of Seiber, but even in a more mature musician like Egon Wellesz, who has composed an English comic opera, *Incognita*, based on a story by Congreve and a number of settings of English poetry, and in Franz Reizenstein, a pupil of Hindemith, who came to England in 1934 at the age of twenty-three. Reizenstein's cantata, *Voices in the*

Night (1951), is a remarkable witness to his sensitive response to English poetic imagery and metres—the text is an anthology ranging from Campian and Charles Cotton to Christopher Hassall who arranged it —and to his ability to compose in the great tradition of English choral music without losing his own individuality. In 1958 he composed a large choral work, *Genesis*, for the Three Choirs Festival at Hereford. Reizenstein, who is also a concert-pianist, has composed some distinguished works for his own instrument—notably a set of *Twelve Preludes and Fugues* and a *Sonata*—as well as a number of orchestral and chamber works. His music combines a severe intellectual control of form, derived ultimately from Hindemith's teaching, with a sensitiveness to texture and to the melodic capacity of the medium, whether vocal or instrumental, which he employs.

Other composers who have adopted, to a greater or less extent, the Schoenbergian method of composition include Elizabeth Lutyens (1906-), whose music, mostly for chamber combinations, clearly shows the influence of Webern. Elizabeth Maconchy (1907-), who has also devoted herself mainly to chamber music, has produced a series of starkly written String Quartets, in which the influence of Bartók's compositions for that medium is apparent. Miss Maconchy makes no concession to sensuousness of sound for its own sake, but her music is intellectually convincing and impressive in its powerful austerity.

A foreign influence of a different kind appears in the music of Alan Bush (1900-), who has allowed a commitment to Communist doctrine to hamstring a considerable talent that produced, as long ago as 1929, such a promising work as the 'Dialectic' for string quartet.

Other composers of importance who belong to no 'school' or sect, whether foreign or native, are William Walton, Edmund Rubbra, Alan Rawsthorne, Michael Tippett, Benjamin Frankel and Benjamin Britten.

Walton (1902-), whose natural musicality brought him to public notice at an early age, had established his reputation between the two world wars with three *Concertos* (for pianoforte, viola and violin respectively) the oratorio *Belshazzar's Feast* (1931) and a Symphony (1932-5). To these works he has latterly added, besides some occasional music, a *Violin Sonata* and a *Violincello Concerto* (1957), besides the opera (his only work in this form to date) *Troilus and Cressida* (1954), to be mentioned later. A second symphony is, at the moment of writing, due for completion shortly. In these later works there is less exuberance than in the earlier works—for example, the famous *Façade* (1922)—and a more mellow poetry in the unashamedly romantic vein of the *Violin Concerto* of 1939 where Walton openly assumes the mantle of Elgar. Vigour and light-heartedness still enliven his quick movements, but the quintessence of his musical personality is enshrined in the lyrical movements that stem from the beautiful *Viola Concerto* of 1928-9.

Rubbra (1901-), who has composed six symphonies, a number of concertos and chamber works, besides a large amount of choral music and songs, is one of the most important composers of the day. Out of choral polyphony he has evolved a symphonic style whose structure depends on the continuous evolution of a single theme, and not on the conflict of opposing tonalities which is the basis of the classical symphony. If he was anticipated in this method by Sibelius, (e.g. in the first movement of his *Fifth Symphony*) and by Carl Nielsen, who has exercised a direct influence on another English composer, Robert Simpson, Rubbra's music shows no resemblance to that of these composers. He has arrived at a similar solution of the symphonic problem in his own way. His earlier symphonies were lacking clarity of texture for the reason that he was using for orchestral music an essentially choral polyphony. In his *Third* and *Fourth Symphonies* his growing mastery of a true orchestral style was accompanied by some loss of grandeur, but in the Fifth (1948) the intensity and nobility of the first two reappeared transfigured by luminous orchestration. Similarly, in his concertante works, Rubbra abandons both the classical and romantic concerto-forms, allowing the music to develop from a lyrical impulse generated by the solo instrument. A typical example of his method is the first movement, called 'Corymbus', of the *Second Pianoforte Concerto in G* (1956), in which a germinal idea is expanded (as the stalks of a corymb lengthen further from the centre of the group of flowers) throughout the piece.

Rubbra is a 'tonal' composer and so is Benjamin Frankel. On the other hand, Rawsthorne's music is like Hindemith's, divorced from any reliance upon the old conventions of key-relationship, but not employing the serial method of the dodecaphonists. For the reason that he cannot resort to the clear-cut contrasts of tonality that are the basis of sonata-form, variation-form is Rawsthorne's chief structural resource. His music has a strong individuality as well as, in the slow movements, a strain of melancholy. Rawsthorne (1905-) is an exception among British musicians in being almost exclusively an instrumental composer who has written little vocal music. In this he is the converse of Rubbra, who approached symphonic composition by way of vocal polyphony. His first major work was the *Symphonic Studies* (1938) which consists of five different aspects of a central theme. The same kind of formal structure appears in the Fantasy Overture *Cortèges* (1945), and again in the second of the two movements of the *Violin Concerto* (1947) while the middle and most substantial movement of the *First Pianoforte Concerto* (1943) is a *chaconne*. On the other hand, in the opening movement of the *Violin Concerto* and in that of his first *Symphony* (1950) to date, Rawsthorne expands the initial themes into paragraphs rather in the manner of Sibelius, achieving in the Symphony a sonata-movement whose tonal centre is G. In his *Second Pianoforte Concerto* (1951), a work conceived in terms of pianistic virtuosity, Rawsthorne displays a command of mordant wit and a feeling for brilliant orchestral colour. His *Second Symphony* (1959) is more restrained and lyrical in its expression of a pastorial mood.

Frankel (1906-) is exceptional in another way, at least at the present day. He approached 'serious' music by way of hard experience as a performer and composer of music for revue, operetta and the films. In the last sphere he has acquired a reputation for producing music that unerringly reflects the action of the film, whether it be comedy or melodrama. Possibly as a reaction against his 'commercial' activities and also on account of his Jewish blood, his other music is characterised by an intense seriousness of purpose, sometimes expressed in rhetorical gestures, and an introspective melancholy. His most distinguished compositions are a *Violin Concerto* (1951) and the fourth of his String Quartets. Michael Tippett (1905-), like Rubbra, has approached instrumental music by way of song and poetry. He consciously applied a madrigalian style of writing to the string quartet in the *Second*

Quartet in F sharp (1942) whose last movement owes its character to his study of the 'sprung' rhythms of Gerard Manley Hopkins. These influences are felt also in the *Concerto for Double String Orchestra* of 1939, the work that first made Tippett's name widely known. He has also produced two Symphonies, the second in 1958 being a work of considerable distinction marred by a too great complexity of texture. Tippett's vocal works include the secular oratorio *A Child of Our Time* (1941), in which he skilfully uses negro spirituals in the manner of chorales in the *Passions* of J. S. Bach, a song-cycle *The Heart's Assurance*, and an opera which will be mentioned later.

Another composer who fits in here, since he belongs to no particular 'school', is Anthony Milner (1925-), who studied at the Royal College of Music and later with Matyas Seiber. Milner's music is almost exclusively vocal, his only instrumental compositions of importance being a *Quartet for oboe and strings* (1953) and a set of *Orchestral Variations* (1958). Most of his works have a religious basis, apart from his settings of the Roman Catholic liturgy. His most important concert works are *The Song of Akhenaten* (1952) for soprano and chamber orchestra, with a text based on the writings of the 'heretical' monotheistic Pharaoh; *The City of Desolation* (1955) for soprano, chorus and orchestra; *St Francis* (1956), a triptych for tenor, chorus and orchestra, and *The Harrowing of Hell*, commissioned by the B.B.C.'s Third Programme in 1956, for double chorus *a capella* with solos for tenor and bass. Milner's music is 'contemporary' in its bold harmonic idiom without being excessively difficult or ungrateful to sing. He has something of Hindemith's direct asperity and clean lines of counterpoint, softened by a more English flexibility of rhythm.

Healthy and abundant though the output of instrumental and vocal music has been—and there is no room for more than a mention of such other contributors as Howard Ferguson, Phyllis Tate, Geoffrey Bush, Kenneth Leighton, Gordon Jacob, Iain Hamilton, William Wordsworth and John Addison—the most remarkable feature of post-war musical life in England has been the operatic activity of composers. This was the natural result of an increased public interest in opera manifested in the establishment of the Royal Opera House, Covent Garden, as a 'National' Opera, subsidised out of public funds. With

Sadler's Wells established as a popular Opera by Lilian Baylis in the 1930s, as a secondary opera-house, London now has two theatres devoted to the presentation of opera and ballet the whole year round. This fact inevitably stimulated native composers to write operas for performance at one or other of these houses. The stimulus to compose ballets had existed ever since the formation of the Sadler's Wells Ballet in the inter-war years and this, too, has continued.

As was to be expected in the handling of this complex and difficult form, even experienced composers were not wholly successful in their first efforts. One problem was to find good librettos, another field in which there was no experienced talent to draw on. J. B. Priestley provided in *The Olympians* (1949), composed by Arthur Bliss, an admirable idea for music—the classic deities incarnated in a company of strolling players and interfering in the lives of mortals—but failed to dramatise it satisfactorily. Michael Tippett, acting as his own librettist, produced a muddled and humourless allegory based on transcendental ideas about life, which an imaginative score could not redeem.[1] Vaughan Williams produced a noble and long-meditated drama based on Bunyan's *Pilgrim's Progress* (1949), which he styled a Morality, even as he had called *Job*, not a Ballet, but a Masque. Here again the result was too solemn and 'religious' for a public nourished on Italian opera.

More successful as operatic craftsmanship, if less lofty in intention, were Arthur Benjamin's *Prima Donna*, an excellent burlesque in one act, and his full-scale melodrama *A Tale of Two Cities* (1957), based on Dickens, both with excellent librettos by Cedric Cliffe; and Walton's *Troilus and Cressida* (1954) which in its text by Christopher Hassall, based on Chaucer, and in its music, rises to real tragic heights. Walton's music is not strikingly original, but uses well-tried operatic conventions in its own way, with good effect. Yet the opera just missed achieving the final (and indefinable) touch of greatness that might have given it a place in the international repertory. Other distinguished essays were Lennox Berkeley's *Nelson* (1953) and John Gardner's *The Moon and Sixpence* (1957), based on Somerset Maugham's novel, both of which achieved some success at Sadler's Wells Theatre without travelling further afield.

[1] *The Midsummer Marriage* (1955).

One composer, Benjamin Britten (1913-), has shown a real genius for opera, and has evolved a new form of his own, independent of the larger theatres. Britten's first and most widely successful opera, *Peter Grimes* (1945), was ready for production when Sadler's Wells re-opened after the war. It showed at once that capacity for presenting dramatic action and character through music which is the basis of opera. The characters, derived from George Crabbe's *The Borough*, are mostly unpleasant in their idiosyncrasies and the central figure, Peter Grimes, arouses little sympathy in the spectator. But there is no denying the power with which his story is presented nor the complete success of Britten's musical creation of the atmosphere of a seaside town in Suffolk.

Britten perceived that opera on the grand scale was too expensive to be a practical proposition for a composer who wished to devote himself mainly to the theatre. He proceeded to form a small company of half-a-dozen singers with a chamber-orchestra, for which he has written his most characteristic works—*The Rape of Lucretia* (1946), *Albert Herring* (1947), and *The Turn of the Screw* (1954). In addition he composed, for production at Covent Garden, *Billy Budd* (1951) and *Gloriana* (commissioned for the Coronation Gala of 1953). Neither of these larger operas has achieved a place in the repertory, as *Peter Grimes* has done. Indeed, *Gloriana*, despite a good libretto by William Plomer, was in the nature of a 'mock-up', a freely sketched design for an opera with some brilliant strokes, but not carried through to completion.

The quintessential Britten is, therefore, to be found in his chamber-operas, and in his songs and choral music, notably the *Serenade* for tenor, horn and strings, the setting of Rimbaud's *Les Illuminations* and the two song-cycles on Sonnets by Michelangelo and John Donne. He is not a symphonic composer, though his mastery of orchestral effect and his individual use of instrumental colour are among the striking features of his music. He appears to be obsessed with twisted and perverted characters as subjects for opera—with the sadistic Grimes, Obey's brutal Tarquin, and the horrible Peter Quint and Miss Jessel of Henry James's story. *The Turn of the Screw* is the best of these operas, a complete resolution of the drama into music—an astonishing feat to have performed with such apparently intractable material. This work also manifests Britten's extraordinary gift for writing music for children—two of the chief characters are a boy and a girl about twelve to fifteen years old—which children can sing without its sounding childish, and incidentally of finding and training children who can adequately perform it. Of this gift he has given further proof in the charming children's opera *Let's Make An Opera* (1949), in *Noye's Fludde* (1958), a setting of the old Chester morality play, and in *Spring Symphony* (1949) a setting of a cycle of poems about spring for soloists, boys' chorus, full chorus and orchestra. The cantata, *St Nicolas*, composed in 1948 for the centenary of Lancing College, and the earlier *Ceremony of Carols* (1942) bear further witness to this delightful side of his art. Altogether, except in the sphere of purely instrumental music to which his most significant contributions so far have been the *Sinfonia da Requiem* and the *Second String Quartet*, Britten is the most important and successful English composer who has come to the fore in the period under review.

(2) ENGLISH MUSIC 1945–1965

by Colin Mason

IN THE years since the first edition of this book was published, the English musical scene has been dominated by the composers who were already in or near their fifties, and by a new generation now in their thirties, rather than by the middle generation, who have not generally gained ground. The recent emergence and remarkable early achievement of the richly and diversely talented group of composers born during the 1930s is comparable to that thirty years earlier of the chronologically close-knit group of composers (Walton, Tippett, Rawsthorne, Berkeley, Rubbra, Bush) born in the first few years of this century.

Three of these young composers did in fact first make their mark as members of a 'school', namely the Manchester New Music Group (with which the pianist-composer John Ogdon was also closely associated). Under the stimulating guidance of their composition teacher Richard Hall at the Royal Manchester College of Music they were among the first in this country to move towards pointillist and other post-Webern techniques. The most thorough-going and assured in his radicalism among them, and the first to assert his powerful and original creative personality, was Peter Maxwell Davies (born 1934), who was chosen to represent England at the annual festival of the International Society for Contemporary Music in three successive years (Strasbourg 1958, Rome 1959, Cologne 1960). While still in his twenties he won a great deal of attention not only for his own compositions but also for his outstanding success in using *avant-garde* material and methods in his educational work as music-master at Cirencester Grammar School. The most notable product of this phase in his career was the sequence of carols with instrumental interludes, *O Magnum Mysterium*, written for performance by the school. Although he soon gave up his work in school, the experience had considerable influence on his later development. It led to his being commissioned to write several other ambitious school works, including the cantata *Veni Sancte Spiritus* (1963), one of his most important compositions, written for the Princeton High School Choir when Davies was on a fellowship in the United States, and *The Shepherd's Calendar* (1965), written for the U.N.E.S.C.O. Conference on Music in Education held in Sydney in that year.

Vocal music generally forms a large and significant part of his output, perhaps partly because, like many other composers in an age when unlimited new technical possibilities seem to be available, he finds in this most elemental and enduring form of music-making a readier communication with listeners and performers than through 'abstract' instrumental music, and also a means of controlling and directing his invention into a channel of more clearly defined limits than are imposed by instruments. Among his other major vocal works are Five Motets for double chorus and chamber ensemble, and *Leopardi Fragments* for soprano and contralto soloists with chamber ensemble. This last is one among many of his works initially inspired by some aspect of pre-classical or medieval music, in this case Monteverdi's *Vespers*, which also contributed to the inspiration of his *String Quartet* and *Sinfonia* for chamber orchestra. He has also written two orchestral

H

'Fantasias' on an 'In Nomine' of John Taverner, the second of which (1964), an extended single movement of some 40 minutes' duration, is one of his most ambitious and momentous works.

The other two members of the 'Manchester' group are Alexander Goehr and Harrison Birtwistle. Goehr (born 1932) is less radical than Davies, and is temperamentally closer to Schoenberg than to the post-Webern school, but his work shows no less individuality and purposefulness. It is in the orchestral field that he has had his most notable successes, among them a so-called 'Little' Symphony (in fact a large-scale work of original design, lasting nearly half an hour), a Violin Concerto, and the symphony-like *Pastorals*, interestingly scored for strings (no violas), brass and two solo woodwind, one of the outstanding works of the 1965 Donaueschingen Festival, for which it was commissioned. His other important works include a Suite for seven instruments, a Piano Trio, *Five Poems and an Epigram of William Blake* for unaccompanied chorus and solo trumpet, a large-scale choral cantata *Sutter's Gold* written for the revivified Leeds Triennial Festival, and a chamber cantata *The Deluge*—an interesting feature of these last two being that the texts of both are film scenarios of Eisenstein.

Harrison Birtwistle (born 1934) has been slightly less prolific and slower to find his feet. Like Davies, by whom he was at first much influenced, he has sought inspiration in early music, an important example being his six-movement fantasy *The World is Discovered*, after a canzonet by Heinrich Isaak. A wind quintet entitled *Refrains and Choruses* and a chamber cantata *Monody for Corpus Christi* are among his other notable early works, already revealing considerable individuality of musical thought, and he has followed these up more recently with more ambitious works such as *Entr'actes and Sappho Fragments* for soprano and six instruments, *Tragoedia* for large chamber ensemble, and *Three Movements with Fanfares* for orchestra, and *The Visions of Francesco Petrarca*, an originally planned quasi-dramatic work for baritone, mime, chamber orchestra and children's orchestra. All of these are exceptionally imaginative in form, rich in material, and have confirmed him as a composer of a creative vitality as powerful and original as that of any of his generation in this country.

At the time of writing (1965) none of the 'Manchester' group has produced an opera, although all three have one in progress, Birtwistle's being nearest to completion. Their three most important contemporaries outside the group have less in common, but are united in that all have made interesting and successful forays in this field. Youngest among them is Richard Rodney Bennett (born 1936), whose *The Mines of Sulphur* (1964), commissioned for the Sadler's Wells company, was staged exactly a year later at La Scala, Milan, and is also going into production at several other foreign opera-houses. Although hampered by a dramatically defective libretto the music is impressively fluent and skilful, rewarding to sing, beautifully scored, and shows a sense of theatrical effectiveness. Bennett's other works include an earlier one-act opera *The Ledge* and a large quantity of orchestral and chamber music.

The subject of Nicholas Maw's (born 1935) comic opera *One Man Show*, based on a story by Saki, has proved a more serious hindrance to the proper appreciation of a superbly sustained and inventive work that has a more strongly personal musical style than Bennett's, and a greater weight of musical substance. Maw's seems essentially a lyrical talent, but one of great stamina and force, and in this respect he is slightly akin to Michael Tippett, though the similarity does not hold true of their actual musical language or technique. The nature and strength of Maw's gifts are also magnificently exemplified in his *String Quartet*, a huge single movement lasting some 40 minutes, and in his *Sinfonia* for small orchestra, the first work to be commissioned from the fund set up by Benjamin Britten from his Aspen Award. *Scenes and Arias* for orchestra, and *Chamber Music* for five players are among his most notable earlier works.

The oldest, most prolific and most multifariously gifted of this young generation is the Australian-born Malcolm Williamson, who works with (and sometimes combines) an amazing variety of techniques and idioms, ranging from the strictest, subtlest and most ingenious kinds of serialism, including such manifestations of it as isorhythm, at the one extreme, to 'pop' tunes at the other. His first opera *Our Man in Havana*, based on Graham Greene's novel, well exemplifies the diversity and vitality of his talent, and contains some brilliant choral numbers in mock-Cuban style which rank with Milhaud's best inventions in this genre. Since then he has written a vastly entertaining quasi-opera in two acts, *English Eccentrics*, based on Edith Sitwell's book of the same title, composed for the English Opera Group, as well as two successful operas for children: *The Happy Prince*, based on Oscar Wilde, and *Julius Caesar Jones*. At the time of writing his latest opera, *The Violins of St. Jacques* (again on a Caribbean theme) is awaiting production at Sadler's Wells.

He has been immensely fertile in other fields too, and is capable of producing half a dozen major works in a year. The enormous list of his works includes two ballets (*The Display* and *Sun into Darkness*), three piano concertos, very much contrasted in character and dimensions, two attractive and interesting early piano sonatas notably showing his ability to reconcile an extreme technical 'intellectualism' with a spontaneous and continuous flow of melody, a Symphony for solo organ and several other organ works including a Concerto with orchestra, a Violin Concerto written for Menuhin, a Concerto for wind quintet and two pianos/eight hands, a *Sinfonia Concertante* for three trumpets and strings, a set of Symphonic Variations for orchestra written for the 1965 Edinburgh Festival, a *Concerto Grosso* for the 1965 Promenade Concerts, and a *Sinfonietta* written for the full opening of the B.B.C.'s 'Music Programme', these last two works being outstanding examples of the highly original and rewarding latter-day-Prokofiev vein that Williamson has recently and richly struck.

Before leaving this rising generation of composers mention should also be made of Gordon Crosse (born 1937), who came into some prominence with a very successful entertainment for children *Meet My Folks*, and has confirmed his promise notably in a one-act opera for stage or television, based on Yeat's *Purgatory* (1966), and in a large-scale choral cantata, *Changes*, performed at the Three Choirs Festival in the same year. Cornelius Cardew (born 1936) and David Bedford (born 1937) represent what might be called the 'school of Cage' in England. Bedford, like Davies and Birtwistle, has been music master in a secondary school, and has successfully introduced music composed with current compositional techniques into the curriculum.

From the under-35s we must turn to the over-50s for any significant contribution to the recent musical scene, and principally of course to

Benjamin Britten, who has continued as fertile and original as ever. His major popular success has been the *War Requiem* written for the opening of the rebuilt Coventry Cathedral 1962, which made an impact on the public unrivalled by any work of his since his opera *Peter Grimes* two decades ago. With a text consisting of the sections of the Latin mass for the dead interleaved with the anti-war (and in some cases anti-clerical) poems of Wilfred Owen, this awoke a deep and widespread response in probably a larger section of the British musical public than Britten had ever reached before.

Whether the music, brilliantly and imaginatively as this highly effective scheme is carried through, is always equal in force and originality of expression to the demands of the text, is a matter of debate, and some may feel that the essential nature of Britten's genius finds truer expression in his enchanting Shakespearean opera *A Midsummer Night's Dream* (1960) or the full-length fairy-tale ballet *The Prince of the Pagodas* (1956). These are among the many works during the past decade or so in which this fundamentally 'tonal' composer has made extremely ingenious use of certain superficial features of twelve-note or serial technique. One of the most important and successful of these is the magnificent *Canticle No. 3* 'Still falls the rain', a setting of part of a poem by Edith Sitwell, for tenor, horn and piano, composed in memory of Noel Mewton Wood, which ranks among the very finest examples of Britten's genius. The delightfully witty *Cantata Academica*, a dazzling *jeu d'esprit* written for the 500th anniversary of Basle University, is another of his successful exercises in pseudo-serialism.

Britten has also continued the long line of song-cycles which have been a major feature of his output from the beginning, in *Winter Words* (Hardy, 1953); *Songs from the Chinese* (with guitar, 1957); *Nocturne* (various English poets, 1958) for tenor and orchestra, a sequel to the popular early *Serenade*, but with obbligati for a succession of different solo instruments; *Six Hölderlin Fragments* (1958); *Songs and Proverbs of William Blake* (1965), written for Fischer-Dieskau; and *The Poet's Echo* (six poems of Pushkin, 1965), written for Galina Vishnevskaya and her husband Mstislav Rostropovich. The art of Rostropovich himself has also inspired three major works from Britten, particularly significant in that they are his first ventures into the field of pure instrumental composition for many years—first the Sonata for cello and piano (1961), followed by the Symphony for cello and orchestra (1963), which even after twenty years shows remarkable affinities with the *Sinfonia da Requiem*, and then the Suite for unaccompanied cello (1965).

In his latest phase Britten has turned twice to a new kind of chamber opera, written for the English Opera Group but using even fewer instruments than his earlier works for them, and both intended for church performance. The first of these was *Curlew River*, based on a Japanese No-play, the scene of which is transferred in William Plomer's adaptation to East Anglia in medieval times. Among the many extremely interesting and novel musical features of this work is the use of both plainsong and quasi-oriental thematic material, and the almost continuous use, in a variety of guises, of a kind of heterophonic texture and technique, in keeping with the Oriental source of the work, though also exemplifying with very characteristic originality Britten's receptiveness to, and ability to put to more conservative and very personal use, ideas current among the *avant-garde*. His second such work, *The Burning Fiery Furnace*, is based on the biblical book of Daniel.

Among Britten's older (and younger) contemporaries Michael Tippett is the one who has most significantly added to his output. His greatest work, somehow overlooked in the first edition of this book, is his first opera *The Midsummer Marriage* (1954), a joyously lyrical Wagnerian comedy in which Tippett's genius finds its most perfect expression. His Piano Concerto is another beautiful work in the same vein, to which he has since returned in his cantata *The Vision of St. Augustine* (1965), after the more angular declamatory style of his second opera *King Priam*, also a powerful and arresting work. His very individual, not to say eccentric style, in which the core of pure lyricism is enclosed in a cloudy profusion of notes, is not easy to come to terms with, and is easy to deride, like, say, Messiaen's, Ives's or Janáček's, to whom Tippett might well be compared in stature as well as in individuality.

Alan Rawsthorne too, after many years during which he seemed content to exploit the very personal but rather limited idiom that he arrived at very early in his career without attempting to increase his resources or range of expression, has lately done so with notable success in such works as his Third Symphony, Quintet for piano and wind, Second String Quartet, and Sonata for violin and piano. Among this generation Elisabeth Lutyens and the Spanish-born Roberto Gerhard have also belatedly won the prominence due to them. Both among the pioneers of serial writing in England, they have also remained alert to more recent techniques of composition, and have produced some persuasively euphonious and inventive examples, especially in the field of chamber music. Among the most memorable of Elisabeth Lutyens's works are her Six Tempi for 10 Instruments, Wind Quintet, and *Wittgenstein Motet* for unaccompanied chorus. Gerhard has a wider emotional range, and a still greater inventiveness in sound, and behind the novelty of the sound and texture an essentially classical spirit, and sometimes a Haydnesque wit, are clearly discernible. The best of his recent works include a Second String Quartet, superbly original in its treatment of this traditional and nowadays unfashionable medium, Hymnody for eleven players, a Nonet for wind and an entertaining *Concerto for 8* (both of which brilliantly and amusingly incorporate the piano accordion into the instrumental ensemble), and a Concerto for Orchestra.

XIX

MUSIC IN THE UNITED STATES

By Robert Layton

It was not until recently that Europe was made aware of the growing importance of American music. For long, America has been regarded as an appendage to the European scene, and it will doubtless be some time before the somewhat patronising attitude of the European will give way to a rightful assessment of developments in the New World. At the present moment, the United States offers a diversity and range of achievement that can well withstand comparison with that of the Old World. It has produced a number of important composers that conceive music in relation to a world of experience that is specifically American, and who have freed themselves of the subservience to European models that has marked previous generations. This world of experience embraces impulses from a wide variety of sources ranging from indigenous folk music of all kinds to the syncopations of jazz. It has been enriched by intimate contact with some of the most influential twentieth-century composers including Stravinsky, Schoenberg and Hindemith, who sought refuge in America from the upheavals in Europe. But whereas the earlier American composer of the century presented a compound of ill-digested influences, the contemporary composer has been far more successful in assimilating Stravinsky and Hindemith into his own language.

A tradition is not formed overnight, and there is no doubt that American music owes a debt of some magnitude to Charles Ives (1874-1954), whose liberating influence made possible the work of so many of his successors. His disregard for the accepted conventions of musical procedure, his cheerful iconoclasm led him into paths that often startle and bewilder; his work shows an extraordinary admixture of sheer genius and downright incompetence. His experiments at the turn of the century often foreshadow the most radical developments of Bartók and Schoenberg before 1914, but they are empirical rather than systematic in nature, and they appear alongside passages of hair-raising banality. Always vital, stimulating and often amusing, completely unpredictable, thoroughly uneven, wildly prolific and entirely uninhibited, Ives is a 'sport' in the biological sense of the word, a figure unique in the history of music. Both he and Carl Ruggles (1876-) are interesting pioneer figures, but it is the generation that came into prominence during the thirties and forties that set American music firmly on its feet. The most important of them are Walter Piston (1894-), Roger Sessions (1896-), Roy Harris (1898-) and Aaron Copland (1900-). With the exception of Sessions, all of them studied with Nadia Boulanger during the twenties; it is however, a measure of their individuality that few traces of French influence can be discerned in their work.

At first Walter Piston succumbed to the heady wine of French influence; his Gallic sympathies emerge in the attractive and high-spirited ballet score, *The Incredible Flutist* (1938). But already in the *Violin Concerto* (1939) it is evident that he was turning from the cosmopolitan to the indigenous, though there is nowhere a deliberate and self-conscious cultivation of an American national style. The linear diatonicism and rhythmic vitality that is the hallmark of so much modern American music is clearly discernible in this fine score and in the impressive series of symphonies that have since followed from his pen. It was the *Second Symphony* (1943) that established him as a major symphonist, but only in the Third (1947) did the full extent of his powers become apparent.

Piston carefully eschews sensational orchestral effects, and aims rather for the utmost clarity of texture. His powers of sustained writing are nowhere better demonstrated than in the first movement of the *Third Symphony*. Here his skill and restraint in handling the massive climax of the movement, his brilliant disposition of the brass in preparing moments of climax, the resourceful treatment of the thematic material, the polyphonic interest of the texture and the sense of organic growth that informs the whole, add up to a formidable achievement. His *Fourth Symphony* (1950) is probably his finest work; a warm and gentle lyricism illumines its pages. The first movement is proportioned with a classical feeling for symmetry and design, its scherzo is full of invention and vitality, while the third movement contains some inspired writing of the utmost poetry and imaginative resource. The line is firmly sculptured and moves with a real sense of purpose. A virile and exciting finale ends the work, which is far more compelling than the *Sixth Symphony* (1956), which is better known in this country. The same fine craftsmanship and feeling for the medium distinguishes his chamber music; the *Piano Quintet* (1949) is a masterly contribution to the literature of American chamber music, and there is a diverting *Sonatina for Violin and Harpsichord* (1945). Piston does not court public favour by colourful harmonies or striking tunes, and his unsensational but nevertheless individual style is never likely to gain a wide following: he is, essentially, a musician's musician.

If Piston is the scholarly and academic composer of his generation, Roger Sessions, a pupil of Bloch, is the radical. Like Piston he is an influential teacher and is widely respected in the United States. He originally attracted attention by the series of *avant-garde* concerts that he gave in collaboration with Aaron Copland during the twenties. His idiom is distinctly less American than that of Roy Harris or Aaron Copland; his melodic lines are highly angular and he often writes for long stretches without a clearly defined key centre. His scores are extremely elaborate and often congested; the *Second Symphony* (1944-46) affords a good example of this.

Neither he nor Copland has been so fascinated by the problems of the symphony as Roy Harris. His *First Symphony* (1933) is a remarkably mature work, powerful in impact and concentrated in design, although the lyrical slow movement tends to sprawl. The *Third Symphony in One Movement* (1937) is a taut, intense work and well deserves its fame; for here in contrast with Barber's *First Symphony* (1936 r. 1943), we have an entirely successful approach to the one-movement structure. The music moves forward relentlessly from the very opening bars until the eloquent and massive epilogue. Its integration of material, its compelling sense of purpose, its seemingly inexhaustible vitality and drive, its original handling of the orchestra and the rugged strength of the melodic line, are all distinguishing features of an undoubted masterwork. His harmonic palette is richer and more varied than that of Piston; his feeling for organic growth greater than that of Copland. His unmistakably American personality emerges, too, in the *Third String Quartet* (1937), a set of four preludes and fugues, modal in character and revealing a scholarly but fresh approach to the medium. The rhythmic variety of the second fugue and the insistent melancholy of the expressive prelude to the third are both highly personal. Every bar of the work bears the indelible imprint of Harris' style. His output during the forties and fifties has not appreciably diminished, but his style does not seem to have undergone any major development. The *Seventh Symphony* (1951) shows no advance musically or spiritually on its predecessors, though it is a fine work in one continuous movement, characteristic in utterance and full of powerful sweeping paragraphs and impressive climaxes.

Despite Harris' achievements as a symphonist, it is Aaron Copland who has captured the popular imagination as the most characteristic of American composers. Certainly his style embraces a wider range than that of either Harris or Piston; impulses from the world of jazz, the folk music of New England, and even Latin American sources have fertilised his style. However, the high-powered, robust humour of his most popular scores like *El Salon Mexico* (1936) or *Rodeo* (1942) do not give the whole picture. Copland's musical personality is a complex mixture of moods and styles. The cerebral *Piano Sonata* (1939-41) with its fascinating sonorities, the contemplative *Quiet City* (1940) and the magnificent *Third Symphony* (1946) give an idea of his wide emotional spectrum. Stravinsky has undoubtedly left an imprint on Copland (just as Hindemith has on younger men like Bernstein and Dello Joio) which is clearly visible in the Sonata. The jagged rhythms and angular line of the earlier *Sextet* (1937)[1] shows the more radical and experimental side of his nature. But the ballet, *Appallachian Spring* (1944), shows just how well Stravinsky's influence has been absorbed into the main stream of his style. This score, with its rich and gentle

1 This is an arrangement for clarinet, piano and string quartet of his *Short Symphony* (1933), the second of the three.

fantasy on the one hand and its fabulous vitality on the other, has been with some justice declared the most beautiful work to come out of America. The *Third Symphony*, with its proliferation of diverse rhythmic patterns, is evidence of his mastery in constructing a large-scale musical edifice; this is a copiously inventive score from a mind rich in imaginative resource and of wide human sympathies. It is a comprehensive musical experience.

There are other composers of this generation who have made an important contribution to the literature of the American symphony. They include Howard Hanson (1896-), Henry Cowell (1897-) and Randall Thompson (1899-). Hanson writes in a frankly Romantic style often indebted to Scandinavian nationalism in general and Sibelius in particular, as witness his *Third Symphony* (1938). He has also been drawn to the one-movement symphony, and in his *Fifth* (1954), subtitled *Sinfonia Sacra*, there are some individual touches. Cowell is an extremely prolific composer, who like Ives is uneven and unpredictable. He, too, has a streak of the undisciplined experimenter in him, but in a work like his *Fourth Symphony* (1946) he is well in command of his material. Elsewhere in some of his piano music and in the *Eleventh Symphony* (1953), subtitled *The Seven Rituals of Music*, his inventive exuberance gets the better of his good judgment.

Considerations of space prevent more than a mention of the work-manlike Thompson or such interesting figures of the generation as Douglas Moore (1893-), the composer of an opera, *The Devil and Daniel Webster* (1938), and a symphonist as well, Virgil Thomson (1898-) and Howard Swanson (1899-).

Probably Samuel Barber (1910-) is the most innately musical of American composers, though his achievement does not match that of say, Harris or Copland. He first attracted wide attention during the late thirties with the *Adagio for Strings* (from his String Quartet) and a *Symphony in One Movement*, both dating from 1936. The one-movement symphony still shows him responding to influences such as Sibelius and Strauss, and the seams in its structure are well visible. There is an abundance of lively invention in this score but even in its revised form it is not as closely-knit and unified in feeling as a one-movement work should be. That he has a perfect sense of balance and proportion emerges in an earlier work, the Overture, *The School for Scandal* (1933), a graduation piece, which is a little masterpiece, full of sparkle and warmth. His fresh, engaging lyricism is a prominent feature of the *Cello Concerto* (1945) and the finely sustained slow movement of the *Second Symphony* (1944 r. 1947). Like Copland he also came for a time under the spell of Stravinsky, whose personality can be felt roaming the pages of the *Capricorn Concerto* (1944), but this was not a lasting influence. It is surprising, in view of his lyrical gifts and the fact that he was trained as a singer, that Barber has not shown himself more sensitive in his treatment of words. His output of songs is uneven and relatively unimportant. Amongst the finest, however, are the post-war *Hermit Songs*, which take a place of honour in the literature of American song.

William Schuman (1910-) has less lyrical inclination and seems to have turned to the symphony as the main vehicle for his trenchant and hard-hitting style. It was with his *Third Symphony* (1941) that he gained critical renown. An original piece, it is one of the few modern scores to employ fugal textures effectively; there is a similarly successful passage in his *American Festival Overture* (1939). It is a spacious work on the whole, with a deeply-felt and highly poetic slow movement called *Chorale* and a final *Toccata* that must be accounted a considerable feat of orchestral virtuosity. The *Symphony for Strings* (his Fifth) which followed in 1943, and the one-movement *Sixth Symphony* (1948) have firmly consolidated his position as one of America's leading symphonists. The last work has not perhaps the sense of purpose and cohesion that one encounters in Harris, but it has the intensity of a fiery imagination. Schuman's symphonic style is easily recognisable; there is a rich harmonic colouring, an extremely keen sense of rhythm and for the most part, a genuine sense of forward movement. However, at climaxes his scoring, which is otherwise most highly effective, seems to be brash and occasionally verges on the hysterical. His other music, including a *Fourth String Quartet* and a ballet, *Undertow* (1945), does not quite match the quality of the symphonies.

But there are many other composers of this generation who have made names for themselves. Composers like Norman Dello Joio (1913-) and Ellis Kohs (1916-) have responded to the stimulus of

Hindemith's music, although the work of the former often wears a more sunny and Gallic aspect. French influences (and particularly that of Milhaud) have also played their part in moulding the style of the highly extrovert and dynamic Paul Bowles (1911-). More widely known outside America is Paul Creston (1906-), who allows himself a more opulent and Romantic harmonic palette. His symphonies, however, often come perilously close to the stock gestures and common-place language of the film screen. Two of the younger composers of the generation, both born in 1915, are David Diamond and Vincent Persichetti; both are fairly traditional in outlook. David Diamond is often content with material of insufficient character to sustain the superstructure he imposes on it; thus, his *Fourth Symphony* (1945) testifies to a splendid command of craftsmanship but leaves a final impression of mere facility. His best-known works are the incidental music to *Romeo and Juliet* (1947), which has some attractive and poetic touches, and the *Rounds for Strings* (1944), a score terse in utterance, vital in conception and optimistic in feeling.

Persichetti's scores often contain music of striking power. His *Fourth Symphony* (1951) opens with a pregnant figure but unfortunately he seems unable to sustain it in the remaining part of the first movement. American works often set out brilliantly but do not always arrive; Dello Joio's *St Joan Symphony* is an instance in point, where the promise of the opening pages is not fulfilled. Persichetti's score offers many incidental beauties, though it is not as serious in content and as organic in feeling as a Piston or a Harris symphony. He seems happier in a work like the *Psalm for Band* (1952), which has a moving and dignified opening. Although both Diamond and Persichetti are still comparatively unknown outside the United States, they are figures who inspire respect, and it would be wise to suspend an assessment of their importance until more of their music becomes available in scores or on records.

Similarly, little of Elliot Carter's work is known here, so that again it is only possible to form an imperfect picture of his stature. Born in 1908, he studied with Piston and Nadia Boulanger, and has evolved in his later works a language of some rhythmic complexity and thematic economy, a good instance of which is to be found in the

String Quartet (1951). He is not the only experimenter of his generation, for we must include the name of John Cage (1912-), whose cheerful antics on prepared pianos have hugely diverted European audiences since the war. It is difficult, however, to discover any musical significance whatsoever in his dreary and uneventful *String Quartet* (1950). A far more serious figure is Wallingford Riegger (1885-), who belongs to the generation before Piston and Harris, and is a contemporary of Charles Griffes (1884-1920). Riegger's inquiring mind led him into serial paths at a comparatively late stage in his career, though his *Third Symphony* (1948), for all its brilliance of texture and fascinating sonorities, does not wholly measure up to symphonic proportions.

Amongst the younger generation of composers the most notable are Leonard Bernstein (1918-), Harold Shapero (1920-), Lukas Foss (1922-) and Peter Mennin (1923-). Bernstein and Foss are both fine executants; the former is immensely gifted and extremely versatile, appearing as a conductor and pianist. He has composed ballet and film scores, Broadway musicals as well as symphonies. His *Age of Anxiety* (1949) hardly sustains its claims as a symphony in terms of concentrated musical thinking, but it does contain music of outstanding fantasy. Bernstein has a genuine melodic gift, a penchant for evocative textures and a flair for the orchestra. Alongside this brilliance, there is also music of real feeling in the closing pages of this symphony. Lukas Foss is a composer whose work has the same healthy affirmative features but his writing has more concentration and tautness. Stravinsky has influenced him a little in his *A Parable of Death*, though this influence is by no means as marked as it is in Harold Shapero's *Symphony for Classical Orchestra* (1948). This work is important not so much for its achievement but for its exceptional promise. The rhythmic vitality of Stravinsky does not obscure his admiration for classical models and the resultant synthesis is both stimulating and original. This score is typically American and in its first movement offers musical thinking of real lucidity. Both the *Symphony* and a *Sonata for Piano* (Four Hands) augur well for the future.

The youngest and most prolific of the four is Peter Mennin, whose *Third Symphony* (1946) was written when he was only twenty-three. Mennin has a capacity to conceive music in long paragraphs, and his well-knit first movement makes a great impact on the listener by its astounding assurance. Here is a composer who knows what he wants to say and says it without striking any false attitudes. The slow contemplative second movement (in which the shades of Vaughan Williams make themselves felt) is a splendid foil to the bracing vigour of the first and contrasts splendidly with the finale, a long sustained series of climaxes of seemingly inexhaustible energy. Its indebtedness to Walton's *First Symphony* is obvious and this inclination is confirmed by a later work, the *Concertato for Orchestra* (1951). Mennin often tends to overscore (there is an instance of this in his *Sixth Symphony*) but for the most part his effects are carefully and simply calculated. Though his music can be a veritable powerhouse of activity, he can be serenely contemplative as in the opening of the slow movement of the *Fifth Symphony*. His work with its positive philosophy, its sense of purpose and its fine craftsmanship is indicative of the healthy state of much American music of this generation of composers.

But America is a vast continent and many more composers than can possibly be accommodated here clamour for attention. Many of them like Ingolf Dahl (1912-) or Ben Weber (1916-) are highly accomplished artists, whose future development must be watched with interest. Suffice it to say that music is flourishing in the United States in a way that it has never done before, and that the foundations of a common musical language of a specifically American stamp have been laid by Harris, Piston, Copland and their younger colleagues. Theirs is a solid achievement which compares favourably with the instability of the post-war European musical world, and it is not a bad inheritance to pass down to the younger talents that are rising in the second half of the century.

What these younger talents have achieved is now described in:

THE NEW MUSIC IN A NEW WORLD

By Wilfrid Mellers

IT HAS been difficult for European composers, with so much past behind them, to release themselves from what Hardy called 'the pain of consciousness'. But we can trace how it gradually happened in considering how Schoenberg is Wagner's successor, and Webern, Schoenberg's: how Messiaen follows Debussy: and how Webern and Messiaen effect the transition to Boulez and Berio. In all of them there's a partial retreat from the West, and an affiliation with techniques and philosophies having contact with pre-Renaissance Europe and, still more, with Oriental cultures. But the transition has been hard, and is still uneasy: whereas the American retreat from the West has been more empirically spontaneous. This is natural enough, both because America had less consciousness of the past, and also because her polyglot culture, Janus-wise, faced East as well as West. Even in the central figures of the American scene one finds elements that are in part a denial of the West: consider the final movements of Ives's *Concord Sonata* and of the *Piano Sonata* of Copland, both the creation of great American humanists. So it isn't surprising that *avant-garde* tendencies should have been manifest in American music way back in the years of the First World War: nor that they should have more to do with Debussyan empiricism than with Webernian serialism. One of the key-works in the early history of 'progressive' music in America is the extraordinary *Piano Sonata* that Charles Griffes (1884–1920) wrote towards the end of his short life. This employs static Debussyan harmonies and Sciabinesque 'raga' formations to generate, from Eastern techniques, a peculiarly Western frenzy. Sophisticated though the idiom is, this music of the asphalt jungle could have been created only in America; still more typical is a phenomenon like Henry Cowell (born 1897) who is what Debussy might have been, shorn of most of his genius, and brought up in the streets of San Francisco and on farms in the Mid-West, by parents who believed that children, like plants, should be left to grow.

Cowell was familiar with Chinese theatre music, Japanese children's street songs, and the fiddle music of the American folk before he knew anything about Brahms or Beethoven. He played the fiddle by ear at the age of five, and began his composing career at the age of eight, not so far behind Mozart. He composed empirically, experimenting with the noises he could extract from an upright piano. Debussy's moment of sensation becomes, with him, the (American) Moment of Sensation, with a capital M and S. But although the composition in the piano pieces Cowell produced during his teens is rudimentary, their sound-sensation remains invigorating after forty odd years. In a piece called *The Banshee*, a piano's strings become a harp capable of an infinite gamut of pitches; the experiment has become the experience. This is the work of an aboriginal, the American boy in the woods, who didn't lose his innocence when grown up, he acquired some academic know-how. Cowell's vastly prolific later output is not very good music, and he's a figure of historical rather than of intrinsic interest. None the less we can see from his youthful piano pieces why he has become a father-figure to the American *avant-garde*; and it's this quality of aboriginality that sometimes makes American *avant-garde* music more congenial than its European counterpart.

Certainly the quality is present in the major figure of the older generation, Edgard Varèse (1885–1965) who was (significantly) born in Paris, and became an American citizen in 1916. He called the first work to which he owns *Amérique*, because it was a New World of sound; but if one listens to his *Offrandes*, written in 1921, one can hear how this new world—like that of his friend, colleague and contemporary, Charles Griffes—is related to the world of Debussy. Varèse has told us that, as a young man, he admired Debussy above all composers —'for his economy of means and clarity, and the intensity he achieved through them, balancing with almost mathematical equilibrium timbres against rhythms and textures, like a fantastic chemist'. The chemical metaphor is significant, and links up with Varèse's complementary admiration for Satie, who wrote 'some rather remarkable music, such as the Kyrie from his *Messe des Pauvres*, a music which always reminds me of Dante's Inferno, and strikes me as a kind of pre-electronic music'. Varèse thus saw Debussy and Satie as a starting-point for his own experiments, since if one liberates the chord from antecedence and consequence, the logical step is to proceed to the liberation of the individual sound. This is not just a technical procedure; it is also a new (and at the same time very old) musical philosophy. Varèse must be the earliest composer to reject the Renaissance conception of art as expression and communication; music he composed during the twenties anticipates by thirty years some of the discoveries of the mid-twentieth century *avant-garde*. Bypassing twelve-note serialism (which he regards as a musical 'hardening of the arteries' because of its dedication to notated, equal tempered pitch), he makes manifest the prophecies of Busoni in his *Entwurf einer Neuen Aesthetick der Tonkunst*, becoming at once a magical composer like Messiaen and a scientific composer like Stockhausen: and demonstrating that the two types are in fact complementary in that they effect a revelation, rather than an incarnation, of natural law. Dedekind said of mathematicians: 'We are a divine race, and possess the power to create.' Certainly to live in a scientific-mathematical universe is inevitably to lose consciousness of self; and it is significant that Varèse—who had some scientific training and as a youth considered the possibility of becoming a mathematical engineer—should, in naming one of his works *Arcana*, specifically relate the revelation of natural order to the activities of the alchemists.

So it is not surprising that Varèse's highly sophisticated music should be also primitive (and often Oriental) in the sense that it does not involve harmony, but rather consists of non-developing patterns and clusters of noises in varying timbre and tension: which interact in a manner that Varèse has compared (in detailed if inaccurate analogy) to rock-formation and crystal mutation. ('I was not influenced by composers as much as by natural objects and physical phenomena. As a child, I was tremendously impressed by the qualities and character of the granite I found in Burgundy . . . And I used to watch the old stone-cutters, marvelling at the precision with which they worked. They didn't use cement, and every stone had to fit and balance with every other . . .') This conception of music as sound-architecture survives when the development of electronic resources finally gave Varèse an opportunity to 'realise' his theories. Whether through indirect human agency or electronics, composition for Varèse is 'process'. 'I am fascinated by the fact that through electronic means one can generate a sound instantaneously . . . you aren't programming something musical, something to be done, but using it directly, which gives an entirely different dimension to musical space and projection. For instance, in the use of an oscillator, it is not a question of working against it or taming it, but using it directly without, of course, letting it use you. The same pertains to mixing and filtering. To me, working with electronics is composing with living sounds, paradoxical though that may appear.' Nothing could be further from the mathematically determined electronic composers such as Milton Babbitt. 'He (Varèse has said) wants to exercise maximum control over certain materials, as if he were *above* them. But I want to be *in* the material, part of the acoustical vibration, so to speak. Babbitt composes his materials first and then gives it to the synthesiser, while I want to generate something directly by electronic means. In other words, I think of musical space as open rather than bounded, which is why I speak of projection in the sense that I want simply to project a sound, a musical thought, to initiate it, and then let it take its own course.'

None the less, Varèse's music does not take the ultimate step to completely open forms and improvisation. In one sense his music is more closely rooted in traditional concepts than is the recent music of Messiaen and Boulez, let alone Stockhausen, for it still implies some kind of dichotomy between Nature and the Self. The structure of a comparatively recent work such as *Deserts* (1953) may seem to be independent of the will's volition, but the controlling force is still the human imagination: which achieves a powerful image of man's isolation, while enabling him to come to terms with the alien universe in which he exists. The music explores the deserts of wind, of sand and sea and rock, of the city street, and those vaster deserts within the human mind. Normal orchestral wind instruments interact with electronically processed natural sounds (of wind, sea, street and factory), while a large percussion band serves as liaison between the human and the non-human world. The humanly operated 'noise' of the percussion doesn't seem to save the human from being threatened by the non-human in a series of cumulatively increasing tensions, and the end of the work, in which noise fades into the eternal silence, is grim rather than assuaging. None the less, there is grandeur, as well as excitement, in Varèse's attempt to emulate, through human means, the processes of Nature; and if the music is frightening (because it admits that the human mind has lost touch with natural order) it is also unafraid (because the admission helps us to live again).

Maybe only God can make a tree, but Man may at least make sounds behave like crystals: so there is a powerful affirmation behind Varèse's bringing together of the aural disparities of the natural world. Whereas Ives (1874–1954), who in some of his music attempted something comparable, was content to be humanly amorphous, Varèse sought the scientist's precision: which could not ultimately be achieved because an artist, being human, is humanly fallible. In this respect, Varèse has more in common with a visual artist like Jackson Pollock than with Ives, or with any earlier musician, and both Varèse and Pollock seek to *reveal* the (basically mathematical?) order inherent in the natural world. This is the artist's new social justification, if justification is necessary: as Harry Partch (born 1901), another senior 'progressive', seems to think it is. Like Cowell—and unlike Varèse, whose background is both sophisticated and European—Partch is an American aboriginal, brought up in the parched and parching wastes of Arizona and New Mexico. From his earliest years he rejected the paraphernalia of harmonised music: rediscovered the justly intoned monody and the rhythms of primitive and Oriental cultures: and designed his own instruments, which are tuned to a forty-three-tone to the octave scale, and are capable of fairly extensive mono-phonic, if not harmonic, tonal organisation. But this turn to the East is as instinctive, as non-wilful, as that of Varèse: as we may see if we compare Varèse's *Deserts* with Partch's *Windsong* which was written as an accompaniment to a cinematic version of the Apollo and Daphne story, and deals specifically with the metamorphosis, indeed the loss, of human identity in the contemplation of the immense solitudes of (American) Nature—of the non-human world. Varèse's score sometimes reminds us of the distonated screach of Japanese *gagaku* music, while Partch's score reminds us of the infinitely slow, microtonal wail of Japanese *koto* music; yet in both cases the affinity comes not from imitation, but from the attempt to create musical images for emptiness, space and non-temporality.

Normally, however, Partch is a magic composer who, like Carl Orff in Europe, relates music directly to theatrical action; both want to renew a moribund society by rediscovering the instinctual springs of life. Partch thinks the proper function of music is that which it fulfilled in classical Greek drama; his own 'musicals' may be considered as an American version of the still vital popular tradition of the Japanese *kabuki* theatre, aiming at a renewal of modern life by incantation, by 'spiritual' monody and by 'corporeal' rhythm. In *The Bewitched*, described as a Dance-Satyr, four lost Musicians consult an aged Seer, seeking a remedy for the ills of the modern world, and learn that they already possess—in being true to the moment—the only truth that is humanly apprehensible. 'Truth is a sandflea; another moment must find its own flea.' So the Musicians are also Clowns, divine fools, and outsiders, bums, hoboes—like Partch himself, who for eight years lived by riding the rails. When social satire and musical parody dissolve into what Partch calls slapstick, this dadaism links contemporary non-values to values so old that they seem eternal. Human beings who microtonally yell, moan, shout, wail, guffaw, or grunt in jazzy abandon or hysteria may become indistinguishable from hooting owls, barking foxes, and the wild cats of the woods; but in returning below consciousness to Nature, they may rediscover their true selves. In a prelude to Scene 10 the wailing pentatonic chant evokes an age-old quietude that is none the less full of longing. Significantly, it is based on a cantillation of the Cahuilla Indians—aboriginal Americans who live in the emptiness of the Californian deserts. This weird chant, sounding the more disturbing against the wavering ostinati of Partch's forty-three-note reed organs, reminds us simultaneously of what home means, and of what it means to be homeless.

In Partch's theatre works jazz appears, usually parodistically. But jazz isn't only a negative force; it's also part of our intuitive rediscovery of our passional life, and has had so pervasive an influence because, starting as the outcry of a dispossessed race, it came to stand simultaneously for the protest of man alienated from Nature, and also as a reminder of the corporeal vigour that modern man has surrendered. So it isn't surprising that jazz, in America, has undergone a development parallel to that in the music we have discussed. Ornette Coleman is a jazz saxophonist who couldn't, during the formative years of his career, read musical notation, though he has since taken lessons with Gunther Schullar. His 'composition' was thus inevitably spontaneous, like that of primitive oral cultures. In a piece such as *Lonely Woman* there is, of course, a corporeal beat such as is alien to the music of Varèse, if not Partch; but against the implicit beat the drumming is of almost Asiatic complexity, numerical and additive rather than divisive. Moreover, there is no harmony instrument, and the minimum of harmonic implication. The solo voices, overriding the beat with Charlie Parker-like freedom, collide in dissonant heterophony; and the lines are not only of extreme rhythmic flexibility, they're also fragmented, disrupted by silence. Despite the sophistication, the effect is disturbingly primitive: like a more distraught and nervous version of the field holler, wherein the Negro cried of his isolation to the empty fields. A white jazz clarinetist, Jimmy Giuffre, has carried this process a stage further, for he has dispensed with 'beat' altogether, and created improvised clarinet monody in complex numerical rhythms and with effects of pitch distortion (achieved by split reeds and overblowing) that have affinities with Asiatic techniques. These strange nocturnal bird and animal, as well as human, noises link up with Varèse and Partch: with the sound, if not the philosophy, of electronic music: and with both the technique and the philosophy of the music of John Cage (born 1912).

For Cage's music, no less that the jazz surrealism of the later Ornette Coleman and Jimmy Giuffre, is a descent below consciousness and an abnegation of the Will. The parallel between Partch and Cage's early music is also close, for both discarded harmony and returned to music as incantation, conceived monophonically in line, numerically in rhythm. His 'night music', *She is Asleep* (and maybe dreaming), is scored for wordless voice and prepared piano: and is a ritual murmuring of the unconscious comparable to Partch's aboriginal chants and to Giuffre's solo clarinet. Similarly, Cage's *Sonatas and Interludes* for prepared piano remind us of the Polynesian sounds of Partch's invented instruments, with an occasional hint of disembodied jazz, if the appropriately paradoxical expression be permitted. These pieces are highly musical and very beautiful; but Cage apparently came to think that their 'chronometric' construction on *ragas* and *talas* was no less an evasion than the chromatic serial principle which he had already abandoned in rejecting European harmony. In any case he gave up humanly pre-ordained structures and handed over to chance operations —the toss of a coin, the throw of dice, the noting of accidental imperfections in the manuscript paper. Though these methods produced some exciting noises (for instance, the Carillon pieces which sound like Japanese temple bells tolling a paean not to God but to Nothingness), they are in effect identical with the strict serialist's mathematically pre-ordained order; both seek to free music, as far as is possible, from subjectivity (composer's, performer's and listener's) and from human error.

In later works such as the *Concert* for piano and orchestra Cage completes the composer's abdication. He no longer notates his material, but merely offers hints for improvisation. The succession and duration of the parts are dependent on chance operations, and also on the sub- or semi-conscious reactions of the participants. Each performance is inevitably different; and while the texture of sound is comparable with that of Varèse in that the instruments play microtonally in an infinite gamut of pitches, the chaotic amorphousness tends to be relaxed in effect, as compared with Varèse's impersonal order. Varèse's music seems to be beyond conscious volition, like Nature herself, whereas Cage's music—by this time—in fact is so, for the forest or the city street take over from man.

While we can't help feeling that the loss of Cage's aural sensitivity is regrettable, he would consider our objection in the strict sense impertinent, for he is no longer concerned with 'so-called music'. Indeed, since each player is instructed to play all, any, or none of the notes allotted to him, it is theoretically possible, if improbable, that a performance could result in complete silence: an ultimate condition which Cage has indeed realised in his notorious 4' 32" for piano. Clearly this is an end: which may also be a beginning in that in possessing so completely blank an innocence Cage can be, like Gertrude Stein and Paul Klee, 'as though new born, entirely without impulse, almost in an original state'. However self-destructive such an attitude may be from our Western standpoint, it is interesting that there should be something like a post-Cage generation of composers in the States, some of whom are literally a new race of composers in that they have never received, and have no use for, any training in the harmonic traditions of Europe. Certainly the degree of talent exhibited by this group is in no way dependent on conventional expertise. No orthodox training would be necessary to create Morton Feldman's (born 1926) *Durations*, which are scored for a number of instruments all playing from the same part, so that one couldn't hope for a more complete rejection of dualism. They play mostly single, designated pitches, but although they begin simultaneously they are free to choose their own occurrences within a general given tempo. The instruments, in changing combinations, are thus 'reverberations' from a single sound source. The tones are always isolated, immensely slow, and delicately soft. Such simultaneous sounds as occur through overlapping of the durations are mostly unisonal or concordant. An infinitely slow drone on muted tuba, a third on muted string harmonics, sound as though the players are creating the tones out of eternal silence, and we are being born afresh in learning to listen to them. Music seems to have reached the point of extinction: yet the little that is left certainly presents the American obsession with emptiness completely absolved from fear. The rarefied tenderness seems to have the property of making us saner, rather than more mad.

The element of renewal in Feldman's music lies in the fact that choice is once more very important in his music; his isolated sounds are as scrupulously selected as are the isolated chords of Debussy, the composer with whom Feldman has most in common. A more widely relevant type of renewal may be exemplified in the graph pieces and *Available Forms* of another post-Cage composer, Earle Brown (born 1926) who claims to have learned more from the painting of Pollock and the mobiles of Calder than from any musician, including Cage. His graph pieces (of which the most extreme is *December 1952* for any number and any kind of instruments) notate only high, middle and low registers and densities, and exist only in their mobility, while they are being made; they are not composition, but a stimulus to musical activity, but differ from Cage's later work in that they call for creative instinct on the part of the performers. Brown's later open form works precisely notate pitch, timbre and often rhythm, but leave to the performers or conductor the decision as to the order in which the sound-events take place. Brown prefers to write for very large resources (his *Available Forms II* is scored for 98 instruments with two conductors who preserve independence during performance, though they have carefully rehearsed the sound-events); the sound of his music is thus remote from the hermetic tranquillity of Feldman, and is more comparable with the multiple-group pieces of Ives and Varèse than with the music of Cage. The human agency of the composer (who devised the complex sound-events), of the conductors (who decide when and in what order the events shall occur), and of the players (who must play the notes as written but not necessarily in temporal conjunction with one another) is immensely important. This is true even though Brown prefers to emulate the ambiguities, the 'open ends' of Nature rather than to impose his order on his material, which ranges from noise and 'inarticulate sounds' to sounds produced by highly sophisticated musical techniques.

In re-involving the performer in creation Brown is turning towards action, and in this resembles the composers who seem to have deliberately abdicated human responsibility. At the furthest swing of the pendulum from Europe's post-Renaissance obsession with the will, Cage and his disciples would free us from past and future, inviting us to enter an autonomous Now. Similarly, Robert Rauschenberg at one time painted completely white or completely black canvases, invoking the space, the nothingness within which we may perceive afresh the astonishingly disparate objects (introduced bodily into his later work) of the visible world. For Cage learning-to-hear, for Rauschenberg learning-to-see, are separate from action but not independent of it, since life must be lived in time. This is why 'any relevant action is now theatrical': a belief which has been actualised when Cage and Rauschenberg have collaborated with the dancer Merce Cunningham to complement their aural and visual images with movement in time and space.

This movement, however, like the hearing and seeing, has no before and after. There is no expressionist purpose, only a 'purposeful purposelessness', in the relationship between movement, sound and image in the work of the Merce Cunningham Dance Group. Thus in *Suite for Five* the actions—now gay, now anguished, now grotesque— are as diverse as Nature herself; yet in being purged of causation they are purged too of the nag of memory and the tug of desire. This they achieve *through* their lack of relationship to Cage's music, which is even more devoid of progression or motor rhythm than is Japanese temple music. The softly reverberative sounds of the prepared piano— occurring at chronometric points dictated by chance operations, and separated by immense silences—really do cause one to listen anew; while Rauschenberg's almost-blank costumes and décor help one to see the actions with unblinkered eyes.

This abstraction is preserved even when the ballet, such as *Crises*, seems to involve dramatic implications. Indeed in this ballet the crises of the title are erotic; yet the actions between the man and four women evade climax. The music is Conlon Hancarrow's celebrated studies for three player-pianos. The fantastic complexity of the poly-rhythms, which machines can negotiate when human beings couldn't, transmutes the sexy and nostalgic flavour of jazz and pop into looney hysteria. Yet the sounds preserve, through the mechanisation, a dis-embodied detachment, which communicates itself to the actions. For all the violence of the gestures and the sleaziness of the atmosphere, we are released from our more inchoate appetites in simply accepting them. Even they can take their place with 'the permanent emotions of Indian tradition'; and Merce Cunningham's *Solo* to Christian Wolff's pianistic explosions goes still further, for it induces a thera-peutic calm from the neurotic twitch and spastic shiver that we've come to recognise—at least since *West Side Story*—as gestures typical of our world and time. Both the abstraction of the mechanical and the dadaistic release into an eternal Now recall Satie's *Parade*; small wonder that John Cage, himself a Beckett clown, regards Satie with admiration.

We have seen that a part of the revolution in twentieth-century music has been a return to the unconscious and to levels of being that have affinities with those of primitive societies; and that this is probably a much more significant matter than a mere escape from our perplexities. Marshall McLuhan has suggested that just as the Elizabethans were poised between medieval religious, corporate experience and our modern individualism, so we 'reverse their pattern by confronting an electronic technology which would seem to render individualism obsolete and corporate interdependence mandatory'. Our ordinary perceptions and habits of behaviour are being remade by the new media; and we are finding the process both painful and chaotic because our heritage is of little help to us in dealing with the oral and aural (rather than literate and visual) civilisation which may be latent in the new technology. The modern physicist may have more in common with religious, medieval man, with the mystics of Oriental cultures, with the alchemists and even with the magicians of primitive societies, than he has with the post-Renaissance rationalist. If most of us have failed to grasp the nature of our metamorphosis, the reason may be that the visual chronology of Renaissance tradition has tied us to the conception of an historical past. This was irrelevant to primitive oral cultures; and may be equally so to our future.

On the other hand, we may think that the physical and mental changes we are undergoing—cataclysmic though they may be—can hardly reverse the destiny of the human race. We may be recovering some of the positive qualities of a primitive civilisation, learning to live, as a rural African lives, in the implicit magic, charged with emotion and drama, of the oral word (it is pertinent to note that Carl Orff will not allow children to study music in his school if they have already learned to read and write). But if we are rediscovering the 'rite words in rote order', we should remember that James Joyce's revoking of our remote, fin-like, fishy, Calibanistic ancestry is also a Wake and awakening. Our reborn primitivism has to contend with, not to evade, consciousness, for having thrown up a Shakespeare or a Beethoven we can't pretend they never existed. On the whole, this seems to be borne out by the history of music—'straight', jazz and pop—during the twentieth century.

XX

MUSIC IN THE U.S.S.R.

By Marcel Frémiot

THE HISTORY of the Soviet music differs essentially from that of the
Western countries. In France, for example, during the last twenty-five
years there has been an incessant conflict, and sometimes an inter-
penetration, not only of diametrically opposed aesthetics but of entirely
different languages and techniques. In the U.S.S.R. there has been
nothing of the kind, at least not if we take as our point of departure
the date of Serge Prokofiev's final return to his own country. For from
1934 onwards the main features of a language and an aesthetic common
to all creative artists had already been determined. Those grandiose
and somewhat overblown spectacles in which drama, music and
cinema combined to form an entertainment presented simultaneously
in several different theatres were seen no more; the concerts of the
Society for Contemporary Music came to an end; Stravinsky was
rejected on account of his 'cynical exploitation of Russian exoticism
and antiquity'; the works of the young Prokofiev (or some of them)
were said to be tainted with 'artificiality' and 'nihilist exaggerations';
Milhaud and Hindemith were labelled 'modernist' and the twelve-note
art of Schoenberg 'entirely formalist'; and nothing more was attempted
on the lines of Alexander Mossolov's Steel Foundry (rejected as 'natural-
ist') or M. F. Gnessine's Monument Symphonique. The R.A.P.M.[1] had
come to an end, and with it all these feverish activities and dissipation
of energy which may have been adventurous but were at any rate
dynamic. This whole epoch in fact was closed once and for all by the
declaration of the 17th Communist Party Congress.

And yet Prokofiev decided to go back definitely to the U.S.S.R.

[1] Russian Association of Proletarian Musicians.

A unique event in the musical history of modern times was in fact taking place in that country. For the first time the great mass of the people (and not merely an intellectual élite) was displaying both an interest in and a craving for contemporary music. And the State (and not merely a few private patrons) was encouraging this trend and providing invaluable assistance in the way of finance and organisation. How could any composer conscious of his responsibility as a citizen fail to appreciate this attitude? Prokofiev himself declared: 'When one returns to Russia after having lived abroad one feels that things are very different. Here people feel a need for scenic creation, and there can be no doubt as to what kind of subject will provide them with inspiration: it must be something heroic and constructive, for these are the qualities most characteristic of the present day. . . . Two things have struck me most in the U.S.S.R.: the extraordinary creative activity of the Soviet composers, and the enormous increase in the interest taken by the public in music as revealed in the vast number of new listeners in every walk of life who are filling our concert halls today.'

It was inevitable that a revolution of this kind should have raised some serious problems for composers, as regards both the form and content of their art. In the socialist society of the Soviet Union art is, by definition, a 'party' matter, and is practised 'to further the cause of the proletariat'. Its means of expression must be sought in the national traditions. It therefore seemed indispensable to establish as a fundamental principle the necessity for the artist and the people to draw their inspiration from the same sources. Hence the rejection of what was called 'naturalism'. To recreate in sound the atmosphere of a factory might very well excite the imagination of a composer. But although to a person of a speculative turn of mind the sound of eight horns blaring in the midst of a frenzied orchestral *tutti* may seem impressive, to the workman employed in the foundry it will merely seem ridiculous. And why go to a concert to meet again the deafening noise and stupefying rhythm of the machines, when most people would rather find there an echo of their inmost feelings or of their need for rest or strife? The 'content' upon which socialist realism will insist will be the artistic expression of the *essence* of things, and not of their outward aspect—the expression, that is to say, of the character and internal make-up of human beings. If it was relatively easy to agree about the aim to be pursued, it was far more difficult to see eye to eye with regard to the means to be employed to achieve it. Audiences were both new and vast numerically. The mass of the workers and peasants of which they consisted had up to now known nothing outside their own folk-lore. For the first time in centuries they were being introduced to 'high-brow' music, i.e. to a cultural level to the formation of which they had made no contribution. And their folk-lore, rich though it was, was very inferior in comparison to the rapid evolution that these same masses were in process of undergoing or had already attained in other spheres of life, whether intellectual, technical, moral or political.

Once these basic principles had been laid down, the whole history of Soviet music became the history of the tensions caused by attempts to reconcile these principles with the solutions proposed by the creative artists. Furthermore, all the mistaken judgments of the 'Westerners' in the face of the new Russian music have been due to the fact that they have always been expressed in terms of conflicting and entirely 'personal' aesthetic principles. They have also been due to the reactions of persons living in countries with age-old traditions of 'serious' music, whereas the Russian school has been in existence for barely a hundred years.

*   *   *

Ever since the foundation of the 'Union of Soviet Composers' in 1932 whose aims, as defined in their statutes, were to 'promote the creation of works worthy of the socialist era', a dual obligation was proclaimed: the necessity for musical works to have a 'social content', and the necessity of their being expressed in readily comprehensible language, which meant, in effect, that their idiom should be either classical, or derived from national folk-lore. This was the logical result of the Marxist-Leninist principles applied to art and re-affirmed by the 17th Communist Party Congress in 1934. It should be pointed out here that there was nothing in this that would seem shocking to a Russian composer. This double obligation was already, as it were, a double tradition of Russian music. On the ideological plane a dynamic urge towards the future, generous social aspirations and a desire to remain in contact with the masses were already manifest in the great classical composers, from Glinka to Rimsky-Korsakov, who on that account sometimes even incurred the displeasure of the ruling powers. On the technical plane, the entire Russian school had endorsed the declarations ot Glinka who aimed at 'uniting popular song with the good, old-fashioned Western fugue'. It is worth noting also that Reinhold Glière was born only eighteen years after Glinka died, and that Prokofiev was a pupil of Rimsky-Korsakov.

In point of fact there are a great many works written before the war in response to the demands made by the 17th Congress of the Party that are considered to be among their authors' most successful works and which are often performed in the 'West' at concerts of contemporary music. For example: (1) Prokofiev: *Violin Concerto No. 2* (1935), *Romeo and Juliet* (1935-6), *Peter and the Wolf* (1936), *Alexander Nevsky* (1938), *Piano Sonato Nos. 6 and 7* (1940); (2) Dmitri Shostakovitch: *Fifth Symphony* (1937), *Quintet* (1940); (3) A. I. Khatchaturian: *Piano Concerto* (1936) and *Violin Concerto* (1940); (4) N. I. Miaskovski: *Symphony No. 21* (1940). During the same period more than thirty new operas were produced. Most of these works, however, did not receive the approval of the Party. Accordingly, in fulfilment of a resolution of the Central Committee of February 10th, 1940, an important conference of musicians was held in Moscow. The resolution adopted referred to the 'progressive' role of the classical tradition and of popular art in the development of the 'realist' Soviet culture. It was also stated that 'fundamental theoretical questions were closely bound up with questions of an immediate and practical nature'. In fact, what the political and cultural Government authorities were seeking was a combative art that would produce immediate results. In the 'West' people spoke of an infringement of the liberty of the creative artist. Looking back after a lapse of time it would seem, rather, that these measures were taken in anticipation of international political events as part of a systematically organised and efficient psychological defence made necessary by a war that was now inevitable.

During this war the Composers' Union, in liaison with the military authorities, organised visits to the front by composers who had not been mobilised, and that is how the following works came to be written: The *Trench Symphony* by V. I. Shebalin; *Extreme-Orient* by L. K. Knipper; the *Red Army Symphony* by L. A. Polovinkin; numerous marches including the celebrated Voroshilov March by M. M. Ippolitov Ivanov, and great quantities of patriotic songs that were rapidly printed, broadcast and added to the repertory of the 'musical brigades' at the front. Other works arising out of the war were: the cantata *Avengers of the People* (1942) and the opera *Under Fire* (1943) by Dmitri Kabalevsky; the *Ballad of an Unknown Child* (1943) and *Ode to the End of the War* (1945) by Prokofiev, as well as works that have passed into the international symphonic repertory such as Shostakovitch's *Seventh* ('Leningrad') *Symphony* (1941), *Symphony No. 2* (1944) by Khatchaturian and *Symphony No. 5* (1944) by Prokofiev. All these works have a common content, linked with the destiny of the Fatherland. From a technical point of view none of these composers renounced (in their symphonic works at least) the technical features that characterised their pre-war creations. The predominant feature in the best of these works is not so much the 'noises of war' (which in any case are evoked rather than imitated) as the expression of human feelings. It is interesting to note, moreover, that the events of these years did not prevent the first performance, in 1941, of Prokofiev's ballet *Cinderella* or the composition of his opera *War and Peace* (1941-42).

The years immediately following the end of the war saw the creation of works that were less specifically 'dedicated', e.g. concertos and chamber music. Composers seemed in need of time in which to think over personal problems and an opportunity to indulge in less grandiose, if not less brutal, means of expression and to give fresh thought to problems of musical language. In any case, a Plenary Congress of composers, meeting in 1946, took note of a diminution in the volume of new works since the war ended, observed that 'the contemporary Soviet theme had almost disappeared from the works of composers', and deplored the existence of too many symphonies and chamber music works that were 'drab' and devoid of content. The Plenary Congress reminded members that however peaceful the edification of socialism would be in future, it would not tolerate any slackening off in the 'content value' of musical creations. Typical of this attitude was the criticism made by Khatchaturian with regard to the *Ninth Symphony* of Shostakovitch, which he reproached for 'not being a satisfactory completion of the trilogy of the seventh, eighth and ninth symphonies' consecrated to the war. It is true that this symphony does not end in a triumphant apotheosis. But does not the character of the *finale* point to greater depths—and for that matter, greater realism—in the art of Shostakovitch? For he allows us to feel that nothing is ever definitely accomplished, and that after victory, all the wounds of war have still to be healed. The Congress declared that the new 'content' would call for new forms, but reproached young composers for taking too much interest in the 'abstract' and 'decadent' music of the West, and for being interested only in the 'formal' methods of the great Soviet composers: this was indirectly aimed at Shostakovitch. The Congress reminded members finally that 'Soviet art can have no other aim than the interests of the people and the State'.

*   *   *

In 1948 I. Muradeli's opera, *The Great Friendship*, was produced. The libretto was judged to be historically inaccurate. The musical themes that accompanied the presence on the stage of the various peoples concerned and their national dances (Ossetians, Lesghians, Georgians and Cossacks) did not seem to have any connection with the well-known popular melodies of these people, and the harmonies were considered too discordant. This gave Andrei Zhdanov an opportunity of reminding a Conference of Soviet musicians what constitutes 'realism': the content must reflect faithfully Soviet reality, stressing especially the dynamic side; the language must be accessible and singable, of a high professional standard, and must take full account of the classical tradition and of the national characteristics contained in folk-lore.

It was in response to this proclamation that Shostakovitch wrote in 1949 his oratorio *The Song of the Forests* (on the reclamation of desert lands and the transformation of Nature by the planting of thousands of kilometres of forest trees); this was followed in the same year by Aroutinian's cantata *The Fatherland* (representing the triumphant march of Soviet men towards communism) and, in 1950, by Prokofiev's oratorio *In Defence of Peace* (exalting the Soviet people's ardour in the preservation of peace). To the same category belong symphonic works such as the violin concertos of Kabalevsky and Dvarionas, or Miaskovsky's *Symphony No. 27*. All this music is certainly 'clear' (it proclaims the sovereignty of the common chord), 'optimistic' and full of melody. To the unsophisticated music-lover this was modern music that was easy to understand. Others thought it showed a definite falling off when compared with the earlier works of the same composers—less interesting and less moving, despite its unhampered lyrical character and its individuality.

The pre-eminence of a 'singing' melody as one of the principal technical ingredients of realist music was now reinforced by the theories of B. V. Assafiev concerning the 'specificity' of music. Unwilling for music to be 'reduced to a simple combination of sounds', Assafiev rejected the definition of a musical image as a sound-image. Basing his theory on the 'obvious' part played by intonation in ordinary speech and on a material conception of the nature of art, Assafiev showed that the 'specificity' of music was due to the fact that it reflects reality in the form of 'intonation-images'. Hence the definition of music as 'the art of intonation'. Since melody consists of the union of several different intonations, 'all music is essentially melodic'. Moreover, according to Assafiev, 'all the other aspects of music (harmony, polyphony, instrumentation, form, development . . .) are subordinated to melody'. As to the nature of this melody, Assafiev demands that it should be 'clear, singable and organically linked with popular art' because 'singing is, *par excellence*, the image of melody'. From this he deduced the corollary that vocal music must take precedence over instrumental music. And this explains the relatively considerable number of cantatas, oratorios and operas written during this period.

As regards the reference to folk-lore, it was diversely interpreted. A certain number of composers thought that in future it would be sufficient to use actual folk melodies for their thematic material, but as this view was confined only to the external aspect of the question, it merely led to a new kind of formalism. This was the opinion of the Armenian composer Babadjanian, speaking for the younger generation: 'The exact transcription of popular songs or their intonations without any real understanding of the soul of a people only results in a superficial picture and not in a work of truly national character'.

Folk-lore themes used in their primitive state have no place in a work of 'serious' music unless they have a very definite expressive, intellectual and emotional value for the hearer. It is in this sense that Shostakovitch uses again in his *Song of the Forests* the theme of one of his extremely popular songs of peace. The song in praise of the successful accomplishment of the re-afforestation plan is thus naturally associated with the idea of peace inherent, in the minds of all who heard it, in the melody thus incorporated. Shostakovitch was to make a very systematic use of this procedure throughout his *Eleventh Symphony*, known as the *1905*. The themes of the revolutionary songs of the period constitute, in fact, the melodic basis and ideological substance of this work. But although this symphony was warmly applauded by the public in the U.S.S.R., it met with a very different reception in the 'West' from audiences knowing nothing of these songs. Thus the caustic Soviet criticism of an 'anti-national modernism' has in this case resulted in the creation of a truly national work, even if it is unable to make its full appeal outside its national frontiers.

The declarations of Zhdanov had still further consequences. Starting from the assumption that their country's main aim was to ensure the fullest development of human faculties, to abolish all conflict between man and man or between man and society, and to allow every manifestation of the human spirit a free outlet in an atmosphere of joy and enthusiasm, some composers formulated a theory of 'absence of conflict', which resulted in a sudden outpouring of works proclaiming a state of collective well-being and complacent optimism. They had also by-passed true realism, for personal dramas and human suffering cannot be entirely suppressed. Error and doubt as well as joy and hope are always present in every man, although it is true that in a harmonious and fraternal society, conceived with a view to human happiness, the positive elements may triumph more easily. And this, it would seem, was the answer conveyed by Shostakovitch in 1953 in his *Symphony No. 10*, a work with an intensely personal message, full of anxiety, but also of a cheerful dynamism. It is written in a very different style from that of the *Song of the Forests*, although remaining throughout in the classical Russian tradition. Having rejected the atonal, polytonal and dodecaphonic techniques, and being unable to confine himself to the tonic-and-dominant tonal system, Shostakovitch has forged for himself a language characterised by a maximum use of all the resources of 'modality'. And here again he is true to the Russian tradition.

*   *   *

Referring to the 24 *Preludes and Fugues*, op. 87, of Shostakovitch, a Soviet critic wrote as follows: '. . . alone with his abstract musical thoughts, the weight of his past has once again made itself felt. Once more we have heard those discords that torture the ear, those artificial constructions, those fatiguing and monotonous themes turned and twisted in every direction, those images reflecting an unhealthy nervous tension.' On the other hand, another critic praised this cycle as a work 'rich in content' and 'often of an epic character'. And he went on to recall the Russian tradition in the use and development of the fugue as exemplified in Tchaikovsky, Skriabin and Glazunov. In any case the work of Shostakovitch raises once again the problem of 'programme music': this essential element of realist-socialist music had also never been clearly defined. Some take the view that 'programme music' is music written on a literary theme, or at least having a concrete title. Others, again, hold that it is music inspired by an internal idea expressed in adequate musical forms. Thus Shostakovitch himself has said: 'For me works such as the preludes and fugues in *The Well-Tempered Clavier* hold a very profound meaning and consequently have a "programme" . . .'. And he cites as an example the *Prelude and Fugue in C sharp minor* in which, he says, are expressed 'the suffering and sorrow of the world'.

*   *   *

In an article written in January 1954 Shostakovitch wrote: 'In our discussions the essential argument must always be above all the high ideological and artistic qualities of a work, and not the question as to whether or not the composer belongs to such and such an artistic "movement".' It might be questioned whether, as far as certain critics

I

are concerned, these ideological discussions did not to some extent arise out of the conflict between the partisans of the common chord and the advocates of 'dissonant' music. In fact, the problem here was the problem of what constitutes 'newness' in art. For how many critics there are who condemn 'modernism' and demand with equal vehemence a 'really new spirit and a new art'! A leading article in *Pravda* of November 27, 1953, speaks of the importance of 'respecting the artist's right to be original and bold in his search for something new'. This was one of the problems which seems to have been discussed at the second Congress of the Composers' Union in 1957. Some people, however, take the view that 'newness' is not a matter of innovations in the *language* of music (which are always condemned under the label of 'modernism' or 'formalism'), but in its *'content'*. To this Shostakovitch replies: 'An art rich in content is always closely linked with the discovery of "new" things in life and the indispensable and inevitable search for the means of recording and fixing these new observations and sensations. If these means have not been discovered, then the "new" content has not found its proper expression either.' It would seem that the problem has been encountered more especially in the domain of opera. Out of the 120 operas composed between the two Congresses, only five or six were ever performed in more than one theatre. The reasons for this must be sought 'not in any theoretical objections, but in the atmosphere of boredom which surrounds so many operatic performances'. Hence the suggestion made by Shostakovitch recommending the establishment of 'an experimental theatre for opera which would introduce a breath of fresh air into the style and repertory of our great opera houses'.

*   *   *

It is obvious, and logical in a socialist society, that all these questions should be closely related to the cultural level of the masses. It is true that a gigantic effort is being made in this country to 'democratise' musical culture: schools of music are springing up everywhere and new conservatories; in every town of importance professional orchestras and operatic companies are being formed; and in both town and country there are innumerable societies of amateurs, folk-lore societies, popular orchestras and choirs. All these amateur artists have at their disposal every kind of pedagogic and material means to assist them in their training and, if need be, to facilitate their acquisition of professional status.

It is interesting to note that what seems to count most is not so much the number of music-lovers who listen to music, but the number of those who can make music for themselves. To appreciate the importance of this effort we must remember that in many of the Republics 'professional' music only came into existence after the October Revolution. Just as Glinka is now considered to be the 'Father of Russian music', there are many contemporary composers who will one day receive the same title in their own countries. For example: Jiganov (for his opera *Djalilée*) in the Tartar republic; Toulebaiev (for his *Birjan and Sara*) in Khazakhstan; Vassilenko and Achrafi (for their *Snowstorm*) in Uzbekhistan; Guerschfeld (for his *Grozovan*) in Moldavia; Saifiddinov (for his *Poulat and Gulrou*) in Tadzhikistan; Vlassov, Maldybaiev and Fere (for their *On the Banks of the Issk-Koul*) in Kirghiz.

It is easy to imagine the difficulties that may arise in connection with this effort of democratisation, especially when one realises how widely the Soviet Republics differ in their cultural development, bearing in mind, too, that a certain degree of 'harmonisation' is essential while they are all progressing together.

Moreover, it would be unjust to forget that in these countries where music (for State reasons as well as by popular tradition) is essentially functional (as it was, we must not forget either, in other epochs and for other classes of society) political events have left their mark. The war and subsequent periods of acute international tension acted as a brake on technical progress. For in order to have any effect it was essential for music to remain within the limits of current terminology.

The political leaders themselves were also a restraining influence. By reason of their own musical culture and personal tastes they remained attached to nineteenth-century modes of expression.

Finally, the great majority of the mass of the people (but this a universal phenomenon) showed a palpable lack of enterprise and a similar attachment to ancient modes of expression. There was another factor, too, invariably to be found in these circumstances, and that was the adoption by sections of society on the up-grade of the more enlightened cultural habits of the class or nation in decline.

All these facts, all these problems, these effects, these principles are closely interconnected; it is therefore practically impossible for a 'Westerner', however well disposed he may be *a priori*, to form a just and definite opinion as to the value of the achievements of Soviet music.

* * *

What, then, of the young generation of composers, those who were born after the October Revolution? They are often blamed by critics for their 'modernism' *à la* Shostakovitch or, worse still, *à la* Hindemith. In point of fact, in no score that I have seen is the influence of Hindemith specially discernible.

To discriminate is always delicate and hazardous. But among the composers whose works I have been able to read or hear the following seem to me to merit attention: Taktakichvili, a Georgian composer born in 1924, author of a *Concerto for Trumpet and orchestra* composed in 1955; Babadjanian, Armenian composer, born in 1921. His *Trio for Piano, Violin and Cello* (1952) and his *Rhapsody for orchestra* (1955) reveal a passionate temperament and a concise and taut musical style. He draws on the folk-lore of his country, but manifestly seeks to do more than rely on its rich external colour in order to attain a deeper and more genuine degree of authenticity. Another Armenian, Balassanian, in his *Seven Armenian Songs* for orchestra reminds one of Milhaud's *Carnaval d'Aix*. These two works are very much akin in the harmonic and even rhythmic treatment of the melodies. Finally, I would mention Chedrine, author of a *Concerto for Piano and Orchestra* (1954) and the ballet *The Little Hump-Backed Horse*. It is true he has not yet asserted fully his personality as regards melodic invention, and the influence of Prokofiev at his best is evident in all the other departments of his musical technique, but of all this younger generation his is perhaps the most engaging personality.

The harmonic language of all these composers is still very 'classical', and their lyricism recalls sometimes that of Rachmaninov. But they all possess an exceptional mastery of the orchestra, a suppleness in their handling of harmony-cum-rhythm that would have pleased Paul Dukas, and an evident interest in rhythmic expression.

* * *

In any case Soviet music during the last few years indicates a rupture with the style of the period 1948-1953. This rupture would seem to be confirmed by a leading article in *Pravda* of June 1958. It comments on a 'decree of the P.C.U.S.' dated May 28, 1958, 'concerning the correction of errors committed in the appreciation of the operas *The Great Friendship, Bogdan Kmelnitski* and *With All My Heart* by Muradeli, Dankevitch and Joukovski respectively. This decree defines in the first place the "positive role" of the resolution of February 1948 against the "false spirit of innovation which excluded the art of the people", recalls the "immutability of the fundamental principles expressed in the resolutions of the Party in regard to ideological questions", and also the "Leninist principles of party spirit and national character". On the other hand, the decree points out that the judgment pronounced [on the operas] was in some ways "unjust and unilateral" and that for this reason, "musical opinion has been to some extent misinformed with regard to what really constitutes 'formalism' in music".' In conclusion the document states that 'the new "content" of life urgently calls for the enrichment of operatic forms and the renovation of melody and intonation', and exhorts composers to show 'more boldness in their researches'. In the same conclusion, however, the document blames the 'passion for formal experiments to which certain young composers are prone', and calls for 'the democratisation of musical language'.

For the time being one can only maintain an attitude of expectation. Everything will depend on the way in which these directives will be interpreted in practice and on the attitude adopted towards the problems raised by these seemingly contradictory declarations of intention. J. S. Bach and Mozart—to cite only two examples—also had to bow to rulings of an ideological and material order. But that did not prevent them from writing masterpieces.

* * *

It would at all events be unjust not to stress the extremely positive element in the general history of music provided by the musical creations of Soviet Russia. This element is undoubtedly of an aesthetic order, and is concerned with the rehabilitation of a realist art, reincarnated in men's hearts and reintegrated in their lives.

[*Translated from the French by the Editor*]

XXI

LATIN AMERICA

By Norman Fraser

LATIN AMERICA's contribution to the present world stream of music can be said to have started in 1870 when the Brazilian (of Portuguese parents) Carlos Gomes (1836-1896) had a triumphal success in Milan with his opera *O Guarani*. But Gomes was almost a European. Even more so was Reynaldo Hahn (1875-1947) who left his native Venezuela when he was eleven. However, Teresa Carreño (1853-1917) really was Venezuelan, the granddaughter of composer José Cayetano Carreño (1774-1836), and was probably the first Latin American musician to settle, and more than hold her own, in Europe. One more of these 'Europeans' must be mentioned: Joaquín Nin (1879-1949), the well-known 'Spanish' composer who was actually a Cuban!

Lack of musical organisation, due partly to apathy, partly to ignorance, is the reason for Latin America's late entry into the main stream of music. Until about fifty years ago all but the very few considered a yearly season by a third-rate Italian opera company (and this only in the largest centres) to be all that was necessary to musical culture. The famous Teatro Colón in Buenos Aires with its world-wide prestige only dates back to 1908. Properly organised music teaching started in Rio de Janeiro in 1890 (Instituto Nacional de Musica) and in Buenos Aires in 1893 (Conservatorio Williams). No countries had permanent symphony orchestras until after the First World War.

It is against this very unpromising background that we must examine the quite astonishing musical progress of Latin America today when the large cities have a cosmopolitan musical life which surpasses that of many European cities of equal size and resources.

Although the many countries are at different stages of development, the basic pattern has everywhere been the same. First of all there has been at least one generation of European-trained native professionals who have returned home to agitate for the wider recognition of music as a civilising force. These men like Williams of Argentina, Villa-Lobos of Brazil, Santa Cruz of Chile and Ponce of Mexico, to name only a few, gradually effected a complete change in the musical outlook of their countries. There followed a generation of locally trained but thoroughly competent musicians, and today many of the excellent music schools and faculties are on a level with our own, as can be seen by their products which reach us in ever increasing quantity and quality.

Let us now examine in as much detail as space allows the present-day musical activities of the various republics starting, alphabetically, with Argentina.

As in most countries, all the artistic activities have until recently tended to gravitate towards the capital, Buenos Aires, where there are three large conservatoires (National, Municipal and 'Williams') turning out fully qualified musicians. It must however be noted with regret that since the death of Alberto Williams (1862-1952), pupil of César Franck and first real Argentine symphonist, the splendid conservatoire which he founded is no longer what it was. The large, cosmopolitan public supports seven symphony orchestras, two chamber orchestras and many chamber music groups including an excellent harpsichord ensemble of old instruments directed by Budapest-trained Adolfo Morpurgo (1889-). There are many choirs and madrigal groups. The Colón theatre is no longer dependent on visiting artists and quite recently (1958) a fine chamber opera group, mostly Colón-trained, has been touring Europe with genuine success. Buenos Aires also has a splendidly disciplined Banda Municipal, a first-rate military band with a serious music repertoire which was trained and conducted for many years by José Maria Castro (1892-).

Towering over all other Argentine musicians today is Paris-trained Juan José Castro (1895-), brother of José Maria, who now conducts and tours with the Orquesta Sinfónica Nacional (created for him after Perón, who had banished him, left the country). Castro writes in a virile, contemporary vein and his operas, symphonies and other works deserve more frequent performance than they get. His opera *Proserpina* won the Verdi prize offered by the Scala Theatre in Milan (1951). A remarkable piano concerto awaits performance in England and elsewhere.

Of the younger generation pride of place must be given to Alberto Ginastera (1916-), until recently Professor of Music at the Eva Perón (formerly and again now La Plata) University. Ginastera belongs to the first generation of entirely locally trained musicians and has developed a personal style in which he blends certain traditional *criollo* elements with present-day contemporary techniques. He is the first Argentine composer to win universal approval.

The song writer Carlos Guastavino (1912-) has attained to great popularity with his facile music. Juan Carlos Paz (1899-) remains comparatively obscure with his atonal dodecaphony, but there is no doubt as to his influence on the present-day school, a member of which, Roberto Caamaño, has recently won a Premio Nacional de Música. Paz has for years gathered the young and adventuresome round him. They will one day be heard. Among the young twelve-tonists we must mention C. Rausch, E. Cantón, M. Kazel, F. Kröpfl, M. Davidovsky and S. Baron. Meanwhile, another vital influence since the last war has been Guillermo Graetzer, more or less a follower of Hindemith. He built up and did splendid work with the local Collegium Musicum and now conducts the chamber orchestra and choir of the Associación Amigos de la Música. He has made a most interesting and musicianly performing version of the *Kunst der Fuge*. In the field of ethnomusicology Carlos Vega (1898-) of Buenos Aires University is still the leading figure.

In the Argentine provinces, until so recently barren of any form of serious musical activities, conditions are today quite surprisingly advanced. The Universities of La Plata, Rosario, Córdoba, Mendoza, Tucumán and Bahïa Blanca take music seriously. Mendoza (Universidad Nacional de Cuyo) has a splendid symphony orchestra, conducted by Aquiles Romani, together with a fine choir and excellent chamber music groups. Rosario has a good symphony orchestra and choir (conductor: Washington Castro). Rio Cuarto has a philharmonic orchestra and choir. Córdoba (founded in the early seventeenth century) also has an old-established symphony orchestra, choir, madrigal society, chamber orchestra, etc. The Argentine radio is becoming more and more preoccupied with good music.

In Bolivia no figure of international importance has as yet appeared.

Brazil has musical history. The early Jesuits brought learning to the country and some really interesting eighteenth-century church music has recently been discovered. The Rio conservatoire was first established in 1841 but was completely reformed in 1890. Today it is a very reputable establishment directed (oddly enough for South America) by a woman, Joanidia Sodre (1903-), who also conducts its symphony orchestra. Although the Escola Nacional de Musica in question is a dependency of the University of Brazil, there is also the Orquesta Universitaria, conducted by Raphael Baptista.

The development of musical life in Brazil has not followed the same lines as that in Argentina. Whereas the operatic aria was the passion in the latter country during the nineteenth century, the pianoforte reigned supreme in Brazil.

Brazil's first real symphonist was Alberto Nepomuceno (1864-1920), a remarkable musician who had studied in Europe. But the outstanding talent of that generation was self-taught, Chopin-influenced Ernesto Nazareth (1863-1934), whose *carioca* music prepared the way for that enigmatic figure, Heitor Villa-Lobos (1887-1959), who has done for the music of his country what Bartók and Vaughan Williams have done for theirs. Whether Villa-Lobos's music has the intrinsic value of that of the two great composers mentioned is beside the point. Quite apart from his prolific and indiscriminate production, Villa-Lobos has done a work of precious and lasting value at his Conservatoire Nacional de Canto Orfeónico, from which carefully trained music teachers (accent on choral singing) are provided to Brazilian schools throughout its vast territory. For this gigantic undertaking alone Villa-Lobos deserves a permanent niche in the musical history of the world.

The other large music school in Rio de Janeiro, the Conservatorio Brasileiro de Musica, founded in 1935 by that fine musician Oscar Lorenzo Fernândez (1897-1948), is now in the hands of Antoinetta de Souza who also conducts the orchestra. Incidentally, it is quite astonishing how women, until so recently jealously guarded chattels, are rapidly assuming the lead in South America's musical life.

Brazil has only one opera house: at Manaos, in the heart of the Amazon jungle! The Municipal Theatre in Rio once engaged reputable touring companies and it will always be remembered that Toscanini made his improvised début as a conductor there in 1886. At the time of writing there is little operatic activity in Brazil. There are, however, four symphony orchestras in Rio and one each in São Paulo, Recife, Bahia and Porto Alegre. There is also considerable interest in chamber music and in Rio alone there are two good string quartets (Quarteto de Rio de Janeiro and Quarteto Radio Ministerio da Educação) with other quartets and trios in the larger provincial centres. Choral singing is, of course, much in the ascendant and the best choir in Rio, the Associação de Canto Coral, with about eighty members, is most impressive. The conductor, again, is a woman: Cleofe Person de Matos. The Coro Municipal with about sixty members and the Ars Nova madrigal group, both of São Paulo, are well above average.

Milan-trained Francisco Mignone(1897-) and Paris-trained Camargo Guarnieri (1907-) are still representative composers of the older school. Radamés Gnattali (1906-) is more adventurous and has even experimented with (and turned down) the twelve-note system. Cesar Guerra Peixe (1914-) and Paris-trained Claudio Santoro (1919-) wrote strict tone-row music for many years. The prime mover in this field, Berlin-trained Hans-Joachim Koellreutter (1915-), arrived in Brazil in 1937. His influence among the younger composers has been enormous, both in Rio and São Paulo where he has worked as teacher and flautist.

Before moving our attention on to Chile, mention must be made of Brazil's outstanding ethno-musicologist Oneyda Alvarenga (1911-), who is doing a lasting job in the São Paulo Municipality.

Chile is a tiny country compared to Argentina and Brazil. She has nevertheless made fantastic musical progress during this century. Starting from the cult of operatic aria plus piano salon music, which had reigned since her independence in 1810, she has, within the last fifty years, completely caught up with and almost surpassed her rich neighbours. This fact is almost entirely due to one man: Spanish-trained Domingo Santa Cruz (1899-). With superhuman courage, energy and determination, he set to work after the First World War and gradually coaxed, cudgelled and finally galvanised his amazed colleagues into action. A Bach Society was started; a Faculty of Fine Arts including music was established at the University of Chile; the old, sleepy Conservatorio was taken over and completely revolutionised; a symphony orchestra was created and a proper system of music examinations was decreed: all this within a year or two of whirlwind upheavals! The results have been quite extraordinary. Systematic training has produced not only accomplished professionals but an advanced and discriminating public as well. The Chileans are naturally musical and in the bad old days Milan-trained Renato Zanelli, and Berlin-trained Rosita Renard and Claudio Arrau, were already international figures; and the music of Milan-trained Enrique Soro (1884-1954) and locally trained Pedro Humberto Allende (1885-) was being published in Europe and the U.S.A.

There are now officially recognised music schools in all the larger centres, visited by examiners from Santiago. There is now also a Faculty of Music (present Dean: Alfonso Letelier (1912-), good composer in contemporary tonal style) which controls the Conservatorio Nacional de Música (present Director, Herminia Raccagni, a leading pianist), a most up-to-date establishment, a very fine ballet school, founded by Kurt Joos and run by Ernst Uhtoff (the Chilean National Ballet has recently (in 1958) had the success of the season at the Colón theatre in Buenos Aires); and last to be inaugurated, a serious opera school run by its founder, Argentine soprano Clara Oyuela. Incidentally, Ramón Vinay's great successes at the Scala, Bayreuth, Covent Garden, etc., have acted as a real incentive to his young compatriots with operatic talent.

There are now three Symphony orchestras in Chile: the Orquesta Sinfónica (Santiago, under Victor Tevah), the Orquesta Filharmónica (Santiago, under Juan Matteucci) and the Orquesta Sinfónica (Viña del Mar, under Isidor Handler).

Within recent years the Instituto de Extensión Musical (part of the Faculty of Music in Santiago) has been running a most interesting and original series of competitions for composers of symphonic, chamber and smaller works. About two thousand members of the general concert-going public are asked to adjudicate and they register their names, addresses and occupations together with a promise to attend all the concerts and vote conscientiously on the works presented. There are so many applicants that the season tickets for the orchestral, chamber and recital series are soon sold out. The scores are read and chosen by a committee. These festivals are held in an atmosphere of intense excitement. The works are carefully rehearsed and built into suitable programmes. Nearly every member of the packed houses is a member of the jury and casts his or her anonymous vote after the concert. The best works often but by no means always get the highest number of votes. This novel idea is also due to Santa Cruz and has proved itself to be the most perfect natural stimulus to indigenous production. Incidentally, these concerts have an enormous radio audience throughout the country. Among the promising young composers thrown up by these competitions are Gustavo Becera, Carlos Riesco, Carlos Botto, Alfonso Montecino, Hans Helfritz, Leni Alexander and Roberto Falabella; also a symphonist of solid attainments whose atonal opera *Deirdre* has been much discussed, the naturalised Free Focke.

Chile has a flourishing school of young dodecaphonists among whom are: Juan Mesquida, Miguel Aguilar, José Vicente Asuar, Fernando García, Abelardo Quinteros, Raúl Rivera, and Eduardo Maturana.

The present Director of the Instituto de Extensión Musical, Juan Orrego Salas (1919-), is probably Chile's best all-round musician. He writes in a free but personal tonal style, is much travelled (frequently having works performed abroad), heads the music critics and is a considerable musicologist. However, Chile's leading musicologist is probably Eugenio Pereira Salas (1904-), brilliant historian and art critic, head of the Instituto de Investigaciones Folklóricas.

The Republic of Colombia, which next engages our attention, is in the process of trying to catch up with its advanced neighbours. Before the advent of air travel, Colombian centres of civilisation were almost completely cut off from one another because of the high mountain ranges. As soon as it was possible, Berlin-trained composer and conductor Guillermo Espinosa (1905-) took his National Symphony Orchestra (1936) on tour by 'plane. Since the last war the orchestra has been re-formed by Esthonian Olav Roots, who now conducts it. It was heard recently at the Miami Festival of the Americas.

The composer of the older school who did most to stir up the musical apathy of Bogotá is Guillermo Uribe Holguín (1880-). Having learnt very little at the old Academia Nacional de Música and, fortunately, realising this, he managed to get to New York where his eyes were opened in astonishment. Back in Colombia he agitated for higher standards and finally persuaded the government to send him to d'Indy in Paris (1907). He returned three years later and made a clean sweep of the Academia, refounding it with official recognition as the Conservatorio Nacional de Música (1910; present Director, Fabio Gonzalez). Among Uribe Holguín's colleagues can be named: Madrid-trained Jesús Bermúdez Silva (1884-) who introduced chamber music to Bogotá; Paris-trained Adolfo Mejía (1908-) who teaches in Cartagena; Paris-trained Carlos Posada Amador (1908-), who has done much for music in Medellín; Paris-trained Antonio María Valencia (1904-), founder of the Cali conservatoire (1930; present Director, Santiago Velasco Llanos); Rome-trained José Rozo Contreras (1894-), conductor of the Bogotá National Band. The most promising composer today is Luis Antonio Escobar. Guillermo Espinosa is at present Chief of the Music Section of the Pan American Union in Washington D.C.

The Colombian government has an Institute for the Promotion of Studies Abroad (ICETEX) which helps musicians. Ramón Cardona García, Director of the Manizales conservatoire, was sent to study in Argentina. The Municipalities of such places as Popayán, Cali and Medellin award music bursaries.

About Costa Rica there is little to say. German-trained Guillermo Aguilar Machado (1905-) directs the National Conservatoire in San José. Hugo Mariani conducts the National Symphony Orchestra (1940). The present-day school of composition was founded by Milan- and Brussels-trained Julio Fonseca (1895-) and Brussels- and New York-trained Alejandro Monestel (1865-).

Cuba is one of the advanced Latin American republics. Already in the nineteenth century Brindis de Salas (1852-1910) became world-famous as the 'black Paganini'; José White (1836-1918) was a professor at the Paris Conservatoire; Paris-trained Ignacio Cervantes (1847-1905) was Cuba's first symphonist. Paris-trained Alejandro García Caturla (1906-1940) and Madrid-trained Amadeo Roldán (1900-1939) were the founders of present-day Cuban music, and both left interesting symphonic and other works. In 1943 Barcelona-trained José Ardévol (1911-) and a group of young enthusiasts founded the Grupo de Renovación Musical. This has brought out the works of Virginia Fleites (1916-), Hilario Gonzales Iñiguez (1930-), Harold Gramatges (1918-), Gisela Hernández Gonzalez (1910-), Edgardo Martín (1915-), Julián Orbón (1925-), Serafí Pró (1906-), Esther Rodriguez (1920-) and others.

The Conservatorio Municipal of Havana (Director: Diego Bonilla) was founded in 1837 as a branch of the Madrid Conservatorio. This disappeared for lack of enthusiasm and was re-established in 1877, and again in 1884 by Cervantes. The final establishments (after wars and vicissitudes) were in 1885 and 1899 by Hubert de Blanck (1856-1900). Today there are no less than fifty-three conservatoires in Havana, all recognised by the Ministry of Education! They form collectively the 'Confederación Nacional de Conservatorios y Profesionales de Musica'. There are, of course, dozens more in the provinces. The Orquesta Sinfónica (1924) and Sociedad Coral (1931) are well established now. There is also an Orquesta Filharmónica (conductor: Alberto Bolet), an Orquesta del Instituto Nacional de Cultura (same conductor), and various chamber music ensembles and concert societies. In 1934 Ardévol founded a chamber orchestra which tackles the advanced music of his group. Finally, Cuba has an outstanding ethno-musicologist in Fernando Ortiz.

In Dominica, Ciudad Trujillo has had a symphony orchestra since 1932 (conductor: Enrique Mejía Arredondo, (1901-) and a national symphony orchestra since 1940 (conductor: Madrid-trained Enrique Casal Chapí, (1909-), till 1945, subsequently Mexican-trained Abel Eisenberg now succeeded by Roberto Caggiano). There is also a Conservatorio Nacional de Música (Director: Manuel Simo).

In Ecuador, the first Conservatorio Nacional de Música in Quito was founded in 1870, and re-established in 1900 since when it has continued its modest course. There are two figures worth mentioning: Brussels-trained Pedro Paz (1893-) now conducting the Lansing Symphony Orchestra at Olivet, Mich., and Berlin-trained Belisario Peña Ponce (1902-). Quito has an Orquesta Sinfónica Nacional (conductor:

Ernesto Xancó). Guayaquil has a symphony orchestra and choral society
run by Angel Negri. Cuenca has a symphony orchestra (conductor:
Rafael Sojos Jaramilla).

Guatemala is making great strides in the musical field. Although the
first Conservatorio was founded in 1873, and lasted for three years, bad
salon music has reigned until comparatively recently. Now, however,
since the founding in 1936 of the Orquesta Progresista and in 1944 of
the Orquesta Filharmónica (now the Orquesta Sinfónica Nacional,
under Andrés Archila) by Paris-trained Ricardo Castillo (1894-),
interest in serious music is thoroughly aroused. There is even today a
Ballet Guatemala which tours in Central America. The younger group
of composers formed themselves into the 'Asociación Musical Juvenil
de Guatemala' and published a magazine, Música. Manuel Herrarte,
U.S.A.-trained, has conducted his own music there. Berlin-trained
Salvador Ley (1907-) directs the National Conservatoire since
1944. Another composer is Brussels- and Rome-trained Enrique
Solares Echeverría (1910-). There is also now a Cuarteto de Cuerda
Guatemala.

The capital of Honduras, Tegucigalpa, saw and heard its first Italian
opera in 1930. There are one or two priests who teach music. Only
poor religious and salon music has been produced so far.

Mexico is in a very different position. It at least rivals Argentina in
musical development. Manuel García took opera to Mexico in 1827
and started the craze for Italian opera. By 1868 the Mexican opera
Ildegonda by Melesio Morales (1838-1908) had been given in Florence.
From this time also Mexican artists (starting with Angela Peralta,
1845-1883) have taken their place in the outside world.

Present-day Mexican music starts with Bologna- and Berlin-trained
Manuel M. Ponce (1886-1948). His influence on Mexican musical life
was so great that the concert hall of the Instituto de las Bellas Artes
was named after him after his death. His later music gives hints of the
'Mexicanism' which his pupil Carlos Chavez (1899-) has developed.
Chavez is, of course, the great figure in Mexican music today. His
harsh, dynamic compositions are as representative of pre-colonial
Mexican music as those of Bloch are of ancient Jewish music: in both
cases being inspired guesswork. As conductor of the Mexican Sym-

phony Orchestra which he founded in 1928, Chavez has kept his country right up to date and brought the players to a considerable degree of cohesion and perfection. The Orquesta Sinfónica Nacional is now conducted by Luis Herrera de la Fuente, and the Orquesta Sinfónica de la Universidad Nacional by José F. Vásquez. There is also a chamber orchestra called 'Yolopatli', and a Cuarteto Ponce.

Among the many interesting figures in Mexican modern music must be mentioned: Daniel Ayala (1908-), Salvador Contreras (1912-), Blas Galindo (1910-), Candelario Huizar (1888-), Eduardo Hernández Moncada (1899-), José Pablo Moncayo (1912-), and Silvestre Revueltas (1899-1940), a very important figure.

Mexico has a National Opera and a fine opera house (Palacio de Bellas Artes), and has produced one of the finest operatic contraltos of today, Oralia Dominguez, among many international singers. The outstanding ethno-musicologist is Vicente T. Mendoza (1894-).

Nicaragua need not detain us for long. Milan-trained Luis Abraham Delgadillo (1887-) is a serious composer and symphonist. He has taught composition in the national conservatoires of Panamá and Mexico.

Panamá has a national symphony orchestra, conducted since 1944 by Walter Myers (1891-), also secretary and theory teacher at the newly re-established Conservatorio (1941) under Alfredo de Saint Malo (1898-). They were both trained in the old conservatoire by Narciso Garay (1876-). Today Herbert de Castro (1906-) conducts the national orchestra and Roque Cordero (1917-) the orchestra of the Instituto Nacional de Música. Cordero's second symphony won second prize at the second Festival of Latin American Music in Caracas (1957).

Present-day composers include: Rome-trained Carlos Arias Quintero (1903-), Ricardo Fábrega (1905-), Barcelona-trained Alberto Galimany (1889-), and Mexican-trained Pedro Rebolledo (1895-), president of the Panamá 'Unión Musical'.

Panamá now also has an Escuela Nacional de Ballet.

Paraguay has practically nothing to offer the serious músician. There is an Escuela Normal de Música in Asunción run by Paris-trained Remberto Giménez (1889-), and the Conservatorio de Música del Ateo, run by Juan Carlos Moreno González. They have not as yet produced anything of value.

In Perú, Lima has, since the last war, begun to become more musically organised than it was before. True, the Academia Nacional de Música 'Alzedo' did some good work before it became, in 1946, the Conservatorio Nacional de Música (present director: Roberto Carpio Valdez, 1900-), but there was no symphony orchestra until Theo Buchwald (1902-) formed the Orquesta Sinfónica Nacional in 1938. He has conducted it ever since, only resigning in 1957. The post has not yet (on writing) been filled. Lima has a choral society started by Carlos Valderrama (1887-) and a chamber music group. There is also an opera and ballet company. There are said to be eight recognised conservatoires in the provinces.

The first Peruvian composer of our time was Teodoro Valcarcel (1900-1943), who successfully exploited the tunes and rhythms of his country. Since then Brussels-trained Andrés Sás (1900-), and Paris-trained Rodolfo Holzmann have continued more or less in the same vein but bringing it more up to date. Another nationalist is Paris-trained Raoul de Verneuil (1901-).

Puerto Rico seems to have nothing to offer but the pianist Jesús María Sanromá (1903-), a pupil of Cortot and Schnabel, who lives in the U.S.A.

Salvador has at least tried to do something about musical culture: in 1875 a Philharmonic Society was founded. It had its own symphony orchestra and lasted for years. In 1910 another orchestra, the Sociedad Orquestral Salvadoreña, was founded and conducted by Antonio Gianola. The present symphony orchestra is conducted by Mexican-trained Humberto Pacas (1905-). He was also for a time Director of the Escuela Nacional de Música at San Salvador. There is one outstanding woman musician: Maria M. de Baratta (1894-). There seems now to be a military band, the Orquesta Sinfónica del Ejército, conducted by Alejandro Muñóz Ciudad Real at San Sol in the Círculo Militar there.

The small Republic of Uruguay with its large capital, Montevideo, has benefited by being so near to Buenos Aires. Opera companies and concert artists have stopped there on the way to and from the outer world for over a hundred years. Even so, Montevideo cannot compare with Buenos Aires, Rio de Janeiro or Santiago in its musical culture. The Conservatorio Nacional de Música (Director: Paris-trained Carlos Estrada, 1909-) is of recent foundation. For this reason there are six reputable establishments, and a municipal school of music (Director: Vicente Ascone, 1897-). Of the private establishments the Conservatorio Kolischer (Director: Guillermo Kolischer) has turned out a number of international virtuoso pianists including Hugo Balzo (who now has his own conservatoire), Nybia Mariño (1920-), Mercedes Olivera (1919-) and Marisa Regules. Among the younger generation of pianists are Fanny Ingold and Luis Battle Ibañez.

The only symphony orchestra in Uruguay (a very rough instrument) is that of the official radio, the SODRE, created in 1930. There is no permanent conductor, but most of the famous conductors have given concerts with it. The two composers of the older school to establish Uruguayan music are: Luis Cluzeau Mortet (1894-1957) and Brussels-trained Eudardo Fabini (1813-1950), both of whom have written neo-romantic gaucho-tinged music. Among the younger generation the most gifted is Hector Tosar Errecart (1923-) who has a contemporary style of his own. Also interesting are Paris-trained Carlos Estrada (1909-) and Ricardo Storm.

Uruguay has a studious musicologist in Lauro Ayestarán (1913-) and an indefatigably dynamic one in German-trained Francisco Curt Lange who established the Interamerican Musicological Institute under the Uruguayan Ministry of Foreign Relations (1940). He also founded a co-operative music publishing business which has brought out about seventy contemporary Latin American and U.S.A. works. His massive volumes of the Boletín Latino Americano de Música contain a wealth of musicological information. He has also unearthed and is publishing some very interesting eighteenth-century Venezuelan and Brazilian church music.

There are three established string quartets (the SODRE, Fabini and Kleiber quartets), the Montevideo Wind Quartet and the American Saxophone Quartet. There are a vocal quartet and eight choirs. In the provinces there are about twelve choirs, and four of these under Raúl H. Evangelista gave a choral festival in the capital in 1957. Montevideo also had an important Festival of Latin American Music in the same year.

There is now only Venezuela left on our list. This country has had cultured musicians since the eighteenth century. Teresa Carreño was the daughter and grand-daughter of well-known musicians. Today Caracas is one of the most go-ahead musical cities in the whole of Latin America, witness the recent two Festivals of Latin American Music with their valuable prizes. Winners of these prizes in 1957 were: Enrique Iturriaga of Perú, Roque Cordero of Panamá, Blas Galindo of Mexico and Camargo Guarnieri of Brazil. The two fathers of the present Venezuelan school are Vatican-trained Juan Bautista Plaza (1898-) and self-taught Vicente Emilio Sojo (1887-), founder and director of the Orquesta Sinfónica Venezolana (1930, present conductor, Antonio Estévez), and the Orfeón Lamas of the same date. In 1936 he became Director of the Escuela Nacional de Música. Another established musician is José Antonio Calcano, who directs the Conservatorio 'Teresa Carreño' and the 'Coral Creole'. Perhaps the most interesting nationalist composer is U.S.A.-trained Juan Vicente Lecuna (1899-), though Antonio Estévez (1916-) is still developing a very personal style. One of the youngest symphonists is Inocente Carreño.

The Universidad Central de Venezuela has a fine choral society conducted by Vinicio Adames.

Finally, mention must be made of José Felipe Ramón y Rivera and his wife Isabel Aretz (1909-), internationally respected ethno-musicologists working in the Ministry of Education.

The vast area covered in these very condensed notes is literally seething with possibilities. These are indeed the musically civilised countries of the future. They have not yet lost their New-World enthusiasm. They are becoming politically stable and healthily, not exaggeratedly, nationalistic. The 'Jeunesses Musicales' movement will soon be established in all the larger centres. The foreigner is no longer received uncritically, yet there is no real anti-foreign bias. Indeed, unless disaster overtakes the world, Latin America looks like becoming the musical Mecca of the future.

NOTES ON CONTRIBUTORS

The Editor: Born 1892. Author of *Modern Music, Music in the Modern World, Introduction to the Music of Stravinsky* and critical biographies of *Debussy, Ravel* and *Erik Satie* (the latter translated into French, pub. Gallimard). General Editor of special number of *La Revue Musicale* (June 1952)—*Erik Satie, son Temps et ses Amis*, and of *Music Today* (Journal of the I.S.C.M. for 1949). Contributor to *Grove's Dictionary* (5th Edition) and to numerous musical journals at home and abroad. Officier d'Académie.

Theodor W. Adorno: Born 1903 at Frankfurt-am-Main, where he is now Director of the Institute of Social Research. From 1938-41 took part in the Princeton, U.S.A., Radio Research Project. Teaches at the Darmstadt summer school. Author of, *inter alia*, *Philosophie der neuen Musik* (Schoenberg and Stravinsky) (1949), *Versuch über Wagner* (1952) and *Dissonanzen.*

Eric Blom: 1888-1959. C.B.E., Hon. D.Litt. (Birmingham University). Editor of *Grove's Dictionary of Music* (5th Edition) and of *Music and Letters.* Author of numerous books on music, including *Everyman's Dictionary of Music.* Former music critic of *Manchester Guardian* (in London), *Birmingham Post* (in Birmingham) and *The Observer*, to which he contributed a regular musical article until his death in April 1959.

Paul Collaer: Eminent Belgian musicologist. Former Director of Music of the Belgian Radio. Author of various works on contemporary music and musicians.

Norman Del Mar: Born London, 1919. Studied under Vaughan Williams and Constant Lambert at the Royal College of Music, London. Has been associated since 1947 with Sir Thomas Beecham, and is now Professor of Conducting at the London Guildhall School of Music.

Norman Fraser: Born 1904 at Valparaiso, Chile. Composer, pianist and writer on music, specialising in Spanish and Latin-American music. Editor of South American articles in *Grove's Dictionary of Music* (5th Edition).

Marcel Frémiot: Artistic Director of a French gramophone record publishing firm. Contributor to various French, German and Italian periodicals.

Karl-Heinz Füssl. Born 1924. Austrian composer and former critic. Studied in Berlin, and Vienna, where he now lives. His works include an *Epitaph* for orchestra, one of the works selected for the I.S.C.M. Festival in 1956. At present working on an opera.

Fred. Goldbeck: Well-known Parisian critic and musicologist. Paris correspondent of *The Musical Quarterly* and other periodicals. Author of *The Perfect Conductor.* Contributor to *Grove's Dictionary of Music* (5th Edition) and numerous musical journals. Former Editor of *Contrepoints.*

André Hodeir: Born Paris, 1921. French composer, pupil of Olivier Messiaen. Author of *Jazz: its Evolution and Essence* and *La Musique Contemporaine* (1954)—the latter to be published shortly in the U.S.A. under the title *Modern Music.*

Dyneley Hussey: Born 1893. Former music critic of *The Times.* Radio critic, *The Listener.* Author of books on Mozart, Verdi, etc.

Arthur Jacobs: Born Manchester, 1922. Music critic of *Daily Express,* London, 1947-52. As critic, lecturer and broadcaster has visited U.S.A. (twice), Canada, Australia, New Zealand and various European countries. Author of *Gilbert and Sullivan* (1951); *A New Dictionary of Music* (Penguin 1958). Contributor to various symposia.

Robert Layton: Born 1930. Studied composition at Oxford under Edmund Rubbra and Egon Wellesz. His works include a *Symphony* (1955-57) and a variety of instrumental music. Author of a biography of the Swedish composer Franz Berwald, published in Stockholm in 1956.

Colin Mason: Born 1924. Music critic *Guardian* and *Daily Telegraph.*

Wilfrid Mellers: Born 1914. Composer and author; Professor of Music, York University.

Anthony Milner: Born 1925. Educated at a Roman Catholic school and at the Royal College of Music, London, where he studied with R. O. Morris. Has also studied composition privately with Matyas Seiber. His music is mainly choral, and his works include a *Mass*, a number of cantatas on religious texts, anthems and other Church music. As a member of the teaching staff of Morley College, London, he has both a practical and theoretic interest in adult education.

Maurice Ohana: Born 1914 at Casablanca. Spanish composer.

Claude Rostand: Well-known Parisian critic and writer on music. Author of *La Musique Française Contemporaine, L'Oeuvre de Gabriel Fauré, Richard Strauss, Brahms, Les chefs-d'oeuvre du Piano,* etc.

Humphrey Searle: Born 1915. British composer. (See Chap. XVII, p. 188.) Author of: *Twentieth Century Counterpoint, The Music of Liszt, Ballet Music.* Contributor to *Grove's Dictionary of Music* (5th Edition).

Robert Simpson: Born 1921. D.Mus. Music critic, lecturer, and composer. Founder of The Exploratory Concert Society. Tutor in music, Extra-Mural Dept. London University. Member of Bruckner Society of America. Author of a critical biography of *Carl Nielsen*, etc. Member of music staff of B.B.C.

Frederick W. Sternfeld: Formerly Professor of Music, Dartmouth (U.S.A.). Since 1956 University lecturer in music, Oxford. Ph.D.,

Yale University; Guggenheim Fellow (1954); Member of Institute for Advanced Study, Princeton, Editor, *New Oxford Dictionary of Music*. Author of *Goethe and Music* (New York) and contributor to the *Musical Quarterly* and other musical periodicals.

Malcolm Troup: Born 1930. Pianist and author.

ACKNOWLEDGEMENTS

MY thanks are due to the following publishers for permission to reproduce the music-type examples in Chapter VII:

Messrs Boosey and Hawkes, London (Stravinsky: *Le Sacre du Printemps*).
Universal Edition, Vienna and London (Alban Berg: *Drei Orchester-
stücke*, Op. 6).
(Anton Webern: *Variations*,
Op. 30).
Heugel et Cie. Paris (Darius Milhaud: *Les Choéphores*).

The Editor

INDEX